S0-DVE-614

LAW SUMMARIES

AGENCY & PARTNERSHIP

Fourth Edition — 1982

Editorial Consultant:

Richard J. Conviser
Professor of Law
IIT/Kent College of Law

1995 Supplement
In Back of Book

HARCOURT BRACE LEGAL AND PROFESSIONAL PUBLICATIONS, INC.

EDITORIAL OFFICES: 176 W. Adams, Suite 2100, Chicago, IL 60603

LAW SUMMARIES

REGIONAL OFFICES: New York, Chicago, Los Angeles, Washington, D.C.
Distributed by: **Harcourt Brace & Company** 6277 Sea Harbor Drive, Orlando, FL 32887 (800)787-8717

PROJECT EDITOR
Elizabeth L. Snyder, B.A., J.D.
Attorney at Law

QUALITY CONTROL EDITOR
Ann R. Kerns, B.S.

SUMMARY OF CONTENTS

gilbert
capsule summary
agency & partnership

AGENCY

I. INTRODUCTION

A. DEFINITIONS

Master-Servant Relationship: Master **controls or has right to control** physical conduct of servant in performance of employment duties. It includes employer-employee relationship . . . . [1-4]
Principal-Agent Relationship: Agent acts **for and in behalf of principal** to effect legal relations with third persons. Representative character and derivative authority allow agent degree of discretion which servant lacks, although same person may be **both** agent and servant . . . . [5]
Independent Contractor: One who renders services in course of independent calling; contracts with employer only as to **results** to be accomplished. Employer has no right of control. **Respondeat superior** does not apply to independent contractors. Person may sometimes function as **both** servant and independent contractor . [6-9]

II. RIGHTS AND LIABILITIES BETWEEN PRINCIPAL AND AGENT

A. NATURE OF RELATIONSHIP
Principal-agent relationship is contractual, but does not require consideration. . . . . [10]

B. AGENT'S DUTY TO PRINCIPAL

Duty to Perform: Every employment or agency contract implies an agreement to use reasonable care, skill, and diligence. Failure to perform results in contract liability, and careless performance may impose tort liability (for negligence) as well . . . . [11-13]
—Gratuitous agent: The same duty and standard of care are required of a non-paid agent, but gratuitous agents are liable only in tort (not for breach of contract) . . . . [14]
Fiduciary Duty: Every agent is deemed a fiduciary (owes the principal faithful service). This implies a duty to **notify** principal of all matters concerning the agency and to be **loyal** to principal regarding agency matters (although agent is not obligated to shield **dishonest** principal) . . . . [15-19]
—Conflicts of interest: Agent may not take position adverse to principal without principal's consent. Thus, the agent may not secretly profit

from relationship, nor may purchasing agent or sales agent engage in personal transactions without consent. . . . . [20-23]
—Dual agency: Agent for two principals (*e.g.*, buyer and seller) must have informed consent of **both** Ps or transaction is voidable by either P.[24]
—Remedies: A's violation of fiduciary duty is **both** breach of agency contract and a tort (fraud). P may claim **damages, rescind** transaction or demand **constructive trust** be imposed on A . . . . [25]
Duties Owed by Subagents: If hiring of subagent is **authorized** by P, subagent owes same duty to P as A would have owed. A is responsible to P for violations of duty by subagents. If hiring of subagent is **not authorized** by P, no agency relationship exists between P and subagent, but A is liable to P for subagent's misconduct. [26-27]
Rights and Benefits Acquired During Employment: Generally, everything acquired by A by virtue of employment (except A's compensation) belongs to P. It is usually immaterial that identity of "P" is not disclosed to third party . [28-29]
—Inventions and patents belong to P (employer) unless developing them is **not** primary part of employee's duties. Even if not part of employee's duties, employer may claim "shop-right" to patent if developed on his time or using his materials . . . . [30-31]
Principal's Right to Indemnification: Employer has right of indemnification against employee. P has cause of action against A for losses resulting from A's violation of instructions . . . . [32]

C. PRINCIPAL'S DUTIES TO AGENT

Compensation and Reimbursement: Unless A's services are gratuitous, P must compensate A for agreed value of services (or reasonable value, if no agreement). In absence of agreement, **salesperson** is entitled to compensation at time offer is accepted. **Subagents** are only entitled to compensation from P if their hiring was authorized. Statutes frequently regulate compensation of employees. . . . . [33-37]
Duty of Cooperation: P must assist and cooperate with A in performance of A's duties, and do nothing to prevent such performance. . . . [38]
Negligence: Common law liability of employer for employee's personal injuries is now generally superseded by state Workers' Compensation Acts . . . . [39-40]

Agent's Remedies: When P breaches agency contract, A has most remedies available to contracting parties. Remedies include right of indemnification from P (unless A's acts unauthorized), lien against P's property, withholding further performance, set-off or counterclaim, and right to demand an accounting, **but not** specific performance. Authorized subagents may act against **either** A **or** P . . . . [41-50]

III. CONTRACTUAL RIGHTS AND LIABILITIES BETWEEN PRINCIPAL (OR AGENT) AND THIRD PERSONS

A. CREATION OF AGENCY RELATIONSHIP
If A is to legally bind P, an agency relationship must exist. Such relationship may be found in three ways . . . . [51-52]
Agency by Agreement: Agency relationships ordinarily arise by agreement of the parties. Although neither consideration nor formalities (except where contract to be negotiated by A is under Statute of Frauds) are required, there must be some manifestation of mutual consent, and purpose of agency must be legal. Only person with capacity to contract may be a principal, but any person may be an agent . . . . [53-62]
Agency by Ratification: An agency is created by ratification when P **accepts the benefits** or otherwise **affirms** conduct of one purporting to act on P's behalf. Ratification is deemed to supply consent required for P-A relationship. There must be objective evidence that P knew of A's act and elected to be bound. However, if P ratifies part of the transaction (beneficial to him), he is deemed to ratify the entire transaction. Verbal ratification is sufficient unless Statute of Frauds applies . . . . [63-65]
Agency by Estoppel: Where P intentionally or negligently causes a third person to believe another is his agent, and the third person so relies in dealing with the supposed agent, there is an **ostensible agency,** and P will be bound as if an actual agency agreement existed . . [67-69]

B. AUTHORITY OF AGENT

Source of Authority: A's acts will be binding on P if there is: (1) actual authority; (2) apparent authority; (3) ostensible authority; or (4) a power arising from agency relationship not dependent on authority from P. . . . . [71]
—**Actual authority** refers to the powers of an A to do that which the P has manifested consent that A should do. Such authority may result from **express** instructions of P or may be **implied** from customary usage or from conduct of P. [72-75]
—*Formalities:* Ordinarily, no formalities are required to delegate authority to an agent. Howev-

er, many state Statutes of Frauds require A's authority to be in writing where A is to execute contract for sale of land or contract which cannot be performed in one year. Still other states have **equal dignity statutes** which require written authority for A to engage in **any** transaction covered by the Statute of Frauds. **Failure to comply** with such statute makes A's action **voidable at option of P.** These statutes do not apply to **mechanical acts** of A or to corporate executive officers . . . . [76-80]
—*Mistake by principal:* Even where there is fraud by A, if P manifests intent to create an agency, there is valid actual authority. . . . . [81-82]
—*Manifestation is made to agent* in all cases of actual authority, **not** to third persons. . . . [83]
—**Apparent authority** results when P manifests that another is his A, and such manifestation is made to a **third person.** Formalities are not necessary unless **equal dignity** is required. If a **reasonable person** under the circumstances would believe that an agency existed and **relies** upon it, P will be bound contractually. [84-87]
—*Revocation of apparent authority* occurs when **notice** is given to the **third person** to whom authority was originally manifested. . . . . . [88]
—*Apparent ownership* (where P clothes A with such indicia of ownership that reasonable person would conclude that A owned property) gives A broader powers than apparent authority, and A may deal with property as if he were the true owner. Possession alone is usually not sufficient to create apparent ownership . . . . [89-95]
—**"Ostensible authority"** is an **estoppel** applied to prevent P who has misled another from profiting thereby. Estoppel is invoked where P **intentionally or negligently** causes or allows third person (T) to believe that A has authority to do things which are not authorized and T detrimentally relies thereon. Unlike apparent authority (where P is considered a contracting party), P is liable to compensate **losses to T** relying on P's acts or omissions and has no rights created in himself. . . . . [96-97]
Scope of Authority: Most problems regarding A's authority turn on whether A had **power** to bind P. A's powers are generally strictly construed, and persons dealing with A who **know** of the agency are under a duty to determine its scope (unless **P's conduct** was misleading) . . . . [98-101]
—**Incidental powers:** If P does not expressly grant detailed powers (usual case), A is deemed to have powers **reasonably necessary or customary** to accomplish objective of agency . . [102]
—*Sales agent* is deemed to have power to warrant title, receive payment, deliver goods and negotiate sales in accordance with specified terms . . . . [103-110]

—*Purchasing agent* may pay purchase price from P's funds, accept delivery of goods or conveyance of title, and either procure offer of sale or buy on specified terms . . . . [111]
—*Delegation* of authority to subagent is **not** allowed without P's consent unless: (1) delegated act is purely mechanical; (2) A cannot lawfully perform act but subagent can; or (3) it is customary or necessary to appoint suba-gents. . . . . [112-117]
—*Emergency powers* allow A to protect rights and property of P in unforeseen emergencies. This includes right to delegate authority. . [118]
—**Powers inherent in agency relationship:** A has certain "inherent" powers by virtue of the fact that she is an agent. A has such powers even when P has specifically **denied** them to her. Inherent powers are recognized only when neces-sary to protect **third person**. These include all powers which T would reasonably suppose A to have (unless there was **notice** that P limited A's authority). A has inherent power to make **repre-sentations** concerning subject matter of agency and to make **warranties** (express or implied) which are customary under the circum-stances . . . . [119-139]
—**Limitations on authority:** A has the power to act only in accordance with authority granted by P. Third persons are protected by doctrine of **inherent powers,** so that P is bound even if act was unauthorized. . . . . [140]
Imputed Knowledge and Notice: Both P and A are deemed to have constructive notice of any fact which one party has notice of and ought (exercising ordinary care) to communicate to the other. *Rationale:* Protection of innocent third persons. . . . . [143-144]
—**Authority to receive notice:** Notice will not be imputed to P unless A had actual or apparent **authority** to receive notice of facts in question (*e.g.,* tenant's notice to bookeeper that he planned to move might not be imputed to P, but notice to building manager would be). Generally, only facts acquired **during** agency are imputed, but Restatement considers it **immaterial** when A acquired knowledge. . . . . [145]
—**Test for imputed knowledge** is whether facts concern **subject matter** of agency and are within the **scope** thereof. Imputed knowledge extends only to **factual** matters, not states of mind (*e.g.,* scienter), and A's knowledge will **not** be imputed to P where A acts adversely to P's interest (clearly outside scope of A's authority). However, a **notification** to A (as distinguished from knowl-edge of facts) is imputed to P, even if A acts adversely. . . . . [146-149]
Termination of Agent's Authority: The agency relationship (and authority of A) may be terminat-

ed by: (1) expiration of term of agency; (2) accomplishment of agency's purpose; (3) change of circumstances (*e.g.,* loss or destruction of agency's subject matter); (4) death or incapacity of P or A (terminates agency automatically unless P paid consideration for power, in which case death of P does **not** terminate agency); or (5) act or agreement of the parties. . . . . [150-160]
—**Renunciation by agent:** Where A unilaterally terminates (renunciation of authority) agency re-lationship ends, although A may be liable to P for breach of contract. . . . . [161]
—**Revocation by principal:** P can usually termi-nate agency or authority granted to A, but P may be liable to A for breach of contract. *Exception:* "Powers coupled with an interest" (*i.e.,* where agency or power was created for benefit of A or T, rather than for P). Powers coupled with interest must be supported by consideration. Such power does not terminate upon death or incapacity of P. P's attempt to revoke will be treated as a nullity (unless P was defrauded by A). . . . . [162-168]
—**Notice required to terminate:** Only death or incapacity of P will terminate agency without notice to A. In cases of **apparent authority,** T must receive notice (from P or other source) that A's authority has been terminated (unless P dies or is incapacitated) . . . . [169-171]

C. RATIFICATION

In General: Ratification is affirmance by a person of a prior act supposedly done in his behalf by another but which was not authorized. The un-authorized act is then treated as if it has been authorized at the outset. Before ratification, T is like offeror in relation to P (agreement with A deemed to be an offer to P). If P never affirms, most courts hold no contract, but upon affirma-tion P is deemed to have "accepted." T is usually free to rescind up to time P ratifies. Ratification may establish both A's authority and **agency relationship** as well. P's ratification may subject him to tort liability for A's acts. [172-177]
Who Can Ratify—Majority: Only purported P may ratify. **Minority:** Unauthorized agent or new party to contract may affirm. . . . . . . [178-179]
Acts Not Capable of Ratification: Neither acts not purportedly done **on behalf of P** nor acts which P **could not have authorized** in the first place (because illegal or against public policy) may become effective through ratification. But, where act is illegal **only because** unauthorized (*e.g.,* A's forgery of P's signature) subsequent ratification is effective. . . . . [180-183]
What Constitutes Ratification: There must be **conduct by P** which manifests her intent (*e.g.,* express notification to A or T by P). . . [184-185]

—Implied affirmation—ratification by conduct: Typically, P does not specifically express an intent to "become bound." If P **voluntarily** retains **benefits** of transaction or **files suit** or **sets up defense** based on unauthorized act, she will be deemed to have ratified. Sometimes P's failure to repudiate unauthorized act will **estop** her from denying affirmation . . . . [186-191]

Knowledge of Principal: There is no ratification unless P was aware of all material facts at time of affirmance. If P was unaware of or mistaken as to facts, she may rescind, unless T has detrimentally relied upon P's affirmance.

—Exceptions include mere mistake as to value of subject matter (some jurisdictions), or failure of P to investigate where reasonable person would have done so . . . . [192-193]

Formalities: Ratification need only be made in manner proper for an original authorization (*i.e.,* no formalities unless equal dignity required). [194]

Effects of Ratification: Under traditional rule, once A's act is ratified, it is treated as if authorized from the outset. All rights and liabilities "relate back" to date of original unauthorized act. . . . . [197]

—Exceptions to "relation back" theory: There is no "relation back" where act is **illegal** or P **lacks capacity** at time of ratification, even though P had capacity or act was legal at time of A's unauthorized act. Even if P has capacity at time of affirmance, there will be no "relation back" if P lacked it at time of A's act. (*Exception:* If P's disability was only partial--*e.g.,* minority--A's acts **can** be ratified if disability is removed.) In addition, there is no "relation back" where rights of innocent third parties acquired in the interim would be prejudiced . . . . [198-199]

Limitations on Power to Ratify

—Whole transaction must be ratified: P cannot only affirm beneficial parts of transaction and refuse to affirm the rest . . . . [200]

—Intervening withdrawal or incapacity of other party: Until affirmation, unauthorized contract is considered merely an **offer;** thus, T is free to rescind. Death or incapacity of T will also end P's power to ratify . . . . [201]

—Change of circumstances: Majority: If ratification occurs **after** a material change in circumstances such that inequity to T would result, T may avoid contract. **Minority:** Ratification merely substitutes P as party to contract, and rights and liabilities should be decided on basis of original contract. . . . . [202-205]

D. LIABILITY ON AGENT'S CONTRACTS

Where Agent Acted Without Authority: Where A purported to act on behalf of a P, but in fact acted without (or in excess of) authority, P cannot be held liable (unless P ratifies) and **A alone** is liable. *Rationale:* A's liability is based upon breach of **implied warranty of authority**. However, T must **rely** upon A's warranty. Under warranty theory, A is liable even if he thought he had authority. If A intentionally misrepresents, he is also liable in tort for **deceit**. . . . . [206-210]

—Disclaimer usually prevents implied warranty of authority from arising. . . . . [211]

—Enforcement of contract: Absent ratification by P, only A may enforce unauthorized contract against T. But if T **relied** on fact he was dealing with P, is estopped to enforce contract [214-215]

—Where third party has performed: T may be able to sue P in quasi-contract for value of benefits conferred . . . . [216]

Where Agent's Acts Were Authorized: Where A acted within scope of authority, P alone is generally party to contract with T and bound thereby . . . . [217]

—Contract in name of principal: Where A negotiates in name of P ("disclosed principal" case), A is **not** party to contract, and A may neither enforce it or suffer liability thereunder. A need not specifically state he is acting for P if T knew (or should have known) that A was doing so . . . . [218-219]

—Where names of both P and A appear liability depends upon interpretation of contract. If nothing indicates agency relationship, P and A are **both** liable. If it is clear A signed in representative capacity, only P is liable. **Extrinsic evidence** is only admissible where there is an **ambiguity**, and is **never** admissible where contract is **negotiable instrument** held by HDC . . . . [220-224]

—Undisclosed principal: If A's signature alone appears on contract (and no statement indicating agency), A is generally liable to T on contract, as T relied on A's credit and reputation. A may have right against undisclosed P under indemnification or quasi-contract theory. . . . . [225-229]

—*Liability of P to T:* If A had **actual authority, P may also be held liable once P's identity is made known. Modern view allows admission of parol evidence to explain capacity in which A signed (except for negotiable instruments) . [230-235]

—*Election by third person:* Although T normally has a right to recover against either undisclosed P or A, he can obtain satisfaction from only one of them. **Minority: T's filing suit against P or A constitutes an election which releases other party. **Majority:** T can file against **both** P and A, and if either defendant objects T must elect **prior to judgment**. However, if T obtains judgment against A without knowledge of P's identity, he can later sue P when his identity is disclosed. Many courts also hold that T may levy upon A's right of

idemnification against undisclosed P. . [236-241]
—*Enforcement of contract against third person:* Since P is entitled to all benefits of contract (as if assignee of A's rights), only he is entitled to enforce it against T. However, T has a right to rescind where A fraudulently represented that he was contracting for himself (or someone other than P) or where enforcement by P would impose an added or different burden on T. Where A has **power coupled with an interest**, he (rather than P) is entitled to recover from T. . . . . [242-247]
—*Tender of performance by principal* may be refused by T, and he may insist upon A's personal performance where A's duties are non-delegable (*e.g.,* credit and personal service contracts). . . . . [248-250]
—*Payment to agent* by P does not relieve him of liability to T in most jurisdictions. But payment to A by T relieves T of liability, so long as T does not know that A was acting as agent of P   [251-255]
—**Partial disclosure:** Where T has notice that A is acting as an agent, but does not know identity of P, the courts generally apply the same rules as in undisclosed principal cases. Parol evidence is generally admissible to establish that the parties intended A **not** to be bound. And if T knows the identity of P (even if P's name is not on the contract), P is considered "disclosed," and A is not a party to the contract. . . . . [256-263]

IV. TORT LIABILITY FOR THE ACTS OF OTHERS

A. LIABILITY OF MASTER FOR ACTS OF SERVANT

Respondeat Superior: A master is liable for all torts committed by his servants while they are acting within the scope of the employment. Thus, injured third parties may sue **both** employer and employee (joint and several liability). However, victim is entitled to only **one recovery,** and a recovery against either party generally bars recovery against the other. Since strict liability is imposed on master (M) to protect third persons, employer may **not** contract with employee to insulate himself from liability, but he usually has a right of indemnification against the servant (S). For respondeat superior to apply there must be (1) a master-servant relationship and (2) S' wrongful act must be committed within the course and scope of his employment. [264-278]
Master-Servant Relationship: M's vicarious liability is based upon his right to control acts of his servants. Since P ordinarily does **not** have right to control physical acts of A (likewise, employer and independent contractor), respondeat superior does not apply to these non-master-servant relationships (although liability may be based on other grounds). . . . . [279-283]

—**Creation of relationship:** Master-servant relationship can exist only if there is an agreement manifesting assent by both parties. Formalities are not required, except where Statute of Frauds applies (employment for period in excess of one year), and agreement may be **implied** from conduct of the parties. If M knows gratuitous services are being rendered and accepts benefits thereof, a master-servant relationship may be implied . . . . [284-289]
—*Duration of employment:* S is presumed hired for length of time adopted for computing wages (hourly, weekly, etc.). If no time period specified, employment presumed terminable at will . [290]
—*Right of M to recover for injuries to S* is rejected by modern cases, (*Exception:* Third person who **intentionally** injures S is liable to M for loss of S' services, as interference with **contract** relationship is tort). . . . . . [291-293]
—**Employment by estoppel:** Where a person ("employer") creates the appearance that another is in his employ, **and** the injured party justifiably relies upon such appearance, **an ostensible employment** is created and "employer" is estopped to deny liability. Note, however, that appearance of employment must be created by **purported master** (not purported servant) **and** injury must be sustained in **reliance** on that employment. [294-297]
—**Sub-servants:** Master-servant relationship may be created by **authorized** agent hiring on behalf of the master. If A hires on behalf of undisclosed P, A will be liable to S on the contract, but P will be held liable for S' torts. Employment of sub-servants in emergency situations, and even certain unauthorized hirings, may subject master to tort liability . . . . [298-303]
—**"Borrowed servants":** Where general employer (M) lends services of her employee to special employer (T) question arises as to whether M or T is responsible for employee's torts. Liability usually depends upon who had right to **control** employee. Lessor who rents equipment with an operator is presumed to **retain** control, but if borrowing is for indefinite period, or where T directs S to perform a specific act (and S acts tortiously), lessee (T) is liable. Where there is **division of control,** both M and T may be liable. . . . . [304-306]
—**Independent contractors** are not servants, thus their torts are usually not imputed to their employers. Test is whether employer has right to control party's conduct or has merely bargained for **result**. Test is sometimes difficult to apply in practice, but building contractors, equipment-owning truck drivers, new vendors and collection agencies are generally held to be independent contractors . . . . [307-312, 319-320]

—*Physicians* engaged by employers to treat third persons (*e.g.*, company doctors, resident physicians in hospitals) are usually considered independent contractors (based on high skill required to practice medicine). However, some states do impose liability on their employers (most often in hospital-resident relationship). Many courts hold employer liable where physician's services are **primarily for benefit of employer** (rather than treatment of third person) or where employer authorizes physician to make representations on her behalf. Even under majority rule, employer is liable if she negligently selected physician . . . . [313-318]

—**In exceptional situations, employer is liable for torts of independent contractor** based on her own negligence or for public policy reasons (**not** respondeat superior). Among these situations are those where contractor is to perform highly dangerous acts (*e.g.*, blasting), or duties which are not delegable by employer, or is authorized to make representations on employer's behalf. Employers are also liable if they select independent contractors negligently . . . . [321-326]

Scope of Employment: For respondeat superior to apply, servant must have committed tortious act **within the course and scope of his employment.** Restatement (Second) sets forth general criteria for determination of whether act was within scope of employment, based upon authorization, custom, employer's benefit, etc. [327-328]

—**Authorization by master:** It is **not** necessary to establish that M specifically authorized a specific act as long as it occurred in scope of employee's regular duties and employment. Even acts **specifically forbidden** by M may render him liable unless S goes beyond the duties for which she is hired . . . . [329-333]

—**Intentional torts by servant** may be imputed to M if "related to carrying forth master's business." However, M is not liable if intentional tort was motivated by S' personal reasons. M may not be found **criminally** liable for S' acts, except as to minor regulatory laws or where M is a corporation. In a few areas (*e.g.*, common carriers, defamation), M may be liable for acts of S outside the scope of employment. Liability is based on M's independent, overriding duty to injured person (not respondeat superior)[334-340]

—**Omissions** by S which constitute torts are treated the same as affirmative acts . . . . [341]

—**Smoking** on the job and like activities were once considered for personal pleasure of S and outside scope of employment, but modern trend is to consider such acts necessary for S' comfort and convenience on job (within scope of employment). In any case, M must always exercise at least reasonable care to prevent S from smoking where M is aware risk is created thereby . . . . [342-344]

—**Use of employer's vehicle** by S **outside** scope of employment will **not** render M liable under respondeat superior, but M might be liable under state permissive use statute re automobiles . . . . [345-346]

—**Unauthorized instrumentalities:** Where S uses some vehicle, machine, etc. in performing M's business which is unauthorized by M, M will not be liable if instrumentality used is **substantially different** from that authorized. Test is usually whether **greater risk** is involved. . . . . [347]

—**Servant going to and from work** is ordinarily **outside** scope of employment, unless S' activity **also** involves some service for M ("special errand rule") or S is a traveling salesperson [348-350]

—**Acts of servants on own behalf** must be **substantial deviation** or departure to free M from liability. If **main purpose** of substantial part of activity was on M's behalf, M remains liable. . . . . [351-354]

—**Unauthorized guests of servant** may not recover from M under majority view. Minority view is that M is liable to trespasser or unauthorized invitee as long as S' negligence occurred within the scope of employment. Other courts hold M liable if S' conduct was "wanton and wilful" . . . . [355-358]

Fellow Servant Rule is important exception to respondeat superior. M is not responsible for injuries inflicted by one servant upon a fellow servant while engaged in the same general enterprise. Fellow servant is any other employee who serves and is controlled by the same master **and** is engaged in the "same general enterprise." However, if employer was **negligent** in hiring injury-causing servant, or victim was injured by **superior servant** acting within his authority, rule does not apply . . . . [359-364]

—**Workers' Compensation Acts** have generally eliminated the need for the rule as they bar employees from suing employer and provide fixed compensation to injured workers. However, not all workers are covered by these acts. In Workers' Compensation cases, courts are more likely to find that S acted "in the scope of employment" or as an "employee" rather than an independent contractor . . . . [365-367]

Liability of Principal for Personal Breach of Duty: Aside from respondeat superior, employer is liable for torts of her employee when employer was directly responsible therefor. If employer directs, authorizes or permits employee to perform tortious act, employer will be liable as if she had committed tort herself. The agent or employee who committed the tort is **also** personally liable. (*Exception:* Fraud or duress by

employer) . . . . [368-371]
—Employer's ratification of tortious conduct: If employer (or principal) **ratifies** the conduct of someone not in her employ or of an employee acting outside scope of employment, she becomes liable for such acts **as if they had been authorized** by her. Only acts which could have been authorized originally can be ratified. It is also essential that employee or agent **intended** to act on behalf of employer. Ratification occurs when employer **accepts or retains benefits** obtained through the wrongful act **with knowledge of all relevant facts** surrounding the tortious conduct. . . . . [372-379]
—Independent duty owed to injured party: Employer may be held independently liable for breach of duty of due care in **hiring** the person who caused injury. She is also liable where she has independent duty to injured person (*e.g.,* duty of common carrier to passengers). Since an employer is imputed to have knowledge of all facts employee discovers **within the scope of employment,** notice of a dangerous condition may be so imputed. . . . . [380-384]

B. TORT LIABILITY OF PRINCIPAL FOR REPRESENTATIONS BY AGENT

General Rule: Employer or principal is subject to tort liability for any loss sustained by third persons as a result of misrepresentations made by one in her employ, wherever making of such representations was **expressly or impliedly authorized.** Authority to make misrepresentations is most frequently found when dealing with agents, but servant or independent contractor may also have such authority. . . . . [385-389]
—Remedies: Defrauded person may sue for damages or to rescind contract. . . . . [390]
Authority to Make Representations may be express or implied from circumstances. Where P authorizes another to deal on her behalf in transactions where representations are customary, that person is deemed impliedly authorized to make them. **Attorneys** are generally regarded as agents of clients. **Broker** employed to obtain sale of property who makes misrepresentations subjects P to actions for fraud or rescission. Exculpatory clauses generally held to free P from damage suits, but she is still subject to rescission . . . . [391-399]
—Agent placed in position to deceive: Where third person relies upon A's apparent authority arising from his position (*e.g.,* bank manager), P may be held liable even though she receives no benefits from transaction . . . . [400]
Innocent Misrepresentations by Agent: If A misrepresents with no intent to deceive, P is generally not liable for tort damages. *Exceptions:* Where P knows A lacks knowledge of facts but put A in a position to innocently misrepresent or where A acts negligently. T may rescind contract on ground of mistake. . . . . [401-405]

PARTNERSHIP

Partnership is similar to agency in many respects—*e.g.,* partner is agent of co-partner for certain purposes. Common law has been superseded in most jurisdictions by Uniform Partnership Act (UPA) . . . . [406]

I. IN GENERAL

A. BASIC NATURE OF PARTNERSHIP

Partnership is "association of two or more persons to carry on as co-owners a business for profit." Key elements are **community of interest** and **sharing of profits** . . . . [407]
Distinguished From Other Relationships: Partnership differs from **agency** in that partners are co-owners; from **other unincorporated associations** in that such associations were not considered as partnerships prior to UPA (or may be nonprofit); from **joint ventures** in that such ventures are usually more limited in scope and duration. . . . . [408-410]

B. ENTITY VS. AGGREGATE CHARACTERISTICS OF PARTNERSHIP

Aggregate Theory that partnership is not entity (but aggregate of individuals) is followed at common law, by federal tax law, and by some parts of UPA (*e.g.,* joint and several liability) . . . . [411-414]
Entity Characteristics: For some purposes, UPA and other statutes treat partnership as entity apart from its several members. Partnership is treated as entity for purpose of conveyancing, bankruptcy and "federal question" jurisdiction, but state laws vary on whether it can sue or be sued as entity . . . . [415-419]

C. PROPERTY RIGHTS OF PARTNER VS. PARTNERSHIP

What Constitutes Partnership Property: Under UPA, "all property originally brought into the partnership stock or subsequently acquired . . . **on account of the partnership,** is partnership property." Chief criterion is whether partners **intended** to devote property to partnership purposes . . . . [420-422]
—Evidence of Intention: Where no clear expression of partners' intent, courts must look to circumstances surrounding ownership. Substan-

tial weight is given to purchase with partnership funds, status in partnership books and association of asset with partnership business, but title, use of property and improvements made by firm are also considered. . . . . [423-430]

—**Real property** may be acquired and held in partnership name (common law did not allow this). Many states require filing of **statement of partnership,** listing members of partnership, in order to facilitate conveyancing. Listed partner may validly convey to bona fide purchaser . [431]

Rights of Partner are (1) rights in specific partnership property, (2) interest in partnership, and (3) right to participate in management. . . [432]

—**Rights in specific property:** Partner is **tenant in partnership** with co-partners as to each partnership asset. Each partner has equal right to possession for partnership purposes which is not assignable (without that of other partners), nor is it subject to attachment (except on claim against partnership) or marital rights. Upon partner's death, her right vests in surviving partners . . . . [433-434]

—**Interest in partnership** is partner's share of profits and surplus; it is **personal** property. It is assignable, but assignee only receives profits and capital to which assignor was entitled, he does **not** become partner. Creditors may obtain **charging order** against partner's interest, and such interest **is** subject to family rights . . [435-441]

II. FORMATION OF PARTNERSHIP

A. PARTNERSHIP BY CONTRACT

Partnership is generally based upon agreement of partners (*i.e.,* a contract). Written agreement is **not** required unless there is agreement that partnership must continue for more than one year. Some states require a writing if partnership deals with **third persons** in real estate or other contracts under Statute of Frauds . . . [442-443]

Duration: Where no time is fixed it is "partnership at will." "Partnership for term" requires partners to continue relationship for given period of time or until specified project completed. [444-445]

Capacity to become partner is based upon capacity to contract. Partnership contract including **minor(s)** is voidable. Prevailing view is that **corporation** may not become partner. [446-448]

Consent of All Co-Partners required for membership. . . . . [449]

Rules for Determining Existence of Partnerships: Sharing of profits of business is prima facie evidence of partnership, but exceptions in UPA make this so only when no other business reason exists for the sharing. Other factors (*e.g.,* joint ownership of property, contribution of capital, sharing of gross income and parties' designation)

will be taken into account by courts, but **do not** conclusively establish there is partnership. . . . . [450-455]

B. PARTNERSHIP BY ESTOPPEL

A true partnership relationship depends upon a contract, but parties who are **not** partners may sometimes be bound as if they were in their dealings with third parties. Under no circumstances does this make them partners in fact. . . . . [456]

Liability of Alleged Partner: A person who holds himself out to be a partner in an actual or apparent partnership or who consents to representations that he is such a partner, is liable to third person who extends credit in good faith reliance on such representation . . . . [457-458]

Liability of Partners Who Represent Third Person to be a Partner: Where an actual partner represents that nonpartner is member of partnership, he constitutes the nonpartner as his agent with power to bind him as though nonpartner were in fact a partner. But resultant liability binds only partners who made or consented to the representation . . . . [459]

III. EFFECT OF THE PARTNERSHIP RELATION

A. RELATIONS BETWEEN PARTNERS

Fiduciary Duty: As between themselves, partners are fiduciaries and owe each other same duties as trustee owes beneficiary. Thus partners must account for profits, refrain from engaging in competitive business without consent, and hold partnership assets in own name as trustee for partnership . . . . [460-464]

Other Rights and Duties when not governed by partnership agreement are imposed by law. [465]

—**Management:** UPA provides partners have equal right to management. Ordinary matters require majority vote, but any action in contravention of partnership agreement must be approved unanimously. One partner may be granted greater share of responsibilities, but he has duty to deal fairly on behalf of all partners. . . . . [466-469]

—**Books and records** must be made accessible to all partners. . . . . [470]

—**Profits** are divided as per agreement (with losses in like proportion). In absence of agreement they are to share equally . . . . [471]

—**Distributions from partnership:** Partner is entitled to repayment of capital advances and for reimbursement of expenses where made on behalf of partnership. No partner is entitled to remuneration for his services absent consent of all partners. Under UPA no partner has greater

right to share of profits absent agreement (non-UPA states may be contra)....... [472-473]
Actions Between Partners: Partner may sue co-partners for dissolution and for an accounting, but may **not** sue for damages (a few limited exceptions) .... [475-478]

B. RELATIONS AS TO THIRD PERSONS

Authority of Partner to Bind Partnership: Every partner is **agent** of partnership for purposes of its business, and each partner may execute instruments and other transactions which will bind partnership providing person with whom partner dealing had no notice that partner lacked authority. Rules of agency apply in determining whether partnership is bound by partner's dealings with third parties.................... [479-481]
—**Limitations on authority** under UPA prevent partner (without agreement) from assigning partnership property for benefit of creditors, disposing of partnership good will, confessing partnership liability, submitting partnership claim to arbitration, or doing other act which would make it impossible to carry on business...... [482]
—**Termination of authority:** Single partner generally cannot terminate authority of co-partners short of dissolution, as majority rules on matters of ordinary partnership business. Rules of agency apply re admissions or representations by partner and imputed notice to other partners. [483-489]
—**Real property** may be conveyed by any partner in **ordinary course of partnership business.** Conveyances outside ordinary course of business require showing of authority to convey. Writing is generally **not** required to show authority, but some jurisdictions are contra. "Statement of partnership" protects innocent purchaser against claim of lack of authority .... [490-493]
Liability to Creditors
—**Liability on contracts:** Partners are jointly (but not severally) liable on partnership debts and contracts. Creditors may not proceed against any single partner, but "silent partners" and new partners are subject to liability with all other partners...................... [494-498]
—**Liability in tort** is joint **and** several. Thus, partners may be sued individually, and judgment against one is generally not res judicata regarding others. Liability for torts of co-partners is analogous to rules of agency, but partner may be liable to co-partner for torts inflicted by her on co-partner (no fellow servant rule). In case of intentional torts it must be shown **each** partner sued had wrongful intent............. [499]
Third Person's Liability: Partnership generally has no right to recover from third party for injuries inflicted on member of partnership (*i.e.,* partner is not "servant" of partnership)........ [500-501]

IV. DISSOLUTION AND WINDING UP OF PARTNERSHIP

A. IN GENERAL
Dissolution of partnership is the change in relation of partners caused by any partner ceasing to be associated in the carrying on, as distinguished from the winding up, of the business. Dissolution does not terminate partnership immediately. Partnership relationship **continues** until winding up............................ [502]

B. CAUSES OF DISSOLUTION
Unless otherwise provided by agreement of partners, dissolution of partnership will be caused by expiration of partnership term, expulsion of partner, withdrawal or admission of partner, occurrence of event making it unlawful for partnership to continue in business and death or bankruptcy of partner .... [503-504, 513-516]
Express Choice of Partner: Any or all partners can effect a dissolution merely by expressing their will to do so. In case of partnership at will, this does not violate partnership agreement if done in good faith. However, where partner demands dissolution of **partnership for fixed term** prior to expiration of term, he may be liable for losses caused by dissolution .... [505-512]
Decree of Court: UPA provides court "shall decree" dissolution in case of insanity, permanent incapacity, or improper conduct of partner, where business can only be carried on at a loss, or in other circumstances "rendering a dissolution equitable." Suit for dissolution is equitable in nature and usually includes action for an accounting. Court usually orders partnership assets sold and proceeds applied to partnership debts. Balance is used (1) to repay each partner's capital account and (2) to pay current earnings in accordance with each partner's share of profits...................... [517-526]

C. RIGHTS OF PARTNERS IN DISSOLUTION

Where Dissolution Does Not Violate Partnership Agreement, no partner has claim or cause of action against other partners for loss sustained in dissolution......................... [527]
Where Dissolution Violates Partnership Agreement, "innocent partners" may have right to damages, to purchase business, or to wind up partnership affairs .... [528-531]
Rights and Duties of Surviving Partners: Upon death of a partner, surviving partners are entitled to possession of partnership assets and are charged with winding up of partnership affairs. Surviving partner acts as fiduciary in liquidating partnership and must account to estate of de-

ceased partner for value of decedent's interest
. . . . [532]

D. EFFECTS OF DISSOLUTION
Dissolution in no way affects each partner's liability for partnership debts; joint liability remains until debts discharged or there is a novation. Where, after a dissolution, there is change in composition of partnership (*e.g.,* death of partner, admission of new member) and business continues, new partnership remains liable for debts of previous partnership. *Retired partner* usually has no liability for debts incurred after dissolution. [533-539]

V. LIMITED PARTNERSHIPS

A. IN GENERAL
Limited partnership is partnership having at least one general partner and at least one limited partner. *General partner* has management responsibilities and full liability for partnership debts. *Limited partner* makes contribution of cash or other property but is not active in management, and his liability is limited to amount of his contribution. Limited partnership may carry on same kinds of business as ordinary partnership . . . . [540-555]

B. FORMATION
Formalities are required for formation of limited partnership. Partners must execute a certificate setting forth name of partnership, character of business, location of principal office, names, addresses, and capital contributions of partners and whether such partners are "general" or "limited". Certificate must be filed with appropriate state or local officials. Similar formalities are required when certificate is amended. . . . [556]

C. DISSOLUTION
Limited partnership may be dissolved in the same ways as regular partnership. However, death of *limited* partner does not dissolve partnership, and decedent's administrator is given rights of limited partner for purposes of settling estate. . . [557]

TEXT CORRELATION CHART

Gilbert Law Summary Agency & Partnership	Conrad, Knauss, Siegel Agency, Associations, Employment, Licensing Partnerships 1977 (2nd ed.)	Henn Agency, Partnership and Other Unincorporated Business Enterprises 1972	Hynes Agency and Partnership 1974	Seavey, Reuschlein, Hall Cases on Agency and Partnership 1962	Steffen, Kerr Cases and Materials on Agency—Partnership 1980 (4th ed.)
AGENCY **I. RIGHTS AND LIABILITIES BETWEEN PRINCIPAL AND AGENT**					
A. Agent's Duties to Principal	456-482	77-96	293-314	109-136	
B. Principal's Duties to Agent	456-482	97-103	293-314		
II. CONTRACTUAL RIGHTS AND LIABILITIES BETWEEN PRINCIPAL (OR AGENT) AND THIRD PERSONS	282-312	104-120	139-154	167-199, 289-314	
A. Creation of Agency Relationship	256-281	19-22		56-132	
B. Authority of Agent	282-358	27-37	167-244	133-136	427-438, 446-448
C. Ratification	338-358, 405-433	38-44	273-292	315-361	522-530
D. Liabilities on Agent's Contracts		109-119	154-163	200-289	55-80
III. TORT LIABILITY FOR ACTS OF OTHERS	91-103, 151-184		35-100		144-164
A. Liability of Master for Acts of Servant		105-106	101-136	53-56	211-235, 251-266
B. Liability of Principal for Representations by Agents		120-121, 132-141		29-53	
PARTNERSHIP **I. IN GENERAL**			315-383		605-621
A. Entity vs. Aggregate Characteristics of Partnership		183-185, 202-207			
B. Property Rights of Partner vs. Partnership	522-558	211-214		412-459	621-642
II. FORMATION OF PARTNERSHIP A. Partnership by Contract		296			755-772
B. Partnership by Estoppel	336	207-208	330-337		432, 441-442
III. EFFECT OF PARTNERSHIP RELATION					
A. Relations Between Partners	456-482			488-497	711-712
B. Relations as to Third Persons	588-602		383-402	465-484	
IV. DISSOLUTION AND WINDING UP OF PARTNERSHIP	558-588	214-235	426-434	362-410	773-792
A. Causes of Dissolution	559	215	403-413	362-410	
B. Rights of Partners in Dissolution			414-426		30
C. Effects of Dissolution		224			
V. LIMITED PARTNERSHIPS			345-356	533, 574-575	643-678
A. Formation	72-76	247-249, 265-270			
B. Dissolution		258-260, 263-264, 267-269			

APPROACH

AGENCY

Agency problems concern the liability of one person (the purported principal or master) for the acts of another (the purported agent or servant) allegedly done on his or her behalf. Generally, the issue is liability to a third party; but rights and liabilities between principal and agent may also be involved.

When analyzing agency problems, the following approach may be helpful:

1. **Are there problems between the principal and agent?** Determine first that an agency relationship in fact exists. If so, consider:

   a. Has the *agent breached* any duty owed to the principal—*e.g.,* improper performance, breach of fiduciary duty, breach by subagent?

   b. Is the principal entitled to any *property or benefits* acquired by the agent during the relationship (patents, inventions, etc.)?

   c. Can the principal obtain *indemnification* from the agent where he is liable to a third party (below)?

   d. Has the *principal breached* any duty owed the agent—*e.g.,* compensation, cooperation, etc.?

2. **Is the principal (and/or agent) contractually liable to a third party**, based on the agent's conduct? This is the most frequent type of agency problem, and requires analysis of several factors:

   a. *Is* there an agency relationship—*i.e.,* an agency by agreement, ratification or estoppel?

   b. If so, what is the *nature or source* of the agent's *authority*?

      (1) If actual authority (express or implied), does it have to be in writing ("equal dignity" rule)?

      (2) If no actual authority, is there apparent or ostensible authority?

   c. What is the *scope of authority* (remembering that an agent's powers are strictly construed)?

      (1) Can the conduct be justified as an exercise of incidental or inherent powers?

      (2) Has the authority been terminated—*e.g.,* by expiration of term, death, etc.? If so, has it been properly communicated?

   d. Even if the agent had no original authority to act, has there been a subsequent *ratification* of his acts? Consider whether the conduct is capable of ratification, and whether the ratification is effective to establish liability (*i.e.,* "relation back" theory, partial ratification, etc.).

   e. What is the *nature of liability* on the contract?

      (1) If the agent acted without authority (so the agent alone is ordinarily liable), can a third party recover against the principal in quasi-contract?

(2) If the agent was authorized, was the principal named in the contract?

    (a) If "disclosed" principal, are **both** agent and principal liable?

    (b) If "undisclosed" principal, are both liable? Can the principal enforce the contract against a third party? Can a third party insist on personal performance by the agent?

    (c) If "partially disclosed" principal, is the agent personally liable on the contract?

3. **Is there an issue of tort liability to a third party** because of the acts of another? Distinguish tortious conduct generally (where master-servant relation usually required to impose liability) from misrepresentations (usually made by agent, rather than servant).

    a. For tortious conduct other than misrepresentations, consider:

        (1) Is there a master-servant relationship between the actor and the employer—*i.e., right to control* physical acts of the employee? Also note possible liability for acts of sub-servants or "borrowed servants"; and possible liability where *no* right to control (*i.e.,* highly dangerous acts).

        (2) Was tortious act within the *course and scope of the servant's employment?* Consider the various relevant factors—*e.g.,* authorization by master, motivation (including "mixed motive" acts), "fellow servant" rule, liability *apart from* respondeat superior (common carriers, independent duty to third party, etc.).

    b. For misrepresentations by an agent, consider:

        (1) Was the misrepresentation tortious—*i.e.,* are the requisite elements of scienter, reliance, etc., present?

        (2) If so, was the agent authorized to make such representations—either expressly or impliedly (*i.e.,* "incidental misrepresenations")?

PARTNERSHIP

Partnership problems may involve the effect of the partnership relation itself, or the effect of dissolution of the partnership.

1. **If the effect of the partnership relation is an issue,** consider:

    a. *Is* there a partnership—*i.e.,* an "association to carry on a business for profit, as co-owners"? Note whether the partnership agreement must be in writing, whether all purported partners have the capacity to be partners, and whether there are sufficient indicia of partnership status (*i.e.,* joint ownership of property, sharing of profits, etc.).

        (1) If there is no partnership by agreement, is there one by estoppel?

    b. If a partnership exists, are any of its *general characteristics* relevant to the facts at hand?

        (1) Aggregate characteristics—joint and several liability, taxing of income?

        (2) Entity characteristics—capacity to sue or be sued, conveyance of property, bankruptcy?

        (3) Property rights of partner (as opposed to partnership): Is the property in question that of the partnership? If so, what are partners' rights therein?

c. Is there an issue concerning relations *between the partners*? Consider:

    (1) Has there been a breach of duty (*i.e.,* fiduciary obligations, management and inspection rights, etc.) by any partner?

    (2) If so, what remedies are available to the injured partner(s)—dissolution? Accounting? Action at law?

d. Is there an issue regarding *liability to third persons* (creditors)? Recall that partners function as agents for the partnership and consider:

    (1) Did the partner(s) have *authority* to bind the partnership (*i.e.,* any limitations on, or termination of, authority)?

    (2) Is contract liability involved, so partners are jointly but not severally liable?

    (3) Is tort liability at issue, so partners are jointly *and* severally liable?

2. **If the effect of a dissolution of partnership is an issue,** consider:

a. Is a *cause* for dissolution shown—*i.e.,* expiration of term, withdrawal or admission of partner, choice of partner (at any time), etc.? If there is an attempted judicial dissolution, are proper grounds shown?

b. If the partnership is dissolved, what are the partners' rights? Distinguish rights where no violation of partnership agreement from rights where agreement is violated. If relevant, what are rights and obligations of surviving partner(s) *re* deceased partner's estate?

c. If there is a dissolution, what is the effect on creditors of the partnership? Note liability for existing debts (not discharged without novation), and liability of partners who continue the business.

AGENCY

I. INTRODUCTION [§1]

The law of Agency concerns the rights and liabilities created as to one individual by the acts of another. This encompasses several distinct areas: the contractual rights and liabilities to third persons of parties who have dealt by or through agents; the circumstances in which one person may be liable in tort for the wrongful acts of another in his or her employ; and the various contract and tort duties which the parties to any agency relationship owe to each other.

A. DEFINITIONS

1. **"Master-Servant" Relationship:** [§2]   A *servant* is one who is employed to render services of any type, other than in the pursuit of an independent calling, and who remains under the control of another (the *master*) in performing such services.

   a. **Must have right to control:** [§3]   The essential feature of the master-servant relationship is that at all times the master *controls or has the right to control* the physical conduct of the servant in the performance of his duties of employment. The servant is entirely under the control of the master, and has no independent discretion. [Restatement (Second) of Agency ("Rest. 2d") §2]

   b. **"Employer-employee":** [§4]   The term "servant," as used above, embraces all persons of whatever rank or position, and is therefore synonymous with an "employee" (the two terms being used interchangeably herein). [Darmour Productions Corp. v. H.M. Baruch Corp., 135 Cal. App. 351 (1933)—motion picture actress is a "servant" of her employer]

2. **"Principal-Agent" Relationship:** [§5]   While a servant merely works for his master, an "agent" acts *for and in place of the principal* to effect legal relations with third persons; *i.e.,* an agent is one who may bind her principal in contracts with third persons.

   a. **The agent has authority to perform "legal acts"**—*i.e.,* to represent her principal in contractual or other dealings with third persons which affect the principal's legal rights and obligations. [Rest. 2d §10]

   b. **The distinguishing features** of an agency relationship are its *representative character and derivative authority,* which give the agent a degree of discretion in carrying out the purposes of her principal which a servant would not have. [Wallace v. Sinclair, 114 Cal. App. 2d 220 (1952)]

   c. **An agent for a particular act or transaction** is called a "special agent." All others are "general agents." [Rest. 2d §3]

   d. **The same person may act as both agent and servant,** depending upon the duties and powers assigned to her; *e.g.,* a store manager may function as the servant of the store owner with respect to her duties to keep records, supervise others, etc., but she may also be the owner's agent for purposes of hiring personnel, purchasing goods, etc.

3. **Independent Contractor:** [§6]   An independent contractor is one who renders services in the course of an independent occupation or calling. He contracts with his employer only as to the *results* to be accomplished, not as to the means whereby the work is to be done.

   a. **No right of control:** [§7]   The primary characteristic of an independent contractor is that the employer has *no right of control* over how the work contracted for is performed. [Rest. 2d §2]

b. **Significance:** [§8]   The main reason for distinguishing between an agent or servant and an independent contractor is that the doctrine of *respondeat superior* (*infra*, §264), upon which the tort liability of employers for employee conduct is usually based, does *not* apply to independent contractors.

   (1) There are a few exceptional situations where the employer will be liable for the torts of an independent contractor (*infra*, §§321-326), but these are not based on the theory of respondeat superior.

   (2) The distinction between an ''employee'' and ''independent contractor'' is also important in determining rights to benefits under unemployment insurance laws, workers' compensation laws, etc. [*See* MFA Mutual Insurance Co. v. United States, 314 F. Supp. 500 (W.D. Mo. 1970)]

c. **Dual function:** [§9]   In certain cases, the same person may function as *both* servant and independent contractor for the same employer, and his status therefore will depend upon his activity at the particular time in question. *Example:* M hires X as a distributor of M's goods, and also requires that X help unload all shipments as they arrive. X would be an independent contractor while acting as distributor, but a servant of M when unloading shipments. [Clough v. Estate of Malley, 11 A.2d 398 (Conn. 1940)]

II. RIGHTS AND LIABILITIES BETWEEN PRINCIPAL AND AGENT

A. NATURE OF RELATIONSHIP [§10]

The principal-agent relationship (and the master-servant relationship as well) is a contractual relationship which arises by consent and agreement between the parties. (*See* discussion *infra*, §§52-62.) The agreement need not be supported by consideration. The same rights and duties are involved in a gratuitous agency as in an agency for hire.

B. AGENT'S DUTY TO PRINCIPAL [§11]

The following duties arise by operation of law from the agency relationship and exist whether or not the principal is known or disclosed to any third party. [Rest. 2d §431]

1. **Duty to Perform:** [§12]   As an implied condition in every employment or agency contract, the employee or agent agrees to use reasonable care, diligence, and skill in his work. [Rest. 2d §379]

    a. **Effect of careless performance or nonperformance:** [§13]   Where the agent fails to perform all duties assigned to him, he is generally liable only for breach of agency contract. However, if he performs the assigned duties, but in a careless or imperfect manner, and thereby causes loss to his employer, he may be liable for negligence (tort) as well as for breach of contract. [Darman v. Zilch, 186 A. 21 (R.I. 1936)]

        (1) *Example:* An insurance agent who fails to obtain coverages ordered by the principal, and places orders for wrong insurance, is liable for negligence as well as breach of agency contract. [Colpe Investment Co. v. Seeley & Co., 132 Cal. App. 16 (1933)]

    b. **Duties of gratuitous agent:** [§14]   It makes no difference whether the employee or agent is paid for his services or renders them gratuitously; the same duty to perform and standard of care apply. However, a gratuitous agent cannot be held for breach of contract, and is subject only to tort liability. [Higgins Lumber Co. v. Rosamond, 63 So. 2d 408 (Miss. 1953)]

        (1) Thus a gratuitous agent cannot be compelled to perform. Only after the agent commences performance does he come under a duty of care in performing. [McPhetridge v. Smith, 101 Cal. App. 122 (1929)]

            (a) *Example:* If real estate broker A gratuitously offers to act as P's agent in the sale of Blackacre, P has no cause of action against A for failure to attempt to sell the property. But if A procured T as buyer but neglected to get a signed sales contract, and T later changes his mind and refuses to proceed, P might have a cause of action in tort (negligence) for T's failure to exercise the degree of care reasonably expected of a real estate broker.

        (2) There is some authority, however, that if the principal detrimentally relies on a gratuitous agent's promise to perform, he may recover damages sustained by the agent's refusal to perform. [Rest. 2d §378]

2. **Fiduciary Duty:** [§15]   In addition to his basic duty to perform the contract and render services with reasonable care, every agent is deemed a fiduciary—*i.e.*, he owes his principal the obligation of faithful service. An agent's obligation to his principal with respect to the subject matter of the agency is the same as that of a *trustee* to a trust.

    a. **Duty to notify:** [§16]   The fiduciary obligation requires an agent to notify his principal of all matters which come to his knowledge affecting the subject of the agency.

[Rest. 2d §381] The effect of this rule is that notice of all such matters coming to the attention of the agent is *imputed* to the principal. (*See* discussion *infra,* §§143-149.)

b. **Duty of loyalty:** [§17]   As a fiduciary, the agent or employee owes a duty to be loyal to his principal on all matters connected with the agency.

  (1) **Competing with employer:** [§18]   It follows that the agent is under a duty not to compete himself, or to act for persons who are in competition with his principal or employer, unless he has the consent of the principal. [Rest. 2d §394]

   (a) *Example: "Manufacturers' representatives"* (selling agents for manufacturers) frequently handle competing lines, but by employing an agent in this type of business, the manufacturer is deemed to have consented to this.

   (b) After termination of his employment, the agent *can compete* with the employer or accept employment from a competitor, unless he has agreed otherwise and the agreement is valid. [Karpinski v. Ingrassi, 28 N.Y.2d 45 (1971)]

   (c) On the other hand, a former agent cannot use or disclose *trade secrets or other confidential information* obtained during his employment. [General Aniline & Film Corp. v. Frantz, 50 Misc. 2d 994 (1966)]

    1) In this respect, *customer lists* may be protected trade secrets if substantial time and money of the employer were involved in compiling same. [Arnold's Ice Cream Co. v. Carlson, 330 F. Supp. 1185 (E.D.N.Y. 1971)—breach of fiduciary duty for present or former employees to use such lists in setting up a competing business]

  (2) **Limitation:** [§19]   Note, however, that the duty of loyalty does not obligate an agent to shield a dishonest principal. *Example:* A discovered that his principal, P, had been cheating a third person, T, on various contracts. A disclosed P's actions to T, who then obtained a judgment against P for damages. *Held:* A's duty of loyalty did not extend to concealing P's dishonest acts from persons affected by them. [Willig v. Gold, 75 Cal. App. 2d 809 (1946)]

c. **Conflicts of interest:** [§20]   The agent's fiduciary duty likewise dictates that he may not take a position adverse to that of his principal or employer without the latter's consent.

  (1) **Secret profits, advantages, benefits:** [§21]   Anything which an agent or employee obtains by virtue of his employment belongs to his principal or employer. Therefore, the retention of any benefit, advantage, or profit which he derives through or from his employment, without his employer's consent, is a breach of fiduciary duty. [Sears, Roebuck & Co. v. Kelly, 149 N.Y.S.2d 133 (1956)]

   (a) *Example:* P employs A to purchase certain goods for him on the open market. A places P's order with T, for which T agrees to give A a rebate under the table. Unless P knows and consents to this, acceptance of the rebate violates A's fiduciary duty to P and P may recover the secret profits obtained by A. [Kinert v. Wright, 81 Cal. App. 2d 919 (1947)]

  (2) **Personal purchase by purchasing agent:** [§22]   Similarly, an agent authorized to purchase certain property for his principal cannot purchase for himself without his principal's consent. If he does, the principal is entitled to whatever the agent obtained, on whatever terms the agent acquired it—the agent being deemed to hold the property as constructive trustee for his principal (*see* below).

(a) Even where the agent has not been given specific authority or instructions to purchase certain property, many decisions hold that he owes the principal the *right of first refusal* if he knows that the principal would be interested in purchasing this type of property—*i.e.,* the agent must inform his principal that such property is available, or offer it to the principal on the same terms on which he acquired it. [*See* 20 A.L.R.2d 1140]

(3) **Personal purchase by sales agent:** [§23]   An agent authorized to sell property on behalf of his principal cannot buy the property himself unless the principal consents. And this is true irrespective of the fairness of the transaction or the adequacy of the price—since the agent still might have obtained a better price from someone else. [Hall v. Paine, 112 N.E. 153 (Mass. 1916)]

   (a) Of course, the agent cannot avoid this rule by purchasing the property indirectly through a nominee or dummy.

   (b) Upon discovery of the agent's interest, the principal can rescind the sale and recover the property. If the property has been resold by the agent, the principal can hold the agent liable for its value and any profits realized by the agent thereupon.

   (c) *Exception:* The rule against self-purchase does not generally apply where the agent is authorized to sell property for a certain net price and to keep any excess as his commission. In this situation, no injury to the principal can result from a purchase by the agent. [Allen v. Dailey, 92 Cal. App. 308 (1928)]

(4) **Dual agency:** [§24]   An agent acting for more than one principal (*e.g.,* for both buyer and seller) in negotiations between them may well be representing conflicting interests and such situations clearly present the possibility of fraud. Hence, unless it clearly appears that *both* principals are fully informed of the dual representation and consent thereto, the transaction is voidable at the option of either principal and the agent cannot recover commissions from either—regardless of the fairness of the contract in the particular case. [48 A.L.R. 917]

   (a) *But note:* A broker employed to sell real estate does not become an agent of the buyer merely because he counsels the buyer on terms in procuring an offer. The broker is still the agent of the seller, and no dual agency exists.

   (b) Nor is there a dual agency where a broker represents the sellers of different properties in negotiations with a single purchaser. [Foley v. Mathias, 233 N.W. 106 (Iowa 1930)] *Rationale:* The sellers in this situation are not principals in the same transaction. If the law were otherwise, a broker could list only one property at a time.

(5) **Remedies:** [§25]   An agent's violation of his fiduciary duty is both a breach of the agency contract and a tort (fraud). [Rest. 2d §399] As a result, the principal P often has a choice of remedies:

   (a) The agent may be held accountable for all *damages* proximately caused to his employer or principal—*i.e.,* he may be required to disgorge any secret profits or advantages obtained.

      1) Where malice or bad faith is established, *punitive damages* may also be awarded against the agent. [Ward v. Taggart, 51 Cal. 2d 736 (1959)]

   (b) Regardless of whether the agent derived any personal gain therefrom, any transaction with the principal which violates the fiduciary duty is voidable by the principal; *e.g.,* upon discovering that A was buying or selling P's property for himself, P can *rescind* the sale if he chooses. [Slusher v. Buckley, 174 Cal. App. 2d 324 (1959)]

    (c) And where the agent has obtained property from third persons in violation of his fiduciary duty to purchase, hold, or obtain the same for P, equity may impose a *constructive trust* on the property (or, if it has been resold, upon the profits obtained thereby). (*See* Equity Summary.)

3. Duties Owed by Subagents

a. Authorized subagent: [§26]   Where the principal has authorized the agent to hire subagents, the subagent owes the same duties to the principal as the agent would have owed. In addition, the agent is responsible to the principal for any violation of duty by the subagent, even though the agent exercised good faith in selecting the subagent.

    (1) Likewise, the subagent owes the agent who hired her substantially the same duties; and she is liable to the agent for any loss sustained because of the subagent's improper performance. [Rest. 2d §428]

b. Unauthorized hiring of subagent: [§27]   Where the subagent is employed *without* authority from the principal, there is no agency relationship between the principal and subagent. The principal is not liable to third persons for acts of the unauthorized subagent (*infra,* §301); and, conversely, the unauthorized subagent owes no duties to the principal. The agent, of course, remains responsible to his principal for performance of the duties involved in his agency, and is liable for any loss sustained by the principal because of the subagent's conduct.

4. Rights and Benefits Acquired During Employment

a. General rule: [§28]   In general, everything acquired by an employee or agent by virtue of his employment (except for his compensation) belongs to his principal. All rights, property, or claims which the agent receives or obtains must be held for, and on behalf of, the principal, and the agent owes the principal a duty to account therefor. [Rest. 2d §388]

b. "Undisclosed principal" cases: [§29]   So far as the agent's duties to his principal are concerned, it is ordinarily immaterial whether the agent discloses the identity of his principal to the person with whom he is dealing—*i.e.,* all rights and claims acquired under a contract with a third person belong to the principal, even though undisclosed; and the principal is entitled to enforce the contract (*infra,* §242).

    (1) But there are exceptional situations in which the third person may refuse to proceed with the contract when the identity of the principal is discovered—*e.g.,* where the agent fraudulently concealed the principal's identity (*see infra,* §244).

c. Inventions and patents: [§30]   Where the employee is hired to develop inventions or patents, any and all rights to such developments belong to the employer absent an agreement to the contrary. Where developing such items is *not* a primary part of the employee's duties, any patent or invention is the property of the employee, rather than the employer. [Rest. 2d §397]

    (1) **"Shop right doctrine":** [§31]   Nonetheless, if the patent or invention was perfected on the employer's time (or using the employer's materials), and is related to the employer's business, the employer is deemed to have a "shop right" thereto—*i.e.,* the irrevocable right to use the idea or invention which does not terminate when the employment ends. [Aero Bolt & Screw Co. v. Iaia, 180 Cal. App. 2d 728 (1960)] (*See* further discussion in Equity Summary.)

5. **Principal's Right to Indemnification**

    a. **Tortious acts of employee:** [§32] An employer has a right to indemnification against an employee for any loss sustained on account of the employee's tortious acts. Thus, where the employer is held liable for damages to a third party for the negligent conduct of his employee, he can sue the employee for the amount of such damages (*infra,* §277).

    b. **Violation of principal's instructions:** [§33] Similarly, a principal has a cause of action against his agent for any loss sustained by the principal as a result of the agent's violation of his instructions. For example, P may be held liable for breach of warranty made by A, even though he specifically instructed A not to make warranties (*see infra,* §138). Under such circumstances, P has a cause of action against A for indemnification.

C. PRINCIPAL'S DUTIES TO AGENT

The following duties on the part of the principal are implied by law in every agency or employment contract, absent a provision to the contrary.

1. **Compensation and Reimbursement:** [§34] Unless it appears that the agent's services were intended to be gratuitous, a principal or employer must compensate the agent for the agreed value of those services (or, in the absence of a specific agreement, for the reasonable value thereof). The principal must also indemnify the agent for all expenditures or losses incurred by the agent in discharge of her authorized duties. [McKinnon & Mooney v. Fireman's Fund Indemnity Co., 288 F.2d 189 (6th Cir. 1961)—expenses of defending lawsuit based on acts performed for principal]

    a. **Sales agents:** [§35] The most frequent problems involving compensation of agents involve the time at which a salesperson is entitled to commissions. In the absence of an agreement on this point, a salesperson is entitled to recover when she makes the sale (offer accepted), even though it is not actually carried through or performed. Furthermore, a salesperson is entitled to the commission if her efforts are the effective or procuring cause of the sale, even though others were involved in completing the transaction. [12 A.L.R.2d 1360]

    b. **Subagents:** [§36] A principal is clearly not responsible for compensation to a subagent where no authority to hire subagents was given. And even if authority to hire is given, the principal is not liable unless authority was given to hire *additional* personnel. If the agent was merely allowed to delegate her authority to another—*i.e.,* to use subagents to perform her own duties—the subagent must look solely to the agent for compensation. [Goodwin v. Glick, 139 Cal. App. 2d 936 (1956)]

    c. **Statutes:** [§37] Many jurisdictions now regulate the time, place, and manner of paying wages to *employees*, as well as their hours and working conditions. [*See, e.g.,* Cal. Labor Code §§201 *et seq.*]

2. **Duty of Cooperation:** [§38] A principal or employer must assist and cooperate with the agent or employee in the performance of her duties, and do nothing to prevent such performance.

    a. **Example:** Where an agent is given an exclusive sales territory, and the principal thereafter invades the territory and makes sales, some courts have held that the agent may recover from the principal the profits she would have made on such sales. [Hacker Pipe & Supply Co. v. Chapman Valve Manufacturing Co., 61 P.2d 944 (Cal. 1936)]

b. **But note:** Other courts hold that while a principal cannot interfere with an exclusive agent by appointing another agent to compete, the principal *can* compete with the agent. [Stahlman v. National Lead Co., 318 F.2d 388 (5th Cir. 1963)]

3. **Negligence:** [§39]   The common law liability of an employer for personal injuries to his employees or agents while performing the duties assigned to them is largely superseded today by Workers' Compensation Acts in effect in most states. Only in cases specifically exempted under such acts (*e.g.,* certain domestic servants), or where an employer fails to maintain the required workers' compensation insurance, do common law liabilities still exist.

a. **Duty to furnish safe working conditions:** [§40]   The principal basis for common law liability is a breach of the employer's duty to furnish and maintain safe premises, equipment, and conditions for employees. This includes the duty to inspect the premises or equipment for defects, and to warn of any such defects. [Rest. 2d §492; *and see* Torts Summary]

4. **Remedies Available to Agent:** [§41]   Where there is a breach of the agency contract by the principal, the agent has most of the remedies available to a contracting party.

a. **Indemnification by principal:** [§42]   Unless the agreement specifically provides to the contrary, the agent may be entitled to indemnification for losses or damages sustained in performing for the principal.

(1) **Scope of indemnification:** [§43]   The scope of this right is often defined in the agreement. If not, the courts will indemnify the agent where it appears just to do so, considering the nature of the business, losses incurred, etc. [Bibb v. Allen, 149 U.S. 481 (1893)]

(2) **No right to indemnity for unauthorized or illegal acts:** [§44]   The agent is not entitled to indemnity for losses resulting from acts which are unauthorized and do not benefit her principal. [*In re* Lathrop, 216 F. 102 (2d Cir. 1914)] Nor is there a right to indemnity where the acts in question were known by the agent to be illegal (whether authorized or not), or were the result of her own negligence. [Veltum v. Koehler, 88 N.W. 432 (Minn. 1901)]

(3) **Recovery by subagents:** [§45]   If indemnification is otherwise proper, an authorized subagent can recover against *either* the principal or the agent—since he is a fiduciary of both. If he proceeds against the agent, the latter has a right of indemnity in turn against the principal. [Admiral Oriental Line v. Atlantic, Gulf & Oriental Steamship Co., 88 F.2d 26 (2d Cir. 1937)]

b. **Lien against property of principal:** [§46]   Absent an agreement to the contrary, the agent also has a right to a lien on property of the principal in her lawful possession, up to the amount of her compensation (or right to indemnity). [Washakie Livestock Loan Co. v. Meigh, 62 P.2d 523 (Wyo. 1936)]

(1) **Attorney's liens:** [§47]   With respect to the client-principal, an attorney has broader lien rights than the average agent. For example, the attorney has both a *retaining lien* on all papers, securities, etc., of the client in her possession as the result of her position as attorney, and a *charging lien* on amounts earned in securing a judgment in specific cases. [*In re* Heinsheimer, 214 N.Y. 316 (1915); *and see* Legal Ethics Summary]

(2) **Lien rights of subagents:** [§48]   The subagent has a lien against the agent's property in her possession for services and expenses, and against the principal's property in her possession to the extent of the agent's rights in such property. [Korns v. Thomson & McKinnon, 22 F. Supp. 442 (D. Minn. 1938)]

c. **Other remedies:** [§49]   In addition to the foregoing rights, an agent may be entitled to withhold further performance under the agency contract, to claim a set-off or counterclaim in any action brought by the principal, or to demand an accounting by the principal.

(1) **No right to specific performance:** [§50]   However, the agent is *not* entitled to specific enforcement of the agency contract, since the principal-agent relationship is deemed to be consensual in nature. [McMenamin v. Philadelphia Transportation Co., 51 A.2d 702 (Pa. 1947)]

III. CONTRACTUAL RIGHTS AND LIABILITIES BETWEEN PRINCIPAL (OR AGENT) AND THIRD PERSONS

As noted previously, an agent is one who acts for and on behalf of the principal in such a way as to affect the legal rights and liabilities—*i.e.*, the agent has the power to perform "legal acts" for the principal. Thus, one must consider the circumstances under which the acts of an agent will legally bind the principal (and/or the agent himself).

A. CREATION OF AGENCY RELATIONSHIP [§51]

The first step in determining whether the agent's act will bind the principal is to establish whether an agency relationship actually exists between the supposed principal and agent. Such a relationship may be created in any of three ways discussed below.

1. **Agency by Agreement:** [§52]   An agency relationship is consensual in nature, and therefore ordinarily arises by agreement of the parties.

   a. **Manifestation of mutual consent:** [§53]   An agency by agreement must be based upon some indication by the principal to the agent that she consents to having the latter act on her behalf, and a similar manifestation of consent by the agent to act for the principal. [Eitel v. Schmidlapp, 459 F.2d 609 (4th Cir. 1972)]

   b. **Express vs. implied consent:** [§54]   The agency agreement may be express, or it may be implied from the conduct of the parties; *e.g.*, if farmer P habitually leaves her crops with produce broker A, she has impliedly appointed A as her agent for the purpose of selling the crops at the market price.

   c. **Capacity:** [§55]   Only a person having the capacity to contract may appoint an agent (*i.e.*, be a principal). On the other hand, any person may be an agent, whether or not he has the capacity to contract. [Rest. 2d §21]

      (1) **Minors:** [§56]   Thus, a minor cannot validly appoint another as her agent, except to the limited extent of contracting for the minor's necessities of life. [Casey v. Kastel, 237 N.Y. 305 (1924)]

      (2) **Incompetents:** [§57]   Similarly, insane persons or persons who are otherwise legally incompetent cannot appoint agents. However, it is possible that if the incompetent was in fact capable of performing the functions involved, such person might be appointed as the agent of another.

   d. **Consideration:** [§58]   No consideration is necessary for either party in order to create an agency relationship. [Groh v. Shelton, 428 S.W.2d 911 (Mo. 1968)]

   e. **Formalities:** [§59]   Ordinarily, no formalities are required to create an agency. Hence the principal-agent relationship may generally be created by word of mouth, by conduct, or by a writing.

      (1) **Exception:** Where the sole purpose of the agency is to negotiate a contract which must be in writing under the Statute of Frauds, the authority of the agent must *also* be in writing under the "equal dignity" rule (*infra,* §77).

   f. **Purposes:** [§60]   An agency may be created only for a *legal* purpose. Where the purpose is illegal or contrary to public policy, the purported agency will be disregarded.

      (1) **Public policy:** Likewise, a principal cannot delegate acts to an agent which public policy requires that she perform *personally* (*e.g.*, voting in a public election). [Mansfield v. Scully, 29 A.2d 444 (Conn. 1942)]

(2) **Personal services:** And, performance in a *personal services contract* with a third person cannot be delegated to an agent. [Trenouth v. Mulroney, 227 P.2d 590 (Mont. 1951)]

2. **Agency by Ratification:** [§61]   An agency may also be created by ratification. This results whenever the principal *accepts the benefits* or otherwise affirms the conduct of one purporting to act on her behalf, even though there is no agency agreement. [Rest. 2d §93]

   a. **Objective determination:** [§62]   Ratification is deemed to supply the consent required for the principal-agent relationship. Thus, in order to find such affirmance, there must be some objective evidence that the principal knew of the act in question and elected to be bound thereby.

      (1) **Consent:** [§63]   Of course, an express approval of the transaction is the clearest evidence of such affirmance. But consent will also be found wherever the principal accepts the benefits of the transaction (as by electing to take title to property purchased by an unauthorized agent), or otherwise obtains any advantage therefrom with knowledge of the transaction.

         (a) **Example:** A, without authority to do so, buys property "on behalf of my employer, P." P discovers what A has done, decides that the purchase is advantageous, and indicates approval. P's conduct constitutes a ratification, and P is bound by the purchase.

      (2) **No partial ratification:** [§64]   A principal cannot ratify only the beneficial aspects of the agent's conduct, while refusing to affirm the rest. If she ratifies at all, she ratifies the entire transaction. [McClintock v. Robinson, 18 Cal. App. 2d 577 (1937)]

      (3) **Tort liability:** As discussed *infra,* (§172), ratification may also expose the principal to *tort liability* for the agent's misrepresentations, etc.

   b. **Formalities:** [§65]   A ratification need only be in the form otherwise required for the original authorization. Since in most cases verbal authority would be sufficient, so is a verbal ratification. But the "equal dignity" rule (*infra,* §78) applies to ratification of contracts within the Statute of Frauds. [Rest. 2d §93]

   c. **Unauthorized acts by otherwise authorized agents:** [§66]   The nature and scope of ratification is discussed in greater detail in connection with the ratification of unauthorized acts by agents who were otherwise authorized (*infra,* §172).

3. **Agency by Estoppel—"Ostensible Agency":** [§67]   The general rule requires that an agency relationship be based on actual consent between the principal and agent. However, where the principal intentionally or negligently causes a third person to believe another to be her agent, and the third person so relies in dealing with the supposed agent, the principal will be held estopped to deny the agency. In such a case, there is an "ostensible agency," and the principal will be bound by the acts of the ostensible agent to the same extent as if an actual agency agreement existed between them. [Rest. 2d §267]

   a. **Principal's acts required:** [§68]   The acts relied upon must be the acts of the principal and not the agent, and the reliance of the third party must be reasonable. [Adamski v. Tacoma General Hospital, 579 P.2d 978 (Wash. 1978)]

   b. **Ostensible authority distinguished:** [§69]   An ostensible agency must be distinguished from cases of "ostensible authority." In the latter situation, there is an actual agency between the parties, but the principal's actions cause third parties to believe that the agent has powers greater than those actually conferred upon him. (*See* discussion *infra,* §96.)

B. AUTHORITY OF AGENT [§70]

The second step in holding a principal bound by the acts of the agent is to establish that the agent's act was authorized. In this regard, it is important to determine both the source and scope of the agent's claimed authority, and the effect of any limitations thereon or of any act allegedly terminating the agent's authority.

1. **Source of Authority:** [§71]   An agent's acts will be deemed binding on the principal if there is (i) *actual authority* from the principal, whether express or implied; (ii) *apparent authority* from the principal; (iii) *ostensible authority* (*i.e., estoppel*); or (iv) a *power* arising from the agency relationship and not dependent upon any authority from the principal. [Rest. 2d §140]

    a. **Actual authority:** [§72]   "Actual" (or "real") authority refers to the powers of an agent to do that which the principal has manifested consent that the agent should do—*i.e.,* the powers to carry out whatever the principal has expressly or impliedly engaged the agent to accomplish. [Makousky, Inc. v. Stern, 169 N.W.2d 752 (Minn. 1969)] An agent's actual authority may stem from express instructions given by the principal to the agent, or implied from words or other conduct between the principal and agent. [Arkansas Valley Feed Mills, Inc. v. Fox De Luxe Foods, Inc. 171 F. Supp. 145 (W.D. Ark. 1959)]

        (1) **Express authority:** [§73]   The agent has express authority to do anything which the principal has specifically instructed him to do, and all acts *incidental or necessary* thereto. [Fidelity & Casualty Co. v. Continental Illinois Bank & Trust Co., 25 N.E.2d 550 (Ill. 1940)]

            (a) **Example:** Where authority is conferred upon an agent to "collect" an account owing to his principal, the agent is deemed to have express authority not only to negotiate with the debtor for payment, but also to institute suit, enforce any judgment obtained, and incur reasonable expenses and costs (including attorneys' fees) to this end.

                1) But mere authority to "collect" an account would probably *not* authorize compromising, discounting, or settling the account for less than is due to the principal.

            (b) **Power of attorney:** [§74]   Perhaps the clearest example of express authority is a power of attorney, which is a written instrument conferring authority on an agent.

                1) The power may be "special"—to do certain acts only—or it may be "general"—to transact all business for the principal. Any vagueness or uncertainty as to the scope of a power of attorney is normally construed in favor of the principal—*i.e.,* to *limit* the authority conferred. [Soders v. Armstrong, 44 P.2d 868 (Okla. 1935)]

                2) An agent acting under such a grant of authority is sometimes called an "attorney in fact" for his principal, and the normal form of signature for such an agent is: "John Jones (principal) by Harry Smith, his attorney in fact." However, deviations from this form are usually immaterial. As long as the agent did have authority to sign, the principal will normally be bound.

        (2) **Implied authority:** [§75]   Actual authority may also be impliedly conferred by *custom or usage,* by *conduct* of the principal indicating his intention to confer it, or by otherwise causing the agent to believe that he possesses it. [Rest. 2d §26]

(a) **Example:** For many years, P has delivered his cattle to A, a cattle sales agent, and A sells the cattle for the best price then available. Upon P's current delivery of cattle, and in the absence of contrary instructions, A has implied authority to sell and deliver the cattle.

(b) **Example:** P's secretary, A, without previous authorization, has purchased office supplies, and P has paid for them without objection. A has implied authority to continue the purchase of necessary office supplies for P.

(3) **Formalities—"equal dignity" statutes:** [§76]   Ordinarily, no formalities are required in order to delegate authority to an agent; *i.e.,* actual authority may be given orally, in writing, or may be implied from the circumstances.

(a) **Where writing required:** [§77]   In many states, however, the Statute of Frauds requires that an agent's authority be in writing and signed by the principal if the authority conferred is (i) *to execute contracts for the sale of land,* or conveyances pursuant thereto, or (ii) *to execute contracts which cannot be performed within one year*.

(b) **"Equal dignity" statutes:** [§78]   Other states go further and require written authority from the principal whenever the authority conferred is to enter into any contract required by the Statute of Frauds to be in writing. [*See* Cal. Civ. Code §2309] This would include not only contracts for the sale of land and contracts incapable of performance within one year, but also contracts to sell personal property for more than $500, contracts of suretyship, etc.

(c) **Effect of failure to comply with "equal dignity" statute:** [§79]   If the agent's authority is required to be in writing, but is *not,* any contract executed by the agent is unenforceable against the principal, even though the contract itself is in writing.

   1) **But note:** The contract is voidable *at the option of the principal,* rather than the other party to the contract. If the principal decides to accept the contract, he can subsequently *ratify* it in writing. [Moore v. Hoar, 27 Cal. App. 2d 269 (1938)]

   2) **Example:** P orally authorizes A to sell P's house. A then enters into a contract on behalf of P to sell the house to X for $10,000. X cannot enforce the contract. But if P wishes to enforce the contract, he can ratify it in writing—whereupon it becomes enforceable by *both* parties.

(d) **Exceptions:** [§80]   The "equal dignity" rule does *not* apply in two situations:

   1) Where the agent acts mechanically—*i.e.,* where he does not have discretionary authority to enter into a contract, but is merely authorized to sign the principal's name to a contract already made. *Example:* P negotiates a contract with X, but leaves town before the agreement has been drawn. If P authorizes A to sign P's name to the agreement, the authority is valid even though oral. [Murphy v. Munson, 95 Cal. App. 2d 306 (1949)]

   2) Where the agent is an *executive officer of a corporation,* he need not have written authority from the corporation to act on its behalf. This is

said to be justified by the necessities of modern business practice. [Jeppi v. Brockman Holding Co., 34 Cal. 2d 11 (1949)]

(4) **Effect of mistake by principal in creating authority:** [§81]   As long as the principal objectively manifests his intention to create authority in another, there is valid, actual authority—even though he did not intend to grant the authority. [Rest. 2d §26]

   (a) **Example:** P goes to an office where several brokers have desks, and leaves a note upon the desk of A, believing it is the desk of X. The note states: "I authorize you to sell my 100 shares of Acme Manufacturing stock at the market price." If A finds the note, A has actual authority to effect the sale, even though P intended to give the authority to X, not A.

   (b) **Agent's fraud:** [§82]   The above rule has also been applied where A deceives P into granting him authority. Thus, for example, where A falsely represents his qualifications as a sales agent to P, and in reliance thereon P authorizes A to sell certain goods, A has valid authority and any sale effected by him is binding upon P.

      1) However, if P discovers the fraud *before* any sale, he may rescind (revoke) his authority even where the authority would otherwise be irrevocable (*see infra,* §168).

      2) And, in any case, P can hold A liable for any damages sustained as the result of his granting authority (as where A's lack of qualifications results in the property being sold for less than its fair market value).

(5) **Manifestation made to agent:** [§83]   Note that in all cases of actual authority, the manifestation of authority to act for the principal is made to the *agent* (not to a third person).

b. **Apparent authority:** [§84]   "Apparent authority" results when the principal manifests that another is his agent and such manifestation is made to a *third person,* rather than to the agent himself.

   (1) **Distinguished from actual authority:** [§85]   Thus, the basic difference between "actual authority" and "apparent authority" is that in the former the expression of authority is made directly to the agent, whereas in the latter the expression is made to the third person with whom the agent deals. An agent who is given apparent authority may or may not have actual authority from the principal. [System Investment Corp. v. Montview Acceptance Corp., 355 F.2d 463 (10th Cir. 1966)]

      (a) **Example:** P writes to A, directing him to act as P's agent for the sale of Blackacre. P sends a copy of this letter to T, a prospective purchaser. A has actual authority to sell Blackacre to anyone in the world, and as to T, he has apparent authority as well.

      (b) **Example:** P leaves his car with A, directing A to find a buyer for the car but not to accept any offers without P's approval. Subsequently, X asks P about the car, and P tells X that she should "work out a deal" with A. In this situation, A has no actual authority to sell, but he does have apparent authority as to X, and P is therefore bound if A sells the car to X.

   (2) **Formalities:** [§86]   As in the case of actual authority, no consideration is required for apparent authority, and there is no requirement of a writing except where the Statute of Frauds or "equal dignity" statutes apply (*i.e.,* wherever

actual authority must be in writing under these rules, the principal's statements to the third person must also be in writing in order to constitute apparent authority).

(3) **Reliance by third person:** [§87]   Apparent authority is an application of the objective theory of contracts—*i.e.,* that the principal, as a contracting party, should be bound by what he says to T (the other contracting party). Thus, if P mistakenly asserts that A is authorized to act for him, he will be bound thereby, if T believed in and relied upon such statements. However, if T knew or had reason to know that P was in error, no authority exists. [S.S. Silberblatt, Inc. v. Seaboard Surety Co., 417 F.2d 1043 (8th Cir. 1969)]

   (a) The test for reliance is what a *reasonable person under the circumstances* would have believed—a test which is sometimes difficult to apply. *Example:* Customer C calls P's office, and asks for the price of P's products. P's secretary answers the phone and supplies erroneous prices. If C relies on the prices to her detriment in bidding on a construction contract, is P bound by the erroneous quotation? This depends on whether a reasonable person in C's position would have believed P's secretary was authorized to supply such information (perhaps so, for a small subcontractor; probably not, if the supplier is United States Steel).

(4) **Revocation of apparent authority:** [§88]   As discussed *infra* (§170), apparent authority is not revoked merely by giving notice to the agent. Rather, notice of the termination of apparent authority must be given to the *third person* to whom authority was originally manifested. [Bussing v. Lowell Film Products, Inc., 253 N.Y.S. 719 (1931)]

   (a) *Example:* P appoints A his agent for the sale of Blackacre, and so advises T. If P were to write A, revoking his authority, this would effectively terminate A's *actual* authority. But unless and until P communicated the revocation to T, A's apparent authority would continue as to T; and T would be protected in dealing with A (*i.e.,* any contracts entered into between T and A, on behalf of P, would be binding).

   (b) Of course, if T knew from other sources that A's authority had been revoked by P, A's apparent authority would also terminate—even without direct communication by P to T.

   (c) And, if the apparent authority is orginally *conditioned* as to time or events, an expiration of the time period (or occurrence of the event) will terminate the authority. *Example:* If P advises T that A is his agent in selling Blackacre "for the next sixty days," A's apparent authority ceases as to T after that period of time.

   (d) Likewise, apparent authority generally terminates upon the *death or incapacity* of the principal or agent.

(5) **Distinguished from apparent ownership:** [§89]   An apparent agent merely has authority to deal with third persons to the extent that the principal, by his statements to those persons, indicates that the agent is authorized. However, where the principal has clothed the agent with both possession and *apparent ownership* of the principal's property, the agent's power is much broader: He can deal with the property as if he were the true owner, and the principal (the real owner) is estopped to assert the invalidity of his agent's dealings, where the rights of innocent third parties are concerned.

   (a) **Example:** In order to deceive his creditors, P deeds his home to A, it being verbally agreed between P and A that A will surrender the premises and reconvey the property on P's demand. If A sells the property to T, an innocent purchaser, P is estopped to assert his title. On the other hand, P can always assert his rights to the property against A.

(b) **Relevant factors:** [§90]   "Apparent ownership" requires that the principal clothe the agent with such indicia of ownership that a reasonable person would conclude that the agent actually owned the property involved. [New York Security & Trust Co. v. Lipman, 157 N.Y. 551 (1899)]

1) **Transferring possession:** [§91]   In general, merely transferring possession of tangible real or personal property to the agent is not enough. Possession is not a sufficient indicia of ownership, since the possessor may be a tenant, adverse possessor, manager, etc. [Carter v. Rowley, 59 Cal. App. 486 (1922)]

2) **Delivery of deed:** [§92]   But where the owner delivers a bill of sale or deed to the property in addition to the possession, this is a sufficient indicia of ownership. [Carter v. Rowley, *supra*]

3) **Document of title:** [§93]   Similarly, where the property involved is a *document of title* (stock certificate, bond, etc.), or a negotiable instrument endorsed in blank by the principal, mere delivery of same constitutes sufficient apparent ownership. [Phillips v. Clifford F. Reid, Inc., 3 Cal. App. 2d 304 (1934)]

4) **U.C.C. criteria:** [§94]   Where personal property is entrusted to a *merchant* who deals in goods of *that kind*, this is sufficient to vest the merchant with the power to transfer title to the goods to an innocent purchaser for value. [U.C.C. 2-403; *and see* Sales Summary]

a) **Factors acts:** [§95]   And, under state "factors acts," if goods are consigned for sale to one in the business of selling goods for others, the factor has power to transfer title to an innocent purchaser for value. (*See* Personal Property Summary.)

c. **Authority by estoppel—"ostensible authority":** [§96]   Ostensible authority is not really authority at all. Rather, it is an estoppel applied to prevent a principal who has *misled* another from profiting thereby. Such an estoppel will be invoked wherever the principal has *intentionally or negligently* caused or allowed a third person to believe that his agent has authority to do that which in fact he is not authorized to do, *and* the third person *detrimentally relies* thereon so that it would be unjust to allow the principal to deny the agent's authority. [Hoddeson v. Koos Bros., 135 A.2d 702 (N.J. 1957)—imposter posing as salesman in defendant's furniture store]

(1) **Example:** P learns that A, who has no authority to sell P's skiing equipment is negotiating for its sale with T on the representation that he is P's agent. P does nothing, although he could easily notify T, and T pays A for the goods. P is bound to deliver the equipment to T at the agreed price; and he is also liable to T for breach of any warranty customary in such a sale; *i.e.,* P is bound to perform as if A were in fact authorized to sell the goods, being estopped to deny such authority.

(2) **Distinguished from apparent authority:** [§97]   Like apparent authority, ostensible authority is based on the principal's manifestations to, or withholding information from third persons. But whereas apparent authority makes the principal a *contracting party* with the third person, with rights and liabilities as to both sides, ostensible authority—an estoppel—only compensates *losses to the third party* relying on the principal's statements or omissions and does not create rights in the principal.

(a) **Note:** In most cases, this distinction is academic, since the courts tend to treat cases of apparent authority and ostensible authority interchangeably. This is particularly true where the principal makes actual representation to third persons (as opposed to withholding information, as in the example above).

(b) **Compare:** However, in certain cases there simply is no apparent authority, and the presence or absence of the elements of estoppel is therefore determinative of the third person's right to relief.

   1) **Example:** Without authority, A offers to sell T *real property* which in fact belongs to P. T asks P whether A is authorized to act on his behalf, and P (either intentionally or negligently) leads T to believe that A is so authorized. Thereafter, T pays the purchase price to A, who absconds with the funds; and T demands a deed from P.

      a) Any actual or apparent authority to sell the land would have to be in writing under the "equal dignity" statutes. (*See supra,* §78.)

      b) However, the fact that P misled T, coupled with T's detrimental reliance, is sufficient to invoke an estoppel against P, and the estoppel bars P from denying A's authority *or* from asserting the "equal dignity" statute as a defense. [Rest. 2d §31]

2. **Scope of Authority—Agent's Powers:** [§98] Most problems involving an agent's authority turn not so much on the source of authority, as on whether the acts in question were within the scope of authority granted—*i.e.,* whether or not the agent had the *power* to bind the principal. [Rest. 2d §§6, 7]

  a. **General rule:** [§99] An agent's powers are strictly construed. Thus, an agent is deemed to have only such powers as are specifically given or as are reasonably required to perform in accordance with the authority granted by the principal.

    (1) **Rationale:** [§100] The policy of the law is to protect the principal from contractual liability for the irresponsible acts of his agent. Hence, the courts restrict an agent's powers to those which the principal clearly intended the agent to have.

    (2) **Third party's duty to ascertain scope of authority:** [§101] The courts likewise hold that a third party who deals with an agent, and *knows of the agency,* is under a duty to ascertain its scope. Hence, if the agent acts beyond her actual authority, the third party cannot look to the principal (unless the principal's conduct misled the third party or conferred apparent or ostensible authority on the agent). [Ernst v. Searle, 218 Cal. 233 (1933)]

  b. **Incidental powers:** [§102] In most cases, a principal does not expressly grant detailed powers to the agent. Instead, the agent is given a general authority or objective—to sell P's goods, to purchase property on P's behalf. This grant of authority is then deemed to carry with it the power to do those acts which are incidental to the specific authority granted—*i.e.,* all acts *reasonably necessary or customary* to accomplish the given objective. Such incidental powers therefore spring from the basic authority granted by the principal. [Rest. 2d §35]

    (1) **Agency to sell:** [§103] An agent who is given authority to sell the principal's property is deemed to have certain incidental powers and authority, namely:

      (a) **Warranting title:** [§104] To *warrant* the title of the principal and the quantity and quality of the goods, if the subject matter is personal property, and to give the usual covenants of warranty if real property is involved. [Rest. 2d §63] (*See* detailed discussion of warranties, *infra,* §§123-139.)

(b) **Receiving payment:** [§105]   To receive payment of the purchase price in accordance with the terms authorized by the principal. [Tysk v. Griggs, 91 N.W.2d 127 (Minn. 1958)]

   1) **Note:** Unless otherwise specified, the authority to sell permits a sale for cash only; and the agent is not empowered to accept goods, etc., in payment therefor. [Rest. 2d §65]

(c) **Delivering goods:** [§106]   Where personal property is involved, to deliver the goods on receipt of the purchase price.

(d) **Negotiation:** [§107]   If the terms of sale are specified, the agent generally has the power to negotiate and conclude a sale on those terms.

   1) **Additional terms:** [§108]   However, this does not necessarily prevent the agent from making additional terms (especially where personal property is involved), so long as such terms are more advantageous to—or at least not inconsistent with—the specified terms. [Myers v. Stephens, 233 Cal. App. 2d 104 (1965)]

(e) **Concluding sale:** [§109]   If the terms of sale are not specified, or are incomplete, an authority "to sell" may not include the actual power to negotiate and conclude a sale. Particularly where land is involved, the courts treat a mere authority "to sell" as an authority only to find a purchaser to whom the principal may sell. [Rest. 2d §53]

   1) **Real estate brokers:** [§110]   Where the authority "to sell" is given to a *real estate broker,* it is almost always held that the broker has no actual power to convey title to the principal's property, or even to contract to convey same. And this is true even where the agent is given the "exclusive right to sell" on specific terms, such language being deemed only to protect the agent's right to a commission, not to authorize her to convey title. [Mason v. Mazel, 82 Cal. App. 2d 769 (1947)]

(2) **Agency to purchase:** [§111]   An agent who is given authority to *purchase* on behalf of the principal likewise has certain incidental powers and authority:

(a) **To pay the purchase price** from the principal's funds, or if no funds have been given by the principal, to purchase same on the principal's credit. [Pan American World Airways, Inc. v. Local Readers Service, Inc., 240 N.E.2d 552 (Ind. 1968)]

(b) **To accept delivery and possession** of goods (where personal property is involved) or a conveyance of title (in the case of real property).

(c) **Note** again that an agency "to buy" may be interpreted merely as authority to find property and procure an offer of sale. The less complete the terms of authority, the more likely the agent will be deemed to have power only to solicit an offer to sell.

(3) **Power to delegate authority:** [§112]   Since an agency involves a consensual relationship between the principal and agent, the general rule is that the agent cannot delegate her authority to another unless the principal consents. [Rest. 2d §78] There are certain situations, however, in which the agent is deemed permitted to delegate her authority to another:

(a) **Mechanical or ministerial acts:** [§113]   When the act delegated is purely *mechanical or ministerial.* [Knudsen v. Torrington Co., 254 F.2d 283 (2d Cir. 1958)] *Example:* P authorizes A to inventory P's incoming merchandise and issue receipts therefor. These acts are purely mechanical, and A can therefore delegate the task to a subagent. [Kadota Fig Association v. Case-Swayne Co., 73 Cal. App. 2d 815 (1946)]

(b) **Agent cannot perform act herself:** [§114]   When the act is such that the *agent cannot lawfully perform it herself*, but the subagent can. *Example:* P engages A to auction off P's goods, knowing that only a licensed auctioneer is permitted to conduct such a sale. If A has no such license, she can delegate the authority to conduct the sale to any licensed auctioneer. [Cleaveland v. Gabriel, 180 A.2d 749 (Conn. 1962)]

(c) **Necessity and custom:** [§115]   Wherever it is *customary or necessary* to appoint subagents. *Examples:* Where P employs A as manager of her business and it is necessary to employ salespeople to carry on the business, A has authority to appoint such persons. Or similarly, if P employs broker A to sell his property, and it is customary for brokers to appoint each other as subagents to procure buyers for properties listed with them, A has authority to appoint any other broker as her subagent. Any broker so appointed has the same authority as A to negotiate a sale.

(d) **Subagent not party to agency agreement:** [§116]   Even though an agent has the power to delegate her authority to another, the subagent is not a party to the principal-agent agreement; *i.e.,* the subagent, X, generally has no right to sue P for the compensation which P agreed to pay A for performance of the agency services, X's claim being against A.

   1) **Minority view:** [§117]   Some courts *have* allowed the subagent to sue P directly in quasi-contract for the reasonable value of the services rendered.

(4) **Emergency powers:** [§118]   In an unforeseen emergency, where the agent cannot contact the principal to obtain additional authority, she is deemed to have the power to do all acts which are necesary to protect or preserve the property or rights of the principal (including the right to delegate authority and appoint subagents). [G.H. Mumm Champagne v. Eastern Wine Corp., 52 F. Supp. 167 (S.D.N.Y. 1943)]

   (a) **Example:** P ships his crops to a factor, A. Upon arrival, A notes that the crops are infested and must be treated immediately to prevent their entire loss. If A cannot reach P, A has the power to order the necessary treatment on P's behalf, and P is liable therefor. [Rest. 2d §47]

c. **Powers inherent in the agency relationship:** [§119]   An agent is deemed to have certain powers by virtue of the fact that she is an agent—even where the principal has specifically *denied* her such powers. These powers are referred to as "inherent" powers, because they are in no way dependent upon or connected with any grant of authority from the principal. Such powers are recognized only where necessary to protect third persons with whom the agent may be dealing. [Rest. 2d §8A]

(1) **Scope:** [§120]   "Inherent" powers include all powers which a third person would reasonably suppose the agent to have—*i.e.,* powers which would be customary under the circumstances—unless the third person were put on notice that the principal had limited the agent's authority.

   (a) **Example:** P employs A as general manager of P's business, and specifically directs her to purchase business supplies from X and no one else. A violates these instructions and purchases supplies from T, who had no notice of P's instructions to A. Since a general manager would customarily have the authority to purchase from any supplier, A had the inherent power to purchase from T; and P is bound by the transaction. Of course, P would have a cause of action against A for violating his instructions.

(b) **Distinguished from actual or apparent authority:** [§121] There is obviously no actual authority in the above case, because A is violating P's express instructions. Nor is there "ostensible" or "apparent" authority, since P has made no representations to third persons concerning A's authority. A's power to bind P is an inherent power—springing from her authority as general manager, and recognized solely for the protection of the innocent supplier, T. [Rest. 2d §8A]

(2) **Representations:** [§122] A typical "inherent" power is the agent's power to make representations to third persons concerning the subject matter of the agency. Every agent is generally deemed to have this power, even where she has been specifically instructed by the principal not to make representations (*i.e.,* no authority). Hence the principal may be liable in tort for the agent's misrepresentations to third persons, although they were entirely unauthorized by him. (*See* discussion *infra,* §393.)

(3) **Warranties:** [§123] An agent will also be deemed to have an "inherent" power to make warranties regarding the subject matter of the agency, wherever such warranties are *customary* under the circumstances. [Jackson v. Baldwin-Lima-Hamilton Corp., 252 F. Supp. 529 (E.D. Pa. 1966)]

(a) **Warranties vs. representations:** [§124] As will be seen below, a warranty may be a representation of fact (*e.g.,* "This is No. 1 grade Moroccan leather"), or it may be in the nature of a promise or guarantee (*e.g.,* "We warrant these tires against blowouts for 30,000 miles"). Where the warranty is a representation of an existing fact which is subsequently proved false, the principal may be liable under either a *tort* theory of misrepresentation, or a *contract* theory of breach of warranty.

  1) **Tort:** [§125] Tort liability requires proof of scienter, etc., by either the principal or agent (*see infra,* §387).

  2) **Contract:** [§126] However, no such intent or guilty knowledge need be established for contractual liability, which exists even if the representation was made in good faith and without knowledge of its falsity by either principal or agent.

(b) **Types of warranties**

  1) **Express warranties:** [§127] Any affirmation of a present or future fact regarding the subject matter in questions is an express warranty of that fact.

    a) An agent's statement of identification, description, quantity, or quality of the subject matter are warranties thereof (*e.g.,* "This barrel contains fifty gallons of pure Pennsylvania S.A.E. #30 motor oil").

    b) Statements that the principal "guarantees" or "warrants" satisfaction or performance are also warranties thereof, as are statements that the goods are returnable if unsatisfactory.

  2) **Implied warranties:** [§128] In addition to express warranties, the agent's acts on behalf of the principal may give rise to certain implied warranties.

    a) **Sale of goods:** [§129] Implied warranties of title, fitness, merchantability, and conformity to sample or description are implied in every sale of goods under the Uniform Commercial Code, except where such warranties are specifically disclaimed. (*See* Sales Summary.)

    b) **Agent's authority:** [§130] The agent herself is deemed impliedly to warrant that she is authorized to deal on behalf of the principal. If she was *not* so empowered, and her acts did not bind the purported principal, the third person with whom she has dealt may then be able to hold her for any damages sustained as a result (*see infra,* §§206-210).

(c) **Authority to warrant:** [§131] As noted above, where the rights of third persons dealing with an agent are concerned, the agent is deemed to have inherent power to make warranties concerning the subject matter of the agency, wherever the making of such warranties is customary in connection with the actual or apparent authority given the agent. [Rest. 2d §63]

    1) **Warranties in sale of property:** [§132] An agent authorized to sell property on behalf of the owner is empowered to make such warranties concerning the property as are implied by law or customary in the community in connection with sales of such property. [Lindow v. Cohn, 5 Cal. App. 388 (1907)—agent authorized to sell merchandise can warrant quality of goods sold]

        a) **Real property:** [§133] Customary warranties in the sale of real property include the description, size, character of soil, boundary lines, and title.

        b) **Personal property:** [§134] Customary warranties in the sale of personal property would include size, weight, grade, etc.

        c) **Sale of business:** [§135] In the sale of a business, warranties concerning income, expenses, assets and liabilities are customary.

    2) **Warranties in purchase of property:** [§136] An agent authorized to purchase property on behalf of the principal is generally deemed to be empowered to make warranties regarding the principal's credit, assets and liabilities—*i.e.,* to qualify the principal as a purchaser. [Rest. 2d §63(2)]

    3) **Power to warrant narrowly construed:** [§137] Because the power to warrant may increase the principal's liabilities, courts generally construe narrowly the agent's authority to warrant, finding no power in doubtful cases.

(d) **Limitations on agent's authority to warrant:** [§138] Since the agent is deemed to have the inherent power to make customary warranties wherever necessary to protect third persons (*see* above), a principal does not terminate the agent's power merely by instructing her not to warrant. However, if the principal puts third persons ***on notice*** of the limitations on the agent's power, this will be effective.

    1) **Example:** P authorizes A to act as her agent in the sale of cars, using a form contract supplied by P; the contract contains a provision to the effect that "no agent is authorized to make any promises or representations not contained herein." This is probably an effective limitation on

A's power to warrant (*i.e.,* sufficient notice to third persons), and hence any other warranties made by A in inducing customers to purchase a car would not be binding on P.

(e) **Waiver of warranty:** [§139]   Instead of limiting the agent's authority to warrant, the principal will often insert a "waiver" of warranties in the form contract used by the agent. These are generally effective absent actual fraud (in which case the waiver may be rescinded).

d. **Limitations on authority:** [§140]   Except in the case of inherent powers designed to protect innocent third persons, discussed above, an agent has the power to act only in accordance with the authority granted by the principal. Obviously, then, whatever has been prohibited to the agent is clearly not authorized.

(1) **Limitations vs. "mere advice":** [§141]   A frequent and difficult issue is whether particular directions given by the principal to the agent constitute a limitation on the agent's authority or mere advice to the agent.

(a) **Example:** P owns a factory running at fifty percent capacity due to lack of orders. Before leaving for his vacation, P tells his manager A not to order more than 100 tons of coal for power and heating at the factory. An order comes in the following day which would require more than 100 tons of coal to process promptly. Can A purchase the additional fuel, or is P's directive a limitation on A's authority?

(b) **Result:** There is no automatic answer in this type of situation. It depends on what the principal intended (or may be assumed to have intended). The courts will consider the principal's purposes, whether or not he could be reached to give further directions, and any other relevant circumstances. In the previous hypothetical, P's accessibility for advice, the importance of filling the order promptly (customer involved, etc.), and the like, would have to be determined.

(2) **Third party rights:** [§142]   Of course, where an agent acts and her conduct is later found to have been unauthorized, the doctrine of inherent powers may still be available to a third party in holding the agent's actions binding on the principal.

3. **Imputed Knowledge and Notice:** [§143]   One of the most important consequences of an agency relationship is that the principal may be charged with knowledge of facts disclosed to the agent (and vice versa), where these pertain to the subject matter of the agency.

a. **General rule:** [§144]   With respect to their dealings with third persons, both principal and agent are deemed to have constructive notice of any facts which one party has notice of and ought, in the exercise of ordinary care, to communicate to the other. In such circumstances, the knowledge of the agent is imputed to the principal. [Rest. 2d §272]

(1) **Example:** P authorizes A to negotiate for the purchase of certain ranch property from T, the apparent owner. In the course of the negotiations, A is advised (or discovers) that X claims an interest in the land, but neglects to tell P, who proceeds with the purchase. P takes the land subject to X's claims, and cannot assert them as a defense to his obligation to pay or as grounds for rescission of the sale.

(2) **Rationale:** An agent has a duty to inform the principal of all matters in connection with the agency which the principal would desire to know (*see supra,* §16). But the fact that the agent has breached this duty by failing to communicate

relevant information to the principal is not allowed to prejudice the rights of innocent third persons. As to such persons, the principal is deemed to know all that the agent should have told him. [Columbia Pictures Corp. v. De Toth, 87 Cal. App. 2d 620 (1948)]

b. **Authority to receive notification:** [§145]   Notice or knowledge will not be imputed to the principal unless the agent had actual or apparent authority to receive notice of the facts in question. [Rest. 2d §276]

(1) **Example:** P owns an apartment house, in which T is a tenant. T notifies A that he intends to move. If A is merely a bookkeeper in P's office, this notice would probably not be effective to terminate T's tenancy. However, if A were the *manager* of the apartment house, T's notice would be effective. Moreover, the notice would be effective in the latter case even if P had fired A as manager—assuming T was not aware of this fact.

(2) **Note:** Ordinarily, only those facts discovered by the agent during the period of the agency will be imputed—*i.e.,* the principal is not charged with knowledge of facts learned by the agent before (or after) his employment. [Cooke v. Mesmer, 164 Cal. 332 (1912)]

(a) However, a few cases have imputed knowledge acquired by the agent prior to employment where, because of the close connection of the transactions, such knowledge must have been present in the agent's mind when he acted for the principal. [Blue Diamond Plaster Co. v. Industrial Accident Commission, 188 Cal. 403 (1922)—knowledge of managing officer of corporation, gained while serving with predecessor corporation, held imputed]

(b) Under the Restatement rule, it is *immaterial* when the agent acquired his knowledge. The issue is whether he had the knowledge in mind when it became relevant in his work for the principal. [Rest. 2d §276]

c. **What facts are imputed:** [§146]   The test for imputed knowledge is whether the facts concern the *subject matter* of the agency and are *within the scope thereof.* [Rest. 2d §272]

(1) **No imputation of agent's state of mind:** [§147]   Imputed knowledge extends only to *factual* matters. Thus, states of mind ("scienter," "bad faith," etc.) of the principal cannot be based solely on imputed knowledge.

(a) **Example:** P ships certain merchandise to T, who finds it unsatisfactory and so notifies P's general manager, A. A forgets to notify P, and P files a lawsuit against T. In a subsequent action by T against P for abuse of process (which requires a showing that the action for the purchase price was filed in bad faith), T cannot prevail merely by showing that he gave A notice of rejection—*i.e.,* P's alleged bad faith cannot be based solely on imputed knowledge. [Snook v. Netherby, 124 Cal. App. 2d 797 (1954)]

(2) **No imputation where agent acting adversely to principal:** [§148]   An agent who takes a position adverse to the principal is acting outside the scope of his authority, and knowledge acquired by him while acting in this fashion is therefore not imputed to the principal. *Rationale:* Where an agent is acting in derogation of his employer's interest, there is no reason to suppose that he will keep his employer properly informed, and it would be extremely unfair to impute his knowledge to the principal. [Rest. 2d §282]

(a) **Example:** X, unable to procure auto insurance, conspires with insurance agent A to obtain a policy for his car in Y's name. Where the company P later seeks to have the policy declared void, A's knowledge would not be imputed to P (since he was colluding to defraud P). [Southern Farm Bureau Casualty Insurance Co. v. Allen, 388 F.2d 126 (5th Cir. 1967)]

(b) **Example:** Likewise, where an officer or director of a corporation causes it to enter into contracts in which he has some secret adverse interest, the corporation is generally not bound thereby (*i.e.,* knowledge of the director's adverse interest is not imputed to the corporation). [Mylander v. Page, 159 A. 770 (Md. 1932)]

1) However, some courts *have* imputed knowledge of dishonest acts by corporate officers or directors to the corporation, at least to bar suit against the surety on fidelity bonds of the dishonest officers.

2) And, knowledge will be imputed to the principal if he *retains a benefit* through the act of the agent, which he otherwise would not have received. [*In re* Brainerd Hotel Co., 75 F.2d 481 (2d Cir. 1935)—embezzling cashier of the hotel stole money of guests to replace prior embezzlements from hotel]

(3) **Distinguish imputation of notice from imputation of knowledge:** [§149] A *notification* to the agent—as distinguished from his knowledge of facts—is imputed to the principal, even where the agent is acting adversely. Thus, notices of rescission, termination of tenancy, etc., given to the agent are imputed to the principal, even if the agent was acting adversely to the principal at the time he received the notice. [Rest. 2d §271]

4. **Termination of Agent's Authority:** [§150] The agency relationship, as well as the authority of the agent, may be terminated in any of several ways.

a. **By expiration of the term of the agency:** [§151] Authority conferred for a specified period of time terminates upon expiration of the period. [Shelton v. Lemmon, 268 S.W. 177 (Tex. 1925)]

(1) **"Reasonable time":** [§152] If no time is specified by the parties, a reasonable time is implied, and the authority terminates at the end of a reasonable period. [Beaucar v. Bristol Federal Savings & Loan Association, 268 A.2d 679 (Conn. 1969)]

(a) **What constitutes a "reasonable time"** depends upon all of the circumstances, including the nature of the agency, likelihood of a change in purposes, etc.

(b) **Example:** P authorizes A to sell P's car for her. If ten years elapse without any communication between P and A, the agency would probably be deemed terminated—*i.e.,* A would no longer have authority to sell the car.

b. **By accomplishment of purpose of agency:** [§153] If the agent's authority was to perform a specified act or to accomplish a specific result, his authority terminates upon the accomplishment thereof—even where the authorized performance was by another agent or the principal himself. [Echiade v. Confederation of Canada Life Insurance, 459 F.2d 1377 (5th Cir. 1972)]

(1) **Example:** P engages A and B as real estate brokers to sell Blackacre for her. If A sells the house to X, and B learns of this, both agents' authority is terminated. Thus, neither A nor B is then authorized to rescind the transaction with X or make a new deal with X or someone else. [Rest. 2d §106]

(2) **But note:** As discussed below, the agent's authority would continue until he has *knowledge* that the act, result, or event has occurred. Thus, in the example above, B's authority may continue until she acquires notice that A has sold Blackacre—unless P had originally made it clear to B that others were also being engaged to sell the property.

c. **By change of circumstances**

(1) **Loss or destruction of subject matter:** [§154]   If the subject matter of the agency is lost or destroyed, the agent's authority to deal therewith is terminated. (A *partial* destruction would likewise terminate the authority if further actions by the agent would not be in the best interests of the principal.)

(a) **Example:** P authorizes A to sell P's house. Prior to any sale, the house is destroyed by fire (or lost through mortgage foreclosure, eminent domain proceedings, etc.). A's authority to sell is thereby terminated.

(2) **Change of circumstance affecting value:** [§155]   Similarly, if there is a basic and unforeseen change in circumstances which substantially affects the value of the subject matter, or otherwise makes it apparent that the principal would not wish the agent to proceed, the agent's authority is terminated.

(a) **Examples**

1)   Thus, where P authorizes A to sell land for a certain amount, and minerals are then discovered on the land which treble its value, A's authority to sell for the original amount is terminated. [Rest. 2d §108]

2)   Similarly, where P wires A to charter a steamship to transport certain goods which P was planning to purchase, and A subsequently learns that P did not purchase the goods, A's authority to charter the steamship terminates. [Rest. 2d §109]

3)   Other "unforseen events" which have been held sufficient to terminate an agent's authority include the outbreak of war, the bankruptcy of the principal or agent, changes of law, embezzlement or other disloyalty of the agent, etc. [*See, e.g.,* McKey v. Clark, 233 F. 928 (9th Cir. 1916)—bankruptcy a sufficient "unforeseen event"]

4)   In any case of unforeseen circumstances, the *principal's* knowledge and actions are obviously relevant. For example, if P and A are in close contact, and P is aware of the change in events, A's authority probably continues absent new instructions from P.

d. **By death or incapacity of either principal or agent:** [§156]   The death or incapacity of either the principal or agent terminates any authority previously granted.

(1) **Automatic termination:** [§157]   Such termination is automatic, and does not depend on the agent or third party acquiring knowledge of the principal's death (or vice versa). Any transaction by the agent after the death or insanity of the principal is not binding on the principal or the principal's estate.

(a) **Example:** P authorizes A to collect a debt from T. P then dies. Before A learns of P's death, he collects the money from T and absconds with it. Since A's authority to collect the money terminated automatically on P's death, the debt remains unpaid, and T must pay again. [Weber v. Bridgman, 113 N.Y. 600 (1889)]

(b) **State statutes:** [§158]   Some states reach a different result by statute. For example, California Civil Code section 2356 provides that "any bona fide transaction'' with a third person who had no knolwedge of the death or incapacity of the principal shall be binding on the principal or his estate. *Rationale:* It is unjust to penalize third persons dealing with an agent because of the unknown death (or incapacity) of the principal.

(2) **Exception for agencies ''coupled with an interest'':** [§159]   As noted below, certain agency powers are held to be irrevocable by the principal because *consideration* was received in return for his grant of the power. Such powers do *not* terminate upon the death or incapacity of the principal, and their exercise therefore binds his estate.

e. **By act or agreement of the parties:** [§160]   Because the principal-agent relationship is consensual in nature, it terminates when either or both parties agree (or otherwise act) to end the relationship. And this is true regardless of any previous agreement that the agency or authority would be ''irrevocable,'' or would last for a specified time, *i.e.,* the agency ends whenever either party communicates to the other an intention that the authority shall end. Such a communication effectively terminates the rights, duties, and powers of the relationship. [Sarokhan v. Fair Lawn Memorial Hospital, Inc. 199 A.2d 52 (N.J. 1964)]

(1) **Renunciation by agent:** [§161]   Where the agent terminates the relationship, there is said to be a renunciation of his authority. The fact that the agent is contractually bound to perform, and that his renunciation thus constitutes a breach of contract and exposes him to liability in damages, does not prevent the renunciation from being effective to terminate his authority and duties as an agent. [Century Refining Co. v. Hall, 316 F.2d 15 (10th Cir. 1963)]

(a) **Example:** P hires A as manager of his business for a period of one year. After six months, A resigns. A may be liable to P for the cost of finding a replacement, but his resignation effectively terminates his authority and relieves him of the duties of the principal-agent relationship.

(2) **Revocation of authority by principal**

(a) **General rule:** [§162]   An agency is deemed to be created for the benefit of the principal, and it follows that the principal is usually free at any time to terminate the agency relationship or any authority granted to the agent.

1) **Agent's contract rights:** [§163]   Of course, the principal's revocation may well constitute a breach of contract with the agent. While the revocation is effective nonetheless, and the authority of the agent terminates, the principal in this case may be liable to the agent for breach of contract. [McDonald v. Davis, 389 S.W.2d 494 (Tex. 1965)—principal in this situation has the power, but not the right, to revoke]

(b) **Exceptions—''powers coupled with interest'':** [§164]   Notwithstanding the general rule permitting revocation, there are certain situations in which an agent's authority *cannot* be revoked—*i.e.,* where the agent's powers are deemed to be ''irrevocable.'' These are cases in which the agency or power was created *for the benefit of the agent or a third person,* rather than for the principal. In such situations, it is no longer proper to permit the principal to terminate it at will; and the agent is said to have ''*powers coupled with an interest.''* [Hunt v. Rousmanier, 21 U.S. (8 Wheat.) 174 (1823)]

1) **Requirements:** [§165]   A mere recital that a power is coupled with an interest is insufficient. [Todd v. Superior Court, 181 Cal. 406 (1919)] In order for the power granted to be held irrevocable, it must appear that:

a)   The power or authority was granted in order to *secure the perfor-*

mance of a duty, or to protect the title of, the agent or some third person; *and*

    b) That it was given when the duty or title was created, and *was supported by consideration*. [Rest. 2d §138]

2) **Not terminated by death or incapacity:** [§166] Since a power coupled with an interest is not held for the benefit of the donor of the power (*i.e.*, the "principal"), it is not really an "agency power" in the usual sense. Accordingly, the power generally does not terminate upon the death or incapacity of the donor ("principal") or its holder ("agent"). [Pan American Petroleum Corp. v. Cain, 340 S.W.2d 93 (Tex. 1960)]

3) **Examples**

    a) P and A agree that if A lends P $5,000, A shall have a one-half interest in P's property, Blackacre, and authority to sell Blackacre for $20,000 (A's loan to be repayable out of the sale proceeds). A's power is coupled with an interest (granted at the time of the loan, to secure repayment thereof, supported by the loan), and is hence irrevocable.

    b) P and A, who own Blackacre as tenants in common, agree to sell the property for $20,000 and further agree that A shall have the "exclusive right to sell." P's authority to A is revocable—*i.e.*, not "coupled with an interest"—because it did not arise at the time that title to the property was created.

    c) P engages attorney A to represent him in certain litigation, and it is agreed that A's fee shall be a percentage of the recovery. A's authority is revocable, because his interest is merely in the *proceeds* resulting from exercise of his power (*i.e.*, A has no beneficial interest in the subject matter of the agency). [Fields v. Potts, 140 Cal. 2d 697 (1956)]

    d) Frequently, a power to sell property will be given to a pledgee, mortgagee, or trustee under trust deed as additional security for the payment of a debt. Thus, where A loans $10,000 to P in return for which P gives A a mortgage on P's house with power of sale in the event of a default in repayment, such a power of sale is coupled with an interest, and is therefore irrevocable. [New York Life Insurance Co. v. Doane, 13 Cal. App. 2d 233 (1936)]

4) **Effect of attempt to revoke powers coupled with an interest:** [§167] Because such powers are truly irrevocable, any attempt by the principal to revoke a power coupled with an interest is regarded as a nullity. The agent is entitled to specific enforcement in equity of the principal's promise not to revoke.

    a) **Agent's fraud:** [§168] If P was *defrauded* by A into giving him an irrevocable power, or if there is some other failure of the consideration P was to receive for giving that power, P would have the right to *rescind*, provided no innocent third parties were involved.

f. **Notice required to terminate**

(1) **Notice to agent—termination of actual authority:** [§169] The general rule is that an agent's authority continues until she knows, or has reason to know, of the change relied upon to terminate the authority. Thus, it must appear that the

principal has notified the agent—or that the agent has otherwise discovered the principal's revocation, the loss or destruction of the subject matter, other unforeseen happening, etc. [Robertson v. Cloud, 47 Miss. 208 (1872)]

(a) No particular form of notice is required. Hence, notice is equally effective if the principal informs the agent directly, or if the agent independently learns of the event which terminates her authority.

(b) As noted previously, an agent's authority is generally destroyed *without* notice upon the death or incapacity of the principal (except in the case of "powers coupled with an interest," *supra,* §164). [Rest. 2d §120]

(2) **Notice to third persons—termination of apparent authority:** [§170]   Wherever the principal represents to third parties that another person is her agent and authorized to act on her behalf on certain matters, the agent has apparent authority (*supra,* §84). Such apparent authority continues despite the termination of actual authority, until such time as the third person receives notice—from the principal or any other source—that the agent's authority has terminated. [Bussing v. Lowell Film Products, Inc., 253 N.Y.S. 719 (1931)]

(a) **Examples**

1) Where the principal knows that the agent has been dealing with particular third parties, personal or individual notice to that party is usually required. [Courtney v. G.A. Linaker Co., 293 S.W. 723 (Ark. 1927)]

2) In cases where the agent's apparent authority arose from representations by the principal to the public at large, notice by advertisement, or similar means is generally held sufficient to terminate the apparent authority.

3) If the principal has given the agent *written* authority (*e.g.,* a power of attorney), she must reclaim the writing or notify all persons with whom the agent may deal that the authority has been revoked. In other words, the principal is charged with knowledge that the agent may show the writing to third persons.

a) If the writing has been recorded, the principal must record a revocation of the authority.

b) But if the written authorization indicates specific conditions upon which the agent's authority will terminate, and the third party learns that such conditions have occurred, no further notice is required. *Example:* Broker A shows prospective purchaser B the power of attorney to sell P's house. If the power states that it expires on a certain date, no further notice to B need be given.

(b) **Exception:** [§171]   As in the case of actual authority, apparent authority terminates automatically upon the death or incapacity of the principal— *i.e.,* no notice to third persons is required. [Rest. 2d §120; *and see* discussion *supra,* §§156-158]

C. RATIFICATION

1. **In General:** [§172]   Ratification is the affirmance by a person of a prior act supposedly done on his behalf by another, but which was *not* authorized (and hence would otherwise not be binding upon him). [Higgins v. D. & F. Electric Co., 140 S.E.2d 99 (Ga. 1964)] The essence of ratification is that the prior unauthorized act is treated as if it has been authorized by the "principal" at the outset. [Rest. 2d §82]

a. **Application:** [§173]   Prior to the affirmation, the relation of the third party, T, to the principal is similar to that of an offeror to an offeree—*i.e.,* T's agreement with the agent is deemed to be no more than an offer to the principal.

(1) **No affirmation:** [§174]   It follows that if the principal never affirms, there is no contract. Neither the agent nor the third party can assert rights against the other, having been mutually mistaken as to the crucial fact of A's authority.

(a) **Exception:** [§175]   A few courts would find an enforceable contract between T and A on the theory that if T receives what he was bargaining for and his performance to A would be no more burdensome than T's contemplated performance to P, the mistake as to A's authority shouldn't excuse T from performing.

(2) **Acceptance:** [§176]   Upon affirmation, however, P is deemed to have "accepted" T's offer and become bound by the contract. As a corollary, T is generally free until affirmation to rescind his contract with the unauthorized agent—*i.e.,* to "revoke" his offer to P. [Rest. 2d §88]

b. **Effect of ratification:** [§177]   Note that ratification may establish both the agent's authority and the *agency relationship* as well (*see supra,* §63).

(1) **Example:** P, the owner and publisher of a small newspaper, is taken ill. Without being asked to do so, his friend A takes charge of the paper and publishes several issues, in the course of which he libels T and incurs certain debts for printing supplies furnished by X. If P subsequently affirms A's actions, he has constituted A as his agent (since no such relationship previously existed) and has bound himself by A's conduct during his absence.

(2) **And note:** P's affirmation may subject him to *tort* liability for T's libel (as well as contractual liability for the supplies furnished by X). Thus, a ratification may impose liability on the principal in both contract and tort. (*See* discussion on ratification of tortious acts, *infra,* §§372-379.)

2. **Who Can Ratify:** [§178]   The majority view is that only the purported principal can ratify. If, in dealing with the unauthorized agent, the third party thought he was contracting with the purported principal P, P alone has the power to affirm the contract—*i.e.,* the "offer" can be accepted only by the person to whom it was made. [Gillihan v. Morguelan, 186 S.W.2d 807 (Ky. 1945)]

a. **Example:** Purporting to act on P's behalf (but without authority to do so), A contracts to purchase a rare antique from T at a very reasonable price. X, a stranger to the transaction, who wants the antique, pays A $500 for an assignment of all rights under the contract and then notifies T that he "affirms" A's purchase. This affirmation is ineffective, since the original A-T contract was made purportedly on P's behalf and only P can ratify it.

b. **Minority view:** [§179]   Some courts have held that the unauthorized agent, A, or the new party, X, *can* "affirm" the contract and enforce it against T. *Rationale:* As long as T receives the price he contracted for and his performance to A or X is no more onerous than performance to P, he has no basis for being excused from performance. [Barnett Bros. v. Lynn, 203 P. 389 (Wash. 1922)]

3. **Acts Not Capable of Ratification:** [§180]   Generally, the principal may ratify any act which he could have authorized at the time the act was done. However, certain acts are not capable of ratification (so that affirmation by the principal does *not* make him a party to the contract). [Berk v. Laird, 317 F. Supp. 715 (E.D.N.Y. 1970)]

a. **Acts not purportedly done on behalf of P:** [§181]   Such acts cannot subsequently be ratified by the principal. [Pettit v. Vogt, 495 P.2d 395 (Okla. 1972)]

(1) **Example:** A poses as the owner of Blackacre and sells it to T. Later, P, the real owner, discovers what A has done and decides to affirm the sale to T. No ratification results—and T is not bound to purchase from P—because A was not purporting to act as P's agent. However, P *can* affirm even where A appeared to be acting for himself or a third person, provided A nonetheless *intended* to act on P's behalf.

b. **Acts not capable of authorization:** [§182]   Similarly, an act which the principal could not have authorized in the first place because it was illegal or contrary to public policy (*supra,* §62) does not become effective by ratification. [Andrews v. Claiborne Parish School Board, 189 So. 355 (La. 1939)]

(1) **Example:** Without authority, A purports to represent P in a gambling wager in a state where such wagers are illegal. Later P finds out and affirms the wager. Since the wager could not have been authorized originally, it is not made enforceable by the subsequent affirmation.

(2) **Acts illegal only because unauthorized:** [§183]   And, where the original act is illegal *only because* it was unauthorized, a subsequent ratification will be effective (the act then being treated as legal). *Example:* An agent's forgery of the principal's name can be ratified, since the principal could have authorized the agent to sign his name in the first place. [Volandri v. Hlobil, 170 Cal. App. 2d 656 (1959)]

4. **What Constitutes a Ratification:** [§184]   As indicated previously, a ratification requires that the principal in some way manifest his intention to be bound by the prior unauthorized act—*i.e.,* to become a party to the transaction.

a. **Must be conduct by principal:** [§185]   Ratification requires some conduct by the *principal* which manifests his intent. Statements or conduct by the purported agent or some other third person will not suffice.

b. **Express affirmation:** [§186]   If the principal expressly affirms the prior unauthorized act—*e.g.,* by notifying the agent or third party thereof—this is sufficient to establish ratification. [Fenn v. Dickey, 35 A. 1108 (Pa. 1896)]

c. **Implied affirmation—ratification by conduct:** [§187]   Typically, however, the principal does not specifically express his intention to "become bound" or "go ahead" with the transaction. In such cases, the question is whether there is conduct by the principal which sufficiently evidences his intent to affirm the agreement. [Shimonek v. Nebraska Building & Investment Co., 191 N.W. 668 (Neb. 1922)]

(1) **Retention of benefits:** [§188]   Voluntary acceptance or retention by the principal of the benefits of a transaction purportedly entered into on his behalf will generally establish a ratification by the principal. [Compuknit Industries, Inc. v. Mercury Motors Express, Inc., 72 Misc. 2d 55 (1972)]

(a) **Example:** Without authority, A contracts to sell Blackacre to T on P's behalf. T advises P of the contract and tenders the purchase price to P. If P accepts the tender, he will be held to have affirmed the sale.

(b) **Exception where retention is involuntary:** [§189]   Of course, where the retention is involuntary—as where the "benefits" have been consumed or made an inseparable part of the principal's property—there is no ratification. *Example:* Without authority, A purchases fertilizer for P and spreads it on P's ground. P knows nothing of the transaction until after the fertilizer is absorbed. P's retention of the benefits under these circumstances is not a ratification. [Pacific Bone, Coal & Fertilizer Co. v. Bleakmore, 81 Cal. App. 659 (1927)]

(2) **Bringing suit or maintaining defense:** [§190]   Where the principal institutes an action, or sets up a defense to any action in reliance upon some prior unauthorized act, he will be deemed to have affirmed that act. [Strawn v. Jones, 285 A.2d 659 (Md. 1971)]

    (a) **Example:** Without authority, A purports to sell Blackacre to T on P's behalf. Knowing the facts, P brings an action against T for the purchase price. P thereby ratifies the transaction. The same result would follow if T had sued P on some other matter, and P had set up the unpaid purchase price as a defense or set-off in T's suit. [*See* Cochran v. Bell, 117 S.E.2d 645 (Ga. 1960)]

(3) **Failure to act:** [§191]   Under certain circumstances, the principal's failure to repudiate an unauthorized transaction may constitute a ratification thereof. [*See* N.A.A.C.P. v. Overstreet, 142 S.E.2d 816 (Ga. 1965)] In this type of case, the principal is in effect *estopped* from denying his affirmation.

    (a) **Example:** Without authority, A places an order with T for advertising on behalf of P. P learns of A's act, knows that T is spending time and money to prepare copy, but does nothing to repudiate the transaction. P would be deemed to have ratified the order.

    (b) **Example:** Without authority, Employee forges Employer's signature on a company check. Employer discovers the forgery, but delays notifying the police or the bank because Employee is a key person and Employer wants to obtain a replacement before reporting the forgery. By the time he does so, Employee has absconded with the funds. Employer would be estopped to claim forgery (*i.e.,* repudiate the check as a properly negotiated instrument). [U.C.C. §3-404(2)]

    (c) **Compare:** However, an employer's failure to discharge an employee who committed a tortious act with respect to a *third person* does not in itself constitute a ratification by the employer of the employee's conduct (*see infra,* §376).

5. **Knowledge of Principal:** [§192]   There can be no effective ratification unless the principal was aware of all material facts at the time of the ratification. If he was not—or if he was mistaken as to any such fact—he can thereafter rescind the affirmation unless the third person has changed his position in reliance thereon. *Rationale:* The unauthorized A-T contract is merely an "offer," and there can be no valid "acceptance" by affirmation unless all the terms thereof are known. It is immaterial whether P's lack of knowledge is caused by A's fraud or is an innocent mistake on his part. [Templeton Construction Co. v. Kelly, 296 A.2d 242 (Vt. 1972); Rest. 2d §91]

    a. **Example:** Without authority, A executes a promissory note on P's behalf, payable to T. Mistakenly believing that the note was one of a number which he had previously authorized A to execute, P tells T that the note is good. P then discovers his mistake and advises T accordingly, repudiating his affirmation. If T has not changed his position in reliance on the ratification, P is not liable on the note. [Menveg v. Fishbaugh, 123 Cal. App. 460 (1932)]

    b. **Example:** Falsely purporting to be P's agent, A sells Blackacre to T. P does not know that oil has just been discovered on Blackacre, and affirms the sale. When he learns about the oil, P can retract his affirmation of the sale (assuming no detrimental reliance by T).

      (1) There is some authority, however, that a mere mistake as to the value of the subject matter is not sufficient to justify repudiating a ratification.

    c. **Principal may assume risk of lack of knowledge:** [§193]   However, where the principal's ignorance of the facts arises from his own failure to investigate, under circumstances in which a reasonable person would have made an investigation, he is held to assume the risk of his lack of knowledge—*i.e.,* the ratification is effective in spite of the fact that he did not know certain material facts. [See-Tee Mining Corp. v. National Sales, Inc., 417 P.2d 810 (N.M. 1966)]

        (1) **Example:** Without authority, A purports to sell Blackacre to T on P's behalf. When informed of this, P—without inquiring about the terms of sale—says that he will stand by anything A has done. This probably constitutes a ratification which P cannot later repudiate upon learning of the actual terms of sale.

6. **Formalities:** [§194]   A ratification need merely be made in a form and manner proper for an original authorization—which means that no special formalities are usually required (*see supra,* §76).

    a. **"Equal dignity" rule:** [§195]   In the few cases where the original authorization must be in writing (under the "equal dignity" rule), the ratification must also be in writing. *Example:* Without authority, A contracts to sell Blackacre to T on P's behalf. Any subsequent affirmation by P must be in writing, since the original authorization would have to have been in writing. [Moore v. Hoar, 27 Cal. App. 2d 269 (1938)] (*See supra,* §78.)

    b. **Ratification need not be communicated:** [§196]   It is *not* necessary that the principal notify or otherwise communicate affirmation to the agent, the third person, or anyone else. [Rest. 2d §95]

7. **Effects of Ratification**

    a. **"Relation back" theory:** [§197]   The traditional rule is that once an agent's act is ratified, it is treated as though it had been authorized from the outset. All rights and liabilities are therefore said to "relate back" to the date of the original unauthorized act.

        (1) **Example:** Without authority, A negotiates a loan purportedly on P's behalf on January 1, the agreement providing that interest is payable from that date. The funds are received by P on February 1, and P decides to affirm the transaction. Interest is payable by P from January 1, the date the loan was originally negotiated by A.

    b. **Exceptions to "relation back" theory**

        (1) **Illegality or incapacity** [§198]

            (a) **There is no "relation back"** where the act is illegal, or the principal lacks capacity, at the time of ratification—even though P had capacity or the act was legal previously at the time of the agent's unauthorized act.

                1) **Example:** Without authority, but purportedly on behalf of P, A hires T to supply gambling odds to P's newspaper. The supplying of such information is not then illegal, but becomes so by subsequent legislation. If P then decides to affirm the transaction, there is no effective ratification.

            (b) **If the principal has capacity at the time of his affirmance,** there will also be no "relation back" where he lacked capacity at the time of the agent's unauthorized contract. However, if P's disability was only *partial* (*e.g.,* minority), the agent's acts *can* later be ratified if the disability is removed (*i.e.,* principal ratifies after turning twenty-one).

(2) **Intervening rights:** [§199]   Similarly, the ratification does not "relate back" where this would prejudice innocent third persons who have acquired rights in the transaction during the interim.

    (a) **Example:** Without authority, A purports to sell Blackacre to T on P's behalf for $10,000. Without knowledge of A's transaction, P subsequently sells the land to B for $8,000. Upon learning of the sale to T at a higher price, P attempts to ratify that transaction. *Result:* The ratification will not "relate back" against B; B can compel specific performance of the contract with P, and P may also be liable to T for damages because of his ratification. [Petray v. First National Bank, 92 Cal. App. 86 (1928)]

    (b) **Example:** P offers to sell Blackacre to T for $10,000. Later, A (who is P's real estate agent) finds someone willing to pay more for the property and, although he has no authority to do so, notifies T that P has revoked the offer to sell. T ignores A's notice and advises P that he accepts P's offer to sell. By this time, P has learned of the higher offer and "affirms" A's unauthorized notice of revocation.

        1) Under the general view, A's unauthorized revocation is deemed invalid; and hence there is no "relation back" to cut off T's acceptance. [Rest. 2d §90]

        2) A few courts are contra, however, asserting that the agent's notice of revocation—even though unauthorized—would deprive the other party of the power to accept P's offer.

8. Limitations on Power to Ratify

  a. **Whole transaction must be ratified:** [§200]   A contract or other single transaction must be affirmed in its entirety in order to have an effective ratification; *i.e.,* the principal cannot affirm only the beneficial parts and refuse to affirm the rest. [Lewis v. Martin, 492 P.2d 877 (Colo. 1971)]

  b. **Intervening withdrawal or incapacity of other party:** [§201]   As noted previously, until affirmation the unauthorized contract between the third party and agent is treated merely as an "offer" to the principal. It follows that until the affirmation the third party is free to rescind—to "revoke" the offer—and that any affirmation by the principal thereafter will be ineffective. [Rest. 2d §88]

    (1) **Example:** A purports to buy goods from T on P's behalf, both parties believing that A is authorized when in fact he is not. T then discovers that A was not authorized and notifies A that he withdraws from the transaction. If P subsequently affirms, his ratification is ineffective to bind T. [Salfield v. Sutter County Land Improvement & Reclamation, 94 Cal. 546 (1892)]

    (2) **Note:** The above holds true even where T has *contracted* that he will not withdraw from the contract, or where he rescinds on grounds which would not be adequate to discharge him from the contract had A been authorized.

    (3) **The death or incapacity of T** will also terminate P's power to ratify. [Rest. 2d §88c]

  c. **Change of circumstances:** [§202]   Finally, if P's ratification occurs after a material change in the basic circumstances such that it would be inequitable to subject T to liability thereon, T can avoid the transaction despite the ratification. [Pape v. Home Insurance Co., 139 F.2d 231 (2d Cir. 1943); Rest. 2d §89]

(1) **Example:** Without authority, A purports to sell Blackacre to T on P's behalf. The next day the house on the property burns down. P's subsequent ratification of the sales contract will not bind T.

    (a) **Minority view contra:** [§203]   Some jurisdictions hold that ratification merely substitutes the principal as a party to the contract, and hence that rights and liabilities should be decided on the basis of the original agreement.

    (b) **Insurance exception:** [§204]   In the case of insurance contracts, many cases have held the ratification to be effective even after destruction of the subject matter, unless T has attempted to withdraw from the contract prior to P's ratification. [Marqusee v. Hartford Fire Insurance Co., 198 F. 475 (2d Cir. 1912)]

(2) **After ratification:** [§205]   Of course, a change in circumstances occurring *after* ratification by P will not be sufficient to avoid the ratification.

D. LIABILITY ON AGENT'S CONTRACTS

1. **Where Agent Acted Without Authority:** [§206]   Where the agent purports to act on behalf of a principal, but is in fact acting without authority or in excess of authority (*e.g.,* by making unauthorized representations), the principal cannot be held liable absent a ratification. In such cases, *the agent alone* is liable. [Rest. 2d §329]

    a. **Rationale—agent's warranty of authority:** [§207]   The agent's liability here is *not* under the contract itself (since the agent was not intended to be personally liable thereunder). Rather, her liability is based on *breach of warranty.*

        (1) **When breach occurs:** [§208]   The agent is said to warrant impliedly that she *has* authority to bind her supposed principal. If she actually was not authorized or exceeded her authority, so that the principal is not bound, she has breached this implied warranty of authority. [Zugsmith v. Mullins, 344 P.2d 739 (Ariz. 1959)]

        (2) **Reliance required:** [§209]   It is essential that the third person *rely* on the warranty, *i.e.,* an agent is not liable where the third person *knows* that the agent was mistaken as to her authority. [R.D. Johnson Milling Co. v. Brown, 196 A. 100 (Md. 1937)]

        (3) **Tort liability:** [§210]   Under the warranty (contract) theory of liability, the agent is liable even though he believed in good faith that he was authorized. But if the agent intentionally misrepresents that he has the requisite authority, he may also be held liable in tort for *deceit.* [R.D. Johnson Milling Co. v. Brown, *supra*]

    b. **Effect of disclaimer:** [§211]   If the agent clearly indicates to the third person that she is uncertain of her authority, this will usually prevent any warranty of authority from arising, and hence will protect the agent from liability on the contract if it turns out that she was not in fact authorized. [Rest. 2d §331]

    c. **Warranty of performance:** [§212]   The agent's implied warranty of authority does *not* include a warranty that the principal will perform the contract, or even that he is capable of performing it. [Greenlee v. Beaver, 79 N.E.2d 822 (Ill. 1948)]

        (1) **Warranty of competence:** [§213]   The implied warranty of authority, however, *is* deemed to include the agent's warranty that the principal is not incompetent. [Goldfinger v. Doherty, 276 N.Y.S. 289 (1934)] (If the princiapl were incompetent, he would not have capacity to appoint an agent or grant authority to the agent in the first place; *supra,* §56.)

d. **Who may enforce contract against third person:** [§214]   Unless the principal P ratifies the agreement, he is not a party to the unauthorized contract. A alone is a party thereto (together with T); and she alone may enforce it. [Rest. 2d §292]

   (1) **Exception—deception as to principal's existence or authority:** [§215]   However, where it appears that T executed the contract in reliance on the fact that he was dealing with P, and would have refused to deal directly with A, A will be estopped to enforce the contract.

e. **Liability where third party has performed:** [§216]   Where the agent exceeds her authority, but the other party renders full or part performance under the contract, that party may be entitled to sue the principal in *quasi-contract* for the value of any benefits conferred, even though he cannot enforce the contract itself absent a ratification.

   (1) **Example:** P employs A to sell certain property. In order to induce X to purchase same, A represents that P will give X a "kickback" on the purchase price—whereupon X pays the purchase price to P and obtains delivery of the property. If P later refuses X's demand for the "kickback," X can obtain a rescission of the sale. *Rationale:* Even though A's representations were entirely unauthorized, P could not repudiate A's representations and still retain X's payments. There is no enforceable contract, and X is entitled to restitution of benefits paid in the mistaken belief that there was. [33 A.L.R. 90]

2. **Where Agent's Acts Were Authorized:** [§217]   Where the agent's acts are within the scope of her authority (or are subsequently ratified), the principal alone is generally a party to the contract with T and bound thereby. [Lux Art Van Service, Inc. v. Pollard, 344 F.2d 883 (9th Cir. 1965)] However, the rights and liabilities of the parties may vary depending upon whether the identity of the principal was disclosed.

   a. **Contract in name of principal ("disclosed principal" cases):** [§218]   Where the agent negotiates a contract in the name of the principal, the agent is *not* a party to the contract. She is not liable thereunder, and is not entitled to enforce it against any other party thereto, or otherwise to assert any rights thereunder. [Rest. 2d §320] The other party to the contract is liable directly to the principal. [Rest. 2d §292]

      (1) **Example:** Where A executes a contract as "P Company, by A," it is clear that she is executing the agreement solely on behalf of another. If her acts are authorized, she is not liable for P's nonperformance of the contract, nor is she entitled to assert any rights thereunder. [H & B Construction Co. v. James R. Irwin & Sons, 198 A.2d 17 (N.H. 1964)]

      (2) **Agent need not specifically state she is acting for the principal:** [§219]   It is sufficient if the third party knows (or should know) that the person with whom he is dealing is acting as agent for another specific person. *Example:* T knows that P is A's employer and the owner of a horse which A is offering to sell. If T buys the horse from A, he cannot hold A as a party to the sale. [*See* Hannin v. Fisher, 5 Cal. App. 2d 673 (1935)]

      (3) **Where names of both principal and agent appear:** [§220]   Where the names of both the principal and the agent appear on the contract, it is a question of interpretation whether the agent signed on behalf of the principal, or as a party thereto along with the principal.

         (a) **No agency indicated:** [§221]   If nothing in the contract indicates any agency relationship between the parties in question (*e.g.,* "P Company, Joan Smith"), the contract is usually held binding on each—*i.e.,* the agent is liable as a party thereto, along with the principal. [London v. Zachary, 92 Cal. App. 2d 654 (1949)]

(b) **Representative capacity established:** [§222]   However, where the signature or description of the agent establishes that she signed only in a representative capacity, the principal alone is liable thereupon. [Carlesimo v. Schwebel, 87 Cal. App. 2d 482 (1948)]

1) In this regard, execution of a contract in the principal's name "by" or "per" the agent's name is generally sufficient to show the agent's representative capacity—as is execution in the agent's name, followed by the words "agent for" or "on behalf of" the principal's name.

2) And, where an office designation follows the agent's name ("P Company, Joan Smith, President"), the principal (P Company) alone is usually liable. [Rest. 2d §156]

(c) **Extrinsic evidence:** [§223]   Where the contract clearly falls within either of the categories above, extrinsic evidence is not admissible to show that the parties actually intended a different result except perhaps to reform the contract. (*See* Remedies Summary.) However, where there is any *ambiguity,* extrinsic evidence—*e.g.,* the acts, declarations and relationship of the parties, and the circumstances surrounding execution of the contract—is admissible. [Rest. 2d §323]

1) **Example:** Where a contract was signed, "P Company, Joan Smith, agt.," parol evidence has been held admissible to show whether or not it was intended that Smith be a party to the contract. [Jones v. Mayden, 32 Cal. App. 23 (1916)]

2) **Exception:** [§224]   Where the contract in question is a *negotiable instrument* and is held by a holder in due course, extrinsic evidence is *never* admissible, *i.e.,* no agency relationship can be established by parol, since it must clearly appear on the face of the instrument. (*See* Commercial Paper Summary.)

b. **Contracts in name of agent only ("undisclosed" and "partially disclosed" principals)**

(1) **Undisclosed agency:** [§225]   If the agent's name alone appears on the contract, with no statement regarding the fact of agency or the name of the principal, both the fact of agency and the principal's identity are undisclosed. The Restatement refers to these as "undisclosed principal" cases. [Rest. 2d §4]

(a) **Liability of agent to third party:** [§226]   In this situation, the general view is that the agent is liable as a party to the contract. Following the objective theory of contracts (*i.e.,* third person entitled to hold person with whom he apparently deals), the agent is deemed personally obligated under the contract, since the third party was obviously relying on her credit and reputation. And the agent was responsible for such reliance if she failed to advise the other party that she was acting only as agent for another. [Marver-Gulden-Annis, Inc. v. Brazilian & Colombian Coffee Co., 199 N.E.2d 222 (Ill. 1964)]

1) **Agent's rights against undisclosed principal:** [§227]   Where the agent is held liable by a third party, the agent may have a right over against the undisclosed principal.

a) **Indemnification:** [§228]   If an agency agreement existed between P and A, there is deemed to be an implied promise therein that P will perform any contract which A is authorized to execute on his behalf, so as to prevent A from being held liable thereunder. P's failure to do so would therefore be a breach of her agreement with A.

b) **Quasi-contract:** [§229]   If *no* agency agreement exists (*i.e.,* A was acting gratuitously on behalf of P), but P accepted the benefits of A's contract with the third party, P may be held liable in quasi-contract, in order to prevent unjust enrichment. [Rest. 2d §104]

(b) **Liability of principal to third party:** [§230]   Once his identity is made known, the *principal* may also be held liable under the contract. Provided the agent's acts were authorized (actual authority, never "apparent authority"—because principal does not appear), the agent *had* the power to bind the principal. The third person may therefore hold either the principal or the agent under the contract. [Standard Oil Co. v. Doneux, 192 Cal. App. 2d 608 (1961)]

1) **Formalities:** [§231]   This is true whether the contract is oral or in writing, at least under modern authority.

a) **Early view:** [§232]   Some earlier cases held that where the contract was in writing it would violate the *parol evidence rule* to allow extrinsic evidence to show that one of the signatories was acting as agent for another. [Ferguson v. McBean, 91 Cal. 63 (1891)]

b) **Modern view:** [§233]   But the modern view is that the parol evidence rule does not apply—*i.e.,* the extrinsic evidence is being admitted not to contradict the writing, but merely to "explain" the capacity in which the party (agent) signed. [Chapman v. Java Pacific Line, 241 F. 850 (9th Cir. 1917)]

c) **Caution:** [§234]   Remember, however, that if the contract is required to be in writing under the Statute of Frauds, the agent's *authority* to execute same is also required to be in writing in many states. [Mitchell v. Locurto, 79 Cal. App. 2d 507 (1947); *and see* discussion *supra,* §79]

2) **Exception—negotiable instruments:** [§235]   An exception to the general rule is recognized for negotiable instruments. The U.C.C. provides that only the actual signer can be held liable on a negotiable instrument [U.C.C. §3-401]; and extrinsic evidence is therefore *not* admissible to show that she signed as agent for another, where no indication of the agency appears on the face of the instrument. (*See* Commercial Paper Summary.)

3) **Requirement of election by third person:** [§236]   Although the third person, T, normally has a right against either the undisclosed principal, P, and the agent, A, he can obtain satisfaction from only one of them.

a) **Minority view:** [§237]   The early rule (and a minority view today) held that the third person's *filing suit* against either P or A constituted an election which operated to release the other from liability—*i.e.,* T could not file suit against both at the same time. [Kayton v. Barnett, 116 N.Y. 625 (1889)]

b) **Majority view:** [§238]   The modern rule, however, is that T can file suit against *both* P and A, but that—upon objection of either defendant—T must elect *prior to judgment* which party he wishes to hold liable. In other words, T cannot obtain judgment against both (unless the defendants fail to object). [Conner v. Steel, Inc., 470 P.2d 71 (Colo. 1971)]

    1/ **Single recovery:** [§239] Even if P and A fail to object, and a joint judgment is rendered against them, T is still limited to a *single recovery* on the judgment.

  c) **No "election" where principal still undisclosed:** [§240] Of course, where T obtains a judgment against A *without* knowledge of P's identity, he can later sue P when his identity is discovered. [Hugener v. Greider's Wooden Shoe, Inc., 246 N.E.2d 323 (Ill. 1969)]

  d) **Comment:** [§241] The election doctrine has been criticized on the ground that T may not know who is liable, and therefore could end up with a judgment against the wrong party. To avoid this inequity, many courts hold that T is entitled to levy upon whatever *right of indemnification* the agent would have against the undisclosed principal (*see* above), so that the principal may still be forced to discharge the debt which he authorized. [*See* Rest. 2d §210, comment]

(c) **Right to enforce contract against third person:** [§242] As between the principal and agent, the principal is entitled to all benefits of the contract, the agent acquiring no beneficial interest therein. In this respect, it is immaterial that the third person thought he was contracting only with the agent and knew nothing of the principal's existence. [Rest. 2d §302; American Enamel Brick & Tile Co. v. Brozek, 231 N.W. 45 (Mich. 1930)]

  1) **Effect:** [§243] The principal is treated as if he were an assignee of all rights under the contract, so that rights and benefits nominally flowing to A are deemed to go to P. [Buckley v. Shell Chemical Co., 32 Cal. App. 2d 209 (1939)—provision of contract waiving any warranty by "seller," A, held to bar any claim for breach of warranty not only against A, but also against the manufacturer, P, where A was acting as agent for undisclosed principal, P, in effecting the sale] And even if the agent is allowed to sue on the contract, any recovery must be held by her in trust for the benefit of the principal. [Clifton v. Litchfield, 106 Mass. 34 (1870)—as trust funds, recovery would not pass to agent's receiver in bankruptcy]

  2) **Exception where agent fraudulently conceals identity of principal:** [§244] Where the agent fraudulently represents to the third party that she is contracting on her own behalf (or on behalf of someone other than the real principal), the third party has a *right to rescind*; *i.e.,* upon discovering the agent's fraud, the third party has the option to go ahead with the contract, or be relieved of it entirely. [Casteel v. King, 269 P.2d 529 (Or. 1954)]

  a) **Example:** P knows that T will never sell Blackacre to him, and for this reason employs A to purchase the property. A buys the property in her own name and represents that she is acting for no one else (or that she is acting for X, rather than P). Upon discovering P's interest, T has the right to rescind the contract entirely, and unless T waives this right to rescind, P *cannot* enforce the contract.

  b) **Affirmative representation necessary:** [§245] Although there is some disagreement in the cases, the general view is that T has the right to rescind only where the agent made some positive represenation (by word or conduct) which reasonably misled the third party and concealed the identity of the real principal. Thus, where the agent makes no representations at all—*i.e.,* merely buys the property in her own name, without indicating who she may be acting for—there would be no right to rescind. [Kelly Asphalt Block Co. v. Barber Asphalt Paving Co., 211 N.Y. 68 (1914)]

3) **Exception where performance to principal would impose greater burden on third party:** [§246]   Moreover, an undisclosed principal will be denied the right to enforce the contract (and the third party will have the right to rescind) where enforcement by P would impose an added or different burden of performance on the third party.

   a) **Example:** A signs a contract with T whereby T is to provide "all coal requirements" for A. If T did not know that A was in fact contracting on behalf of P, whose coal requirements are much bigger (or otherwise different from A's), P cannot enforce the contract.

   b) **Example:** Acting for an undisclosed P, A engages T as her butler. The rendering of such personal services involves different burdens as between P and A, so that P cannot enforce the contract and T has the right to rescind.

4) **Exception for powers coupled with an interest:** [§247]   Where the agent's powers are held irrevocable because she has some interest in the subject matter (*see supra,* §164), the agent's rights are considered paramount to those of the principal—so that she, rather than the principal, is entitled to any recovery from T.

   a) **Example:** A loans $5,000 to P, and as security P gives A the authority to sell Blackacre. A contracts to sell Blackacre to T, without disclosing the agency. A's authority to sell Blackacre was "coupled with an interest" and thus irrevocable, since the benefits of the agency were really intended for A. Therefore A, rather than P, is entitled to sue under the contract and to obtain the benefits thereof.

(d) **Third person's right to insist upon personal performance by agent:** [§248]   As already indicated, T can hold A liable for performance of a contract on behalf of an undisclosed principal. Moreover, where the duties involved are *nondelegable* under the law of contracts (*see* Contracts Summary), T can *refuse* a tender of performance from P and insist upon A's personal performance. [Rest. 2d §309]

   1) **Credit contracts:** [§249]   Wherever the contract involves an extension of credit, T can insist upon the credit of A. *Example:* A, acting on behalf of undisclosed principal P, buys T's car for $1,000, the terms of sale being a $250 down payment and the balance secured by a promissory note executed by A. T can refuse a promissory note tendered by P. [Lansden v. McCarthy, 45 Mo. 106 (1869)]

   2) **Personal service contracts:** [§250]   Similarly, where the performance to be rendered by A consists of nondelegable personal services, T can refuse a tender by the undisclosed principal, P. *Example:* A, acting on behalf of undisclosed principal, P, advertises that she will conduct an art tour through Europe. T, who signs up for the tour in reliance on A's reputation in the field, can rescind the contract if P seeks to conduct the tour. [*See* Walton v. Davis, 22 Cal. App. 456 (1913)]

(e) **Effect of payment to agent by undisclosed principal:** [§251]   Another problem is whether P or T must bear the burden of any dishonesty or errors by the agent, A, in handling payments from the principal. *Example:* Suppose A enters into a contract with T, under which A is to pay T $5,000. P gives the money to A, but A absconds with it. Can T sue P for the $5,000?

1) **Majority view:** [§252]   Under the great weight of authority, payment to the agent does *not* discharge the principal from his liability to the third person. *Rationale:* Having created A's authority, P must assume any loss resulting from the agent's violation of duty. [Senor v. Bangor Mills, 211 F.2d 685 (3d Cir. 1954)]

2) **California statute:** [§253]   California is apparently *contra* by statute. California Civil Code section 2335 provides that an undisclosed principal is exonerated "by payment or other satisfaction made by him to his agent in good faith, before receiving notice of the creditor's election to hold him responsible." However, this statute has received little support in the cases.

(f) **Effect of third person's payment or performance to agent:** [§254]   So long as T does not know or have reason to know that A was acting as agent for another, he is protected in dealing exclusively with A (and in making whatever payments are required under the contract).

1) **After agency revealed:** [§255]   However, once T learns that A was acting as agent for P, he must render his performance to P, if so requested. Should T continue making payments to A, he will be liable to P. [Darling-Singer Lumber Co. v. Commonwealth, 195 N.E. 723 (Mass. 1935)]

(2) **Disclosed agency but unidentified principal ("partial disclosure"):** [§256]   In certain situations, the third party may have notice that A is acting as an agent, but not know the identity of the principal (*e.g.,* A signs contract, "A, agent"). The Restatement characterizes such cases as involving a "partially disclosed principal" [Rest. 2d §4]; and the courts generally apply the same rules as in the case of "undisclosed principals."

(a) **Liability of agent:** [§257]   Where the agent signs or describes herself as agent of another, but does not set forth the name of the principal in the contract, the agent is *still personally liable* on the contract, unless otherwise agreed between the parties. [Rest. 2d §321]

1) **Example:** A offers to sell goods to T, stating that she is a representative of the manufacturer but not otherwise identifying the latter. If T accepts, A is liable as party to the contract. *Rationale:* Under the objective theory of contracts, T must be held to have relied on A's reputation and credit unless it clearly appears that he was relying on that of the unidentified principal. [Murphy v. Helmrich, 66 Cal. 69 (1884)]

(b) **Rights and liabilities of principal:** [§258]   As in cases of undisclosed agency, the principal (when his identity is made known) is also liable on the contract; and he is likewise entitled to all rights and benefits under the contract (subject to the same exceptions previously noted in the case of undisclosed principals). [Otoe County National Bank v. Delany, 88 F.2d 238 (8th Cir. 1937)]

(c) **Parties' intent governs:** [§259]   Of course, the parties may indicate their intention that the agent *not* be bound, whereupon the agent does not become a party to the contract (*e.g.,* A tells T that she cannot guarantee the performance of the principal whom she represents and who remains unidentified). [Rest. 2d §321]

1) **Parol evidence admissible:** [§260] Where the contract discloses that A is acting as agent for another, but the principal remains unidentified, extrinsic evidence generally *is* admissible to show the intentions of the parties as to whether or not A is personally bound, unless the contract clearly resolves this issue. [Rest. 2d §323(2)]

(3) **Where P's identity is known to third party:** [§261] Finally, if the third person *knows* the identity of the principal, the principal is "disclosed" even though his name does not appear in the contract; and the agent is therefore not a party to the contract.

(a) **Example:** P instructs A to purchase goods from T on his behalf. A offers to purchase the goods as "A, agent." T discovers by an independent investigation that A is acting for P, and accepts the offer. This would be treated as a "disclosed principal" case—*i.e.,* A is not a party to the contract, and P alone is liable thereunder. [Rest. 2d §149]

(b) **Subsequent knowledge of P's identity:** [§262] And, even where P's identity was not known at the time of the contract, if T thereafter acquires such knowledge, any further dealings by him with A are subject to the rights of the principal.

1) **Set-off against agent:** [§263] Frequently, T may acquire a claim against the agent. Whether T can assert this as a set-off against his liability on the contract will thus depend on whether he had notice of P's identity *at the time* the claim against the agent arose. [Continental Purchasing Co. v. Van Raalte Co., 295 N.Y.S. 867 (1937)]

IV. TORT LIABILITY FOR THE ACTS OF OTHERS

A. LIABILITY OF MASTER FOR ACTS OF SERVANT

1. **Doctrine of Respondeat Superior:** [§264]   Under the doctrine of respondeat superior ("let the master answer"), a master will be liable for all torts committed by the servant while acting within the scope of the employment. Any third person injured by the employee's tortious act can therefore proceed against *both* the employee and the employer—the employee being directly liable for his wrongful act, and the employer being *vicariously liable* therefor. [Rest. 2d §219]

   a. **Background:** [§265]   The doctrine developed at early common law when the servant was considered the "property" of the master. The master was deemed to have absolute control over the servant's acts so that he might properly be held to answer for same.

   b. **Present rationale:** [§266]   A servant is obviously no longer viewed as being the property of his master, but the doctrine of respondeat superior has been retained in our modern law on either or both of the following theories:

   (1) **"Entrepreneur theory":** [§267]   Even though the servant is not the property of his master, the master does have the right to control the servant's acts. Having created the risk that some third person may be injured if the servant acts wrongfully, and having the right to control same, the master must assume full responsibility for any damages caused, including acts beyond the actual or possible control but inherent in or created by the enterprise. [Rodgers v. Kemper Construction Co., 50 Cal. App. 3d 608 (1975)]

   (2) **"Deeper pocket theory":** [§268]   Public policy requires that the person injured by the servant's wrongful act be afforded the most effective relief. Since the master is more likely than the servant to be able to respond in damages, he should be held liable. [*See* 26 Yale L.J. 105]

   c. **Nature of liability:** [§269]   Respondeat superior imposes *strict liability* ("liability without fault") on the master; *i.e.,* the employer is responsible for the employee's wrongful acts, notwithstanding his exercise of due care in hiring the employee or supervising his acts.

   (1) **Waiver ineffective:** [§270]   Since this liability is imposed for the protection of third persons, the master *cannot* contract with his employee to insulate himself from liability. *Example:* M hires S in what is clearly an employment relationship, but has S agree in writing that he is serving as an "independent contractor," and that in "no event shall M be liable for S' tortious acts." The contract between M and S will *not* affect M's liability to third persons injured by S' wrongful acts.

   (2) **Vicarious liability:** [§271]   Respondeat superior is likewise a form of *vicarious liability,* since the employer is held accountable for the acts of another. Such liability is *joint and several* with that of the employee for his own acts. The employer can be sued alone, or he can be sued together with the negligent employee.

   (a) **Single recovery:** [§272]   However, the victim is entitled to only one recovery; and a recovery against either party will bar recovery against the other.

   (b) **Exoneration:** [§273]   Moreover, if the employee is exonerated or released from liability, this generally operates to release the employer as well. [Holcomb v. Flavin, 216 N.E.2d 811 (Ill. 1966)]

1) **Exception:** [§274]   Where the employer was guilty of some negligence or breach of duty to the injured party, independent of the acts of his employee, he could be held liable even where the employee was exonerated. [Barsoom v. City of Reedley, 38 Cal. App. 2d 413 (1940); *and see infra*, §§380-384]

2) **Servant's immunity not imputed to master:** [§275]   And, an employer may be held liable for torts committed by his employee even where the employee is immune from liability—as where H negligently injures his wife, W, while acting in the course and scope of his employment for M. In this situation, the employer M *can* be held liable by W, even though no judgment could be obtained by her against H if inter-spousal tort immunity is retained. [Fields v. Synthetic Ropes, Inc., 215 A.2d 427 (Del. 1965)]

a) **Rationale:** [§276]   H's immunity is *personal,* and does not cover the enterprise by which he is employed. There is no realistic threat to "family harmony" in allowing W to recover against H's employer, particularly since insurance exists in most cases. [Schubert v. Schubert Wagon Co., 249 N.Y. 253 (1928)]

d. **Master's right to indemnification:** [§277]   Where the master is held liable for an employee's torts, the master can hold the servant liable in turn—*i.e.,* he has a right of *indemnification* against the servant for any damages he must pay a third person because of the servant's wrongful acts. [Popejoy v. Hannon, 37 Cal. 2d 159 (1951)]

(1) However, indemnity has been denied where the employee was *immune* from liability in the first place (*see* above).

e. **Analysis:** [§278]   In determining whether the doctrine of respondeat superior applies, two basic elements must be established:

(1) Is there a *master-servant relationship* between the party whose actions caused the injury and the person sought to be held liable therefor?

(2) If so, was the servant's wrongful act committed *within the course and scope of his employment*?

2. **Master-Servant Relationship:** [§279]   The first question in every case is whether a master-servant relationship actually existed between the person who committed the tortious act and the person who is sought to be held vicariously liable.

a. **Right to control physical acts of employee:** [§280]   Liability under the doctrine of respondeat superior is based upon the master's right to control the physical acts of the servant—a right unique to the master-servant relationship. [Gifford-Hill & Co. v. Moore, 479 S.W.2d 711 (Tex. 1972)] As will be seen, a principal ordinarily does *not* have the right to control the physical acts of the agent, or of an independent contractor in her employ; and, accordingly, respondeat superior generally does not apply in principal-agent or employer-independent contractor relationships.

(1) **Example:** P engages real estate broker A to sell P's land. While driving a prospective purchaser to the land, A negligently injures X. P has no right to control the physical acts of A, and therefore is not liable to others for A's negligence.

(a) **Dual status:** [§281]   Keep in mind, however, that the same person may be *both a servant and an agent.* Thus, in the example above, if P had employed A not only to sell the land, but also to drive prospective customers from P's office to the property, A might be deemed P's servant (*i.e.,* subject to P's control) while so driving. In such case, P *could* be liable to X.

(2) **Compare—misrepresentations by agent:** [§282]   There are certain instances in which a principal is vicariously liable for nonphysical tortious acts (usually misrepresentations) committed by the *agent*. However, this liability is predicated upon *authority* granted by (or ratification by) the principal, rather than upon respondeat superior. (*See* discussion *infra,* §386.)

(3) **Compare—independent contractors:** [§283]   There are also certain situations in which an employer may be held vicariously liable for the tortious acts of an independent contractor in her employ. Again, however, these are situations in which the employer is deemed to have been directly at fault in some measure—and hence outside the doctrine of respondeat superior. (*See* discussion *infra,* §§321-326.)

b. **Creation of relationship:** [§284]   The master-servant relationship (like that of principal and agent) is consensual in nature, and can exist only if there is an agreement manifesting assent by each of the parties to the creation of the relationship. [Oleksinski v. Filip, 30 A.2d 912 (Conn. 1943)]

(1) **Formalities:** [§285]   The contract may be oral, except when required to be in writing under the Statute of Frauds (*e.g.,* employment for period in excess of one year).

(2) **Capacity**

(a) **Master:** [§286]   Generally, any person having the *capacity to contract* may employ an agent or servant. Thus, *minors and incompetents*, lacking contractual capacity, ordinarily cannot appoint servants or agents to act on their behalf, and hence cannot be held vicariously liable. [Rest. 2d §20]

(b) **Servant:** [§287]   However, no special capacity is required to *be* a servant or agent; *i.e.,* an adult employer *can* be held vicariously liable for the negligent acts of employees who are minors. [Rest. 2d §21]

(3) **Implied agreement:** [§288]   While the master-servant relationship is usually created by an express agreement (whether oral or written), it may also be *implied* from the circumstances or conduct of the parties. [Rest. 2d §26]

(a) **Example:** At harvest time each year, farmer M has employed S as a farmhand. S returns at the current harvest and places his belongings in the employees' bunkhouse. If M knows of and permits this, an employment relationship arises by implication.

(4) **"Volunteers":** [§289]   Since the relationship is consensual, the servant cannot foist his services on the master without her consent. But the mere fact that one party has not requested the other to render services does not prevent a master-servant relationship from arising, if the "master" *knows* that services are being rendered and accepts the benefits thereof. [Copp v. Paradis, 159 A. 228 (Me. 1931)]

(a) **Example:** M's employees are loading merchandise on a truck in front of her store. X, a passerby, commences to help them. At this point, X is not a servant of M. However, if M observes X's act and allows X to continue (thereby accepting the benefits of his work), a master-servant relationship may be held to exist between M and X, at least so far as to impose liability on M for any wrongful act by X injuring a third party.

(b) **No consideration required:** [§290]   In this respect, it should be noted that consideration is *not* essential to the creation of a master-servant relationship. One may gratuitously undertake to act as the servant of another; and if he assumes the duties involved, he will be held to the same obligations and responsibilities as a servant for hire.

    1) **Example:** M's neighbor, S, volunteers to help rebuild M's house following its destruction in a fire. While working under M's supervision, S negligently injures a passerby, P. M is probably liable to P, provided he had *control* over S' acts at the time of the injury.

(5) **Duration of employment:** [§291] A servant is presumed to be hired for the length of time adopted for computing his wages (hourly, weekly, monthly, etc.). If no time period is specified, the employment is presumed to be terminable at will.

    (a) Many states have statutes limiting the length of personal service contracts. [*See, e.g.,* Cal. Labor Code §2855 specifies that they may not exceed seven years]

    (b) Where the servant remains employed by the master after the original employment agreement expires, it is presumed that his employment has been renewed on the same terms.

(6) **Right of master to recover for injuries to servant**

    (a) **Early view:** [§292] The early common law held that one who injured a servant was liable to the master for the loss of the servant's services, the servant being regarded as a "chattel" of the master and the injury as one to a property interest of the master.

    (b) **Modern rule:** [§293] Modern cases uniformly reject this notion, since the relationship between master and servant is now considered strictly one of *contract*.

        1) Thus, a third person who *intentionally* injures a servant is liable to the master for the loss of the servant's services—because intentional interference with contractual relationship is an actionable tort. (*See* Torts Summary.)

        2) But where the injury was merely the result of negligence by the third person, *no* action will lie. [Snow v. West, 440 P.2d 864 (Or. 1968)]

    (c) **Compare:** Similar rules apply in *partnership* cases; *i.e.,* the partnership generally cannot recover against third parties for negligent injuries to one of the partners. [Sharfman v. State, 253 Cal. App. 2d 333 (1967), *and see* discussion *infra,* §500]

c. **Employment by estoppel ("ostensible employment"):** [§294] As noted previously, the general rule is that the master-servant employment relationship must be founded on an agreement between the parties. However, where a person intentionally or negligently creates the *appearance* that another is in her employ, and a third person *relies* thereon, the first person may be estopped to deny the employment relationship, and would be liable to the third person as though she in fact were the master. This is known as an *ostensible employment.* [Standard Oil Co. v. Gentry, 1 So. 2d 29 (Ala. 1941)]

(1) **Requirements:** [§295] Since this relationship is based on estoppel, it must clearly appear that (i) the "employer" in some way created the *appearance* that the "employee" was in her employ, and (ii) the injured party *justifiably relied* on such appearance in dealing with the employee. Where either element is lack-

ing, the ostensible employer cannot be held liable for the torts of the "employee." [Councell v. Douglas, 126 N.E.2d 597 (Ohio 1955)]

(2) **Example:** D Department Store advertises that it employes a skilled chiropractor, X, offering services to the public at nominal rates. Relying on the ad, P engages the services of X. If P is injured through X's negligence, D may be estopped to deny that the chiropracter was its servant (*e.g.*, that she was in fact an independent contractor). Having created an appearance of employment by its representations, D would be vicariously liable for P's injuries.

(3) **Acts by employer required:** [§296]   Note, however, that the appearance of employment must be created *by the purported master*, not by the purported servant. Thus, if S holds herself out as M's servant, and M neither knows of nor consents to such representations, M would not be liable to a third person injured through S' negligence. [McMurry v. Pacific Ready-Cut Homes, Inc., 111 Cal. App. 341 (1931)]

(4) **Reliance requirement:** [§297]   And note that the injury must be sustained in *reliance* on the appearance of employment. *Example:* D Department Store engages independent contractor IC to deliver its parcels, and requires IC's trucks to carry signs advertising D Department Store. If one of IC's trucks hits P, D is *not* estopped from showing that IC was actually an independent contractor, because P was *not* injured in reliance upon D's sign.

d. **Sub-servants:** [§298]   To create a master-servant relationship, it is not necessary that the employer or principal himself do the hiring of employees. Such status can be created by an authorized agent acting on behalf of the master. [Dickerson v. American Sugar Refining Co., 211 F.2d 200 (3d Cir. 1954)]

(1) **Effect on respondeat superior:** [§299]   If the agent is *authorized* to hire a servant for his principal, the servant is placed in a direct relation to the master, and the master is therefore liable for his tortious acts. [Smith v. Rutledge, 163 N.E. 544 (Ill. 1928)]

(a) **Example:** M authorizes S to hire truck drivers to work in M's business. S hires X, who subsequently injures T while driving one of M's trucks. M is liable for X's negligence notwithstanding the fact that X was hired by S, rather than M.

(b) **Undisclosed principal:** [§300]   If the agent does not disclose that he is hiring on behalf of another, and the servant is not otherwise aware of this, the master is said to be an undisclosed principal (*see* discussion *supra,* §225).

1) In such a case, the agent remains liable to the employee *on the contract* (*e.g.,* for wages due and owing the employee). [Pierce v. Johnson, 34 Conn. 274 (1867)]

2) However, the agent hiring an employee for an undisclosed principal is generally *not* liable in *tort* to third persons injured by the wrongful acts of the employee. *Rationale:* Respondeat superior imposes liability only on the *true master*, and as between P and A, P must be held the master of S.

(2) **Unauthorized hirings:** [§301]   If the agent, S, was *not* authorized to employ a sub-servant, X, there is no relationship between M and X, and ordinarily M would not be liable to third persons for X's torts. [White v. Consumers Finance Service, Inc., 15 A.2d 142 (Pa. 1940)]

(a) **Exception:** [§302]   Nevertheless, if the work in question requires no particular skill or discretion (so that M had attached no special significance to the identity of the servant), *and if* the services of the stranger are within the scope of S' employment for M and are performed *under S' supervision and in his presence*, M may be held liable to third persons. *Rationale:* This situation is tantamount to S having rendered the services himself. [Gibbons v. Naritoka, 102 Cal. App. 669 (1929)]

(b) **Example:** M hires S to act as a flag-person in M's paving business. Without authority, S permits a friend, X, to flag cars in S' presence and under her supervision. M may be held liable for injuries caused by X's negligent actions at the job site.

(3) **Emergency authority to hire:** [§303]   Even an ordinary servant may have authority to hire and employ a sub-servant in an emergency. If an unanticipated situation requires immediate action in order to preserve or protect the master's interests, and communication with the master is impossible or impractical, the servant is deemed to have the authority to employ another to assist him; and in such an event, the master becomes liable for the wrongful acts of the sub-servant.

(a) **Example:** While delivering perishable merchandise for M, S becomes ill and is unable to contact M. S asks X, a passerby, to deliver the merchandise. If X negligently injures P while attempting to make the delivery, M may be liable to P. [Kirk v. Showell, Fryer & Co., Inc., 120 A. 665 (Pa. 1923)]

e. **"Borrowed servants":** [§304]   Frequently, an employer may lend the services of his employee to another, either gratuitously or for compensation. A common example is where M lends or leases a piece of equipment to T and sends along his employee, S, to assist T in its operation. If S commits a tortious act while operating the equipment, who is liable therefor? Who is the "master"—M or T?

(1) **Right to control servant determinative:** [§305]   Liability in these situations usually turns on whether the general employer, M, or the special employer, T, had the right to control the employee, S.

(a) As a general rule, a lessor who rents his equipment with an operator is presumed to *retain* the right of control over the operator. Hence, he (rather than the lessee) would be liable for the operator's torts unless the operator must take orders from the lessee. [Brittingham v. American Dredging Co., 262 A.2d 255 (Del. 1970)]

(b) However, if the primary right of control has been given to T (particularly where the borrowing is for an indefinite period), liability for S' actions also passes to T. [Meyer v. All-Electric Bakery, Inc., 271 Ill. App. 522 (1933)]

(c) And, *regardless* of who has the primary right of control, if the special employer directs S to perform a specific act, he will be liable if S performs it tortiously. [Hilgenberg v. Elam, 198 S.W.2d 94 (Tex. 1947)]

(2) **Compare—joint liability of general and special employer:** [§306]   Where there is a *division of control* over the employee—as where T directs S to perform a specific act which is also within the scope of S' employment by M—*both* M and T may be liable for the tortious performance of the act. *Example:* M loans his truck and driver S to T. T orders S to load dirt on the truck and haul it to T's construction project. S loads the truck in a negligent manner, and as a result the truck overturns en route to the construction site, injuring P. If loading was within the scope of S' employment by M, both M and T may be liable to P. [Rest. 2d §227; 17 A.L.R.2d 1388]

f. **"Servants" vs. "independent contractors":** [§307]   The doctrine of respondeat superior is limited to the master-servant relationship, and does not apply where the tortious acts are committed by an independent contractor (or *his* servants or employees). Thus, an employer ordinarily is not liable for injuries caused by the negligent acts of an independent contractor, even though the contractor is acting for the employer's benefit. [Green v. Independent Oil Co., 201 A.2d 207 (Pa. 1964)] (Of course, the employer may still be liable for the *results* he ordered from the independent contractor; *see infra,* §§368-384.)

(1) **Test is right to control:** [§308]   The chief criterion for whether a given party is a servant or independent contractor is whether the employer has the right to control the party's conduct in the performance of the work. As noted previously, the master-servant relationship requires that the master have the right to control the employee's services and mode of doing the work. Thus where the employer is merely bargaining for a *result*, and retains no such control, the relationship is that of employer-independent contractor. [Parks v. Lynch, 195 So. 331 (Miss. 1940)]

   (a) **Note:** In certain cases, the same person may be *both* a servant and an independent contractor to the same employer; and in such cases his status will depend upon his activity at the particular time in question. (*See* discussion *supra,* §9.)

(2) **Relevant factors:** [§309]   The legal distinction between a servant and an independent contractor is easy to state but more difficult to apply in practice. Frequently, the extent of control by the employer is disputed or unclear, and the distinction between servant and independent contractor may be a matter of degree. The following factors are relevant in determining the status of the individual involved. [Rest. 2d §220]

   (a) **The agreed extent of control** which the employer may exercise over details of the work;

   (b) **Whether the person employed is engaged in an occupation or business distinct from that of the employer;**

   (c) **Whether the work is usually done under the employer's direction, or by a specialist** without supervision;

   (d) **Whether the employer supplies the tools and place of work;**

   (e) **The length of time** for which the person is employed;

   (f) **The method of payment** (whether by time or by completed job); and

   (g) **The degree of skill** required by the person employed.

(3) **Examples**

   (a) **Building contractors:** [§310]   A general contractor who erects a building is clearly an independent contractor, and so is a *subcontractor* who contracts to furnish materials and services for a particular part of the job. Each usually has his own organization and employees, and the property owner generally has no right of direct control over the manner and means used to accomplish the job. [Moriarty v. W. T. Grant Co., 155 N.Y.S.2d 483 (1955)]

   (b) **Truck drivers** [§311] who own their own equipment and hire out for specific jobs are generally independent contractors [Skelton v. Fekete, 120 Cal.

App. 2d 401 (1953)]; whereas those who drive their employer's trucks in the daily course of business are usually servants [Amyx v. Henry & Hall, 79 So. 2d 483 (1955)]

(c) **News vendors** [§312] are likewise generally held to be independent contractors, despite such matters as payment of wages, right of immediate discharge, and some measure of control by the employer. [Skidmore v. Haggard, 110 S.W.2d 726 (Mo. 1937)]

(d) **Physicians:** [§313] A frequent problem arises where doctors are engaged by an employer to treat third persons—*e.g.*, the "company doctor," or the resident physician employed by a hospital. If the doctor negligently injures a patient, can the employer be held liable therefor under respondeat superior?

1) **General view:** [§314]   Most courts hold that highly-skilled persons such as doctors or lawyers are independent contractors, even though employed on a retainer basis. *Rationale:* Medicine is a skilled and learned art, and it would be incompatible to say that a doctor is subject to the "complete control" of another, without which there can be no master-servant relationship. [Giannelli v. Metropolitan Life Insurance Co., 29 N.E.2d 124 (Mass. 1940)]

   a) **Minority view:** [§315]   However, a number of jurisdictions *do* impose liability on the employer, at least in the case of a physician employed by the hospital where she is a resident. [*See* Bowers v. Olch, 120 Cal. App. 2d 108 (1953)]

2) **Compare—where services primarily for benefit of employer:** [§316] Where the physician's services were primarily for the benefit of the employer—rather than for treatment of a third person—many courts have held that the physician should be considered a "servant" and the employer held liable for the physician's negligent injury of such third persons.

   a) **Example:** E hires doctor D to give a physical examination to P, whom E is considering employing. The examination results are to be used by E in determining P's fitness as an employee. In such a case, the examination is primarily for the benefit of E rather than P, and hence E may be liable for any injuries which D negligently inflicts on P in the course of the examination. [Pearl v. West End Street Railway Co., 57 N.E. 339 (Mass. 1900)]

   b) **Representations:** [§317]   A similar result would follow where the employer authorizes the physician to make *representations* to third persons on the employer's behalf. *Example:* E hires physician D to treat an injured employee, P, and for the purpose of minimizing P's claim against him, E directs the physician to assure P that his injuries are not serious. Relying on D's assurances, P returns to work too soon and greatly aggravates the injury. E may be liable for the false representations by the physician. (*See* discussion *infra,* §386.)

3) **Compare—negligent hiring of physicians:** [§318]   Even under the general rule that a physician is an independent contractor whose employer is not liable for his negligence, a contrary result will follow if it appears that the employer was neglient in *selecting* the physician (*see infra,* §325).

   a) **Example:** Hospital D hires X as a resident physician, knowing that he is an alcoholic. While intoxicated, X negligently treats and injures P. D is liable to P. *Rationale:* This is *not* an application of respondeat superior, but liability for the *direct negligence of the employer*.

(e) **Collection agencies:** [§319]   An outside collection agency employed by a creditor to collect a debt is generally held to be an independent contractor, since the agency is usually engaged in a distinct occupation and the creditor reserves no control over the methods of collection. As a result, the creditor generally is not liable for any torts committed by the agency in attempting to collect the claim (*e.g.,* assault, defamation, invasion of privacy).

    1) **Exceptions:** [§320]   Of course, the result would be *contra* if the creditor were shown to have *caused or directed* the collection agent to commit the tort, or if the agent was not self-employed but a full-time employee of the creditor.

(4) **Exceptional situations in which employer is liable for torts of independent contractor:** [§321]   There are certain limited situations in which an employer may be held liable for the tortious acts of an independent contractor in his employ. As will be seen, however, these are not applications of respondeat superior—which is limited to the master-servant relationship. Rather, liability is imposed on the employer because of his *own* negligence or wrongdoing, or the act of the independent contractor is attributed to the employer as a matter of *public policy*.

(a) **Highly dangerous acts:** [§322]   Where the work contracted for is of a highly dangerous nature, the employer will be liable for any injuries caused thereby; and he cannot avoid or delegate such liability by arranging to have it done by an independent contractor. [Giem v. Williams, 222 S.W.2d 800 (Ark. 1949)]

    1) This exception is usually limited to cases in which the activity in question amounts to an "ultra-hazardous activity"—*i.e.,* one in which strict liability ("liability without fault") would be imposed as a matter of law. (*See* Torts Summary.) It is therefore immaterial whether the independent contractor was negligent in causing the injury.

    2) *Example:* E hires IC, an explosives expert, to blast some boulders on E's land. The blast is set off carefully, but a piece of rock is unforeseeably hurled onto P's land, injuring P. E would be liable therefor, even though IC was not negligent. (*A fortiori,* if IC had actually been negligent.)

    3) Other ultrahazardous activities include transporting highly volatile chemicals, use of poisonous gases in fumigation or crop-spraying, drilling of oil wells, etc. (*See* Torts Summary.)

(b) **Nondelegable duties:** [§323]   Similarly, where E is under a duty which is nondelegable as a matter of law or public policy but nevertheless engages IC to perform same, E remains fully liable for IC's conduct.

    1) **Example:** E, who is required to provide a safe place of employment for his factory workers, engages IC to make repairs on the place of employment. IC is negligent and, as a result, one of the workers sustains injuries. E would be liable for the injuries. [Rest. 2d §492]

    2) **Automobile cases:** [§324]   Because of the substantial risk of harm involved, a number of cases hold that the owner of an *automobile* is liable for injuries caused by its defective condition, even though he employed

a reputable garage to repair the car, *i.e.,* the owner's duty to maintain his car in a safe condition is considered nondelegable. [Maloney v. Rath, 69 Cal. 2d 442 (1968); *and see* Torts Summary]

    (c) **Employer negligence in selecting independent contractor:** [§325]   As noted *supra* (§249), an employer may be charged with liability for injuries caused by an independent contractor, where the employer is negligent in selecting the independent contractor or permitting him to undertake the activity in question.

    (d) **Representations:** [§326]   Finally, where the independent contractor is authorized to make representations on behalf of his employer, the employer may be liable for any misstatements made by the contractor (*see* discussion *infra,* §§386-389).

3. **Scope of Employment:** [§327]   Once it is established that a master-servant relationship exists between the employer and the person employed, one must also determine that the employee committed the tortious act *within the course and scope of his employment* in order to hold the employer liable therefor. Basically, this means that the servant must have been engaged in work for the master of a type that he was employed to perform, during working hours.

    a. **Relevant factors:** [§328]   Under the Restatement, the following general factors should be considered in determining whether or not a particular act occurred within the scope of employment [Rest. 2d §229]:

        (1) **Whether the act was authorized** (or incidental to any act authorized) by the master;

        (2) **The time, place and purpose** of the act;

        (3) **Whether the act was one commonly performed by employees** on behalf of their employers;

        (4) **The extent to which the employer's interests were advanced** by the act;

        (5) **The extent to which the private interests of the employee were involved** therein;

        (6) **Whether the employer furnished the means or instrumentality** (truck, machine, etc.) by which the injury was inflicted;

        (7) **Whether the employer had reason to know that the employee would do the act** in question;

        (8) **Whether the act involved the commission of a serious crime.**

    b. **Authorization by master:** [§329]   Very few employers knowingly authorize tortious acts by their employees. Hence, it is *not* necessary to show that the master authorized or permitted the particular act which caused the injury, so long as the act occurred in the scope of the employee's regular duties and employment. [Tucker v. United States, 91 F. Supp. 527 (D. Ala. 1950)]

        (1) **Example:** M employs S to deliver merchandise for M, using M's truck. Instead of driving M's truck, S uses his own private car, and while negligently driving on a delivery, injures P. Even though the particular act (driving his own car) was not authorized, the negligence occurred within the scope of the duties assigned to S (delivering merchandise) and M may therefore be liable.

        (2) **Forbidden acts:** [§330]   On the same theory, even acts which are *specifically forbidden* by the employer may be within the scope of employment, *i.e.,* a master cannot avoid responsibility for the negligence of a servant by telling him

to act carefully, or never to commit some particular tortious act. [National Premium Budget Plan Corp. v. National Fire Insurance Co., 234 A.2d 683 (N.J. 1967)]

(a) **Example:** M, the owner of a sporting goods store, directs his salesperson, S, never to insert a cartridge while exhibiting a gun to a customer. Nevertheless, S does so, and causes injuries to P. Since S' act was directly related to his assigned duties (selling guns) and hence within the scope of his employment, M would be liable to P.

(b) **Violations affecting authorization:** [§331] However, when the servant—in violating his employer's instructions—goes *beyond the duties for which he is hired*, his act may be outside the scope of his employment, and the master relieved of liability for the tortious consequences.

   1) **Example:** M employs S to collect for goods sold by M to third parties, but S is specifically instructed not to attempt repossession of any goods, even peaceably. If S uses force to repossess goods previously sold by M to P, he has exceeded the scope of his employment (*i.e.,* collecting monies); and M is therefore not liable for any tort committed by S during the repossession.

   2) **Analysis:** [§332] Decisions in this type of case are a matter of *degree*: Minor "deviations" from assigned orders generally do not take the act out of respondeat superior, whereas major "departures" would.

   3) **Compare:** [§333] Authorization is of *crucial* importance where liability for the *representations* of another are concerned (*see infra,* §391).

c. **Intentional torts by servant:** [§334] Liability under respondeat superior extends to intentional acts by the servant, provided they occur within the scope of his employment. If the servant's intentional act is related to carrying forth the master's business, the master may be chargeable therefor. [Novick v. Gouldsberry, 173 F.2d 496 (9th Cir. 1949)]

   (1) **Motivation:** [§335] Again, the factual issue is whether the criminal or intentional act is "related to carrying forth the master's business." Probably the most important factor in these cases is whether the infliction of injury was motivated by the servant's personal reasons or whether he was acting to further the business interests of his employer. The more serious or culpable the act, the less likely it will be found to be within the scope of the servant's employment. [Nelson v. American-West African Line, 86 F.2d 730 (2d Cir. 1936)]

      (a) **Example:** M employs S to repossess goods sold to P. P refuses to give up the goods, and S obtains them by the use of excessive and unlawful force. M is civilly liable for S' battery upon P. [*See* Magnolia Petroleum Co. v. Guffey, 102 S.W.2d 408 (Tex. 1937)—forcible detention of customer by gas station attendant]

      (b) **Example:** M sends S to deliver a package to T. When S sees T, he recognizes him as a long-time enemy and strikes T. Even though M's business happened to lead S to the spot where he attacked T, the act was not related to the duties of his employment; and hence M would not be liable.

      (c) **Example:** M employs S as a bouncer to maintain order in M's tavern. When S attempts to evict P, a noisy patron, a fight ensues, and S becomes unreasonably excited and kills P. Even though S' reaction may have been abnormal, and even though he clearly used excessive force, the act was related to the employer's business, and M may be held liable. [34 A.L.R.2d 372]

1) **Compare:** However, where a bartender shot a customer who made advances toward another patron, this was held to be *outside* the scope of his employment. [Howard v. Zaney Bar, 85 A.2d 401 (Pa. 1952)]

(2) **Civil vs. criminal liability:** [§336]   Respondeat superior is a rule of *civil* liability. Except as to minor regulatory laws (*e.g.,* sale of impure food or sale of alcoholic beverages to minors), the doctrine does not apply in criminal law. Thus, even where S acts within the scope of his employment, M cannot be held criminally liable unless he somehow participated therein.

(a) **Compare:** [§337]   But a *corporation* can be held criminally liable for the acts of its officers and employees—the rationale being that the corporation can *only* act through its officers, etc. (*See* Corporations Summary.)

(3) **Master's liability apart from respondeat superior:** [§338]   In a few cases, an employer has been held civilly liable for his employee's tortious and criminal acts, even though such acts were clearly *outside* the scope of employment, where the employer is found to owe an *independent, overriding duty* to the injured party.

(a) **Common carriers:** [§339]   The best example is in common carrier cases, where the carrier is placed under a duty of "utmost" care to its passengers and thus is liable for *any* tortious or criminal acts inflicted by its employees on passengers. *Example:* where P, a passenger on a train, was raped by a Pullman porter, the Pullman Co. was held liable, the court finding it immaterial that the porter's act was clearly outside the scope of his employment. [Berger v. Southern Pacific Co., 144 Cal. App. 2d 1 (1956)]

1) In this area, liability is imposed on the basis of the employer's *own* duty to third persons (passengers). (*See* discussion *infra,* §381.)

(b) **Defamation** [§340] cases are another example. An employer in the business of disseminating information (*e.g.,* a broadcaster, or credit reporting bureau) may be held liable for *publishing* defamations uttered by one of its employees, even though the defamation was neither authorized nor within the scope of the writer's employment. Again, liablity is not based on respondeat superior but on the employer's republication—which makes him directly liable. [Rest. 2d §247]

d. **Omissions by servant:** [§341]   Where an employee's failure to act constitutes a tort, the employer may be held liable under respondeat superior just as if the employee had been guilty of some affirmative wrongful act. *Example:* M Railroad Co. hires S as a switchman, and he is directed to throw a certain switch each day. S neglects to do as instructed, and this causes a train wreck. M Railroad is liable for S' failure to act.

e. **Injuries caused by servant smoking, drinking, etc., on job:** [§342]   Whether the employer is liable for damages caused by the careless smoking, eating, etc., of an employee while on the job is still somewhat unclear.

(1) **Early view:** [§343]   Earlier cases took the position that smoking, eating, etc., was for the personal convenience or pleasure of the employee, and hence was outside the scope of employment—so that the master could not be held liable therefor.

(2) **Modern trend:** [§344]   However, more modern cases view these as *necessary to the employee's comfort or convenience while on the job*—and hence are within the scope of employment. [DeMirjian v. Ideal Heating Corp., 129 Cal. App. 2d 758 (1954)]

(3) **And note:** Even where smoking, etc., is considered to be outside the scope of employment, the employer will be liable if he permits the employee to smoke (or fails to exercise reasonable care to prevent it) while aware of the risk created thereby—*e.g.,* where M observes S smoking around inflammable liquids and fails to put a stop to it. [13 A.L.R. 997]

f. **Servant's use of employer's vehicle, equipment, etc., outside the scope of employment:** [§345]   The mere fact that M has permitted S to use M's truck, machine, etc., is not sufficient to impose liability on M for injuries negligently caused by S in use thereof, if the use was outside the scope of employment. M is liable only when the instrumentality is being used for the purpose of advancing M's business interests, rather than S' personal affairs. [Keener v. Jack Cole Trucking Co., 233 F. Supp. 181 (W.D. Ky. 1964)]

(1) **Examples**

(a) M furnishes S a bicycle for use on the job, and also permits S to take the bicycle home at night for personal use. If S negligently injures P while using the bicycle for recreational purposes, M is not liable.

(b) M Railroad employs S as an engineer. For the sole purpose of scaring P, S blows the whistle, causing P's horse to bolt and injure P. M is is not liable. [Chesapeake & Ohio Railway Co. v. Ford, 166 S.W. 605 (Ky. 1914)]

(2) **Compare—"permissive use" statutes re automobiles:** [§346]   Even where an employer is not otherwise liable under respondeat superior for the employee's ngeligent use of the employer's vehicle, equipment, etc., outside the scope of employment, many jurisdictions have "permissive use" statutes which impose limited liability on the *owner* of a motor vehicle for any damages negligently inflicted by a person driving it with his permission. [*See e.g.,* Cal. Veh. Code §17150—registered owner liable up to $15,000 for injuries inflicted by any person driving car with his express or implied consent] In such jurisdictions, if S were driving M's car with the latter's consent, it is immaterial whether S' acts were within or outside the scope of employment.

g. **Servant's use of unauthorized instrumentalities:** [§347]   A more difficult problem arises where S uses some vehicle, machine, equipment, etc., in performing M's business, where M has not authorized such use. The cases hold that if the instrumentality used is *substantially different* from that authorized, the use thereof must be deemed outside the scope of employment, and M cannot be held liable. What is "substantially different" is generally measured by determining whether *any greater risk* is involved in the instrumentality used. [Spence v. Maier, 59 A.2d 609 (N.J. 1948)]

(1) **Example:** M employs S as a messenger, instructing him to use public transportation. However, S decides to drive his own car, and negligently injures P. The use of a private automobile is "substantially different" from the use of public transportation, and hence M probably would not be held liable. [Barton v. McDermott, 108 Cal. App. 372 (1930)]

(a) If M had given S *no* instructions as to means of transportation, the result would probably be contra.

(2) **Example:** M tells S to drive X into town, using M's car. S chooses to use M's truck instead. Although the instrumentality used was different from that

authorized, it probably would not involve any greater risk of harm. Thus, M probably would be liable for S' negligence in driving the truck.

h. **Servant going to and from work:** [§348]   An employee going to and from work, or to meals, is ordinarily considered outside the scope of her employment for purposes of respondeat superior. [Brown v. Bond, 1 So. 2d 794 (Miss. 1941)]

   (1) **Exception—"special errand rule":** [§349]   However, where S' going to or from work *also* involves some service or purpose for her employer, she may be held to be within the scope of employment. [Boynton v. McKales, 139 Cal. App. 2d 777 (1956)]

   (2) **Exception—traveling salespeople:** [§350]   Likewise, a traveling salesperson compelled by work to be away from home or business headquarters for long periods is generally regarded as within the scope of employment the whole time that he is away, even while not actually at work, as when he is returning home.

i. **Acts of servant done entirely or partially on own behalf:** [§351]   Where the employee temporarily departs from instructed duties and undertakes personal business, is she acting outside the scope of the employment? *Example:* While delivering goods for M, S goes out of her way to visit a friend; and while en route back to work, injures P. Is M liable?

   (1) **Substantial departure required:** [§352]   Again, the cases turn on the *degree* to which S was serving her own interests: Only a *substantial* deviation or departure will take the employee outside the scope of her employment. If the *main purpose* of the activity is still the employer's business, it does not cease to be within the scope of the employment merely because of incidental personal acts, slight delays, or deflections from the most direct route. [Harris v. Oro-Dam Constructors, 269 Cal. App. 2d 911 (1969)]

      (a) **Deviation vs. departure:** [§353]   The term "deviation" is ordinarily used to describe minor deflections, while "departure" indicates the kind of abandonment which takes the acts outside the scope of employment.

   (2) **Examples**

      (a) S, while on an errand for M, picks up a personal friend, drive him three blocks *past* her business destination, and while there, negligently injures X. Since S actually reached *and passed* her business objective, this would probably be considered "departure" from the employment relieving M of liability to X.

      (b) M directs S to sell M's goods in Middletown, but S proceeds instead to Clarksville. While there, P tampers with the merchandise in S' truck, and S uses unreasonable force in getting rid of P. Notwithstanding the change of locale, the particular act causing the injury was directly related to S' duties for M, and M would therefore be liable.

   (3) **"Mixed motives":** [§354]   In many cases, S may be acting partly for her own interests and partly for her employer. If any substantial part of the act was done for the purposes of the employer, that is generally sufficient to impose liability on the employer for all the consequences thereof. [Rest. 2d §236]

      (a) **Example:** M instructs S to deliver goods in town, and S decides to transact some personal business en route. On the way to perform both tasks, S negligently injures P. M is liable.

      (b) **Example:** S, employed in driving a truck for M, gives a ride to a personal friend, X. In order to accommodate X, S drives the truck at an excessive rate of speed and injures P. M is liable. [Cochran v. Michaels, 157 S.E. 173 (W.Va. 1931)]

j. **Liability to unauthorized guests of servant:** [§355]   Where S invites a third person to ride along with her in M's vehicle (or the third person is riding as a trespasser therein), and that person is injured through S' negligence, can M be held liable?

   (1) **Majority view:** [§356]   The general rule is that unless otherwise authorized by M, S' invitation to ride in M's vehicle does *not* constitute an invitation by M. S' invitation is held to be *outside* the scope of her employment, thereby relieving M of any liability for any injuries to the invitee. [Lippman v. Ostrum, 123 A.2d 230 (N.J. 1956)]

      (a) And, this is true even though the conduct which causes the harm—S' operation of the vehicle—is within the scope of the servant's employment. [74 A.L.R. 160; Rest. 2d §242]

      (b) The rule applies *a fortiori* to trespassers riding *without* an invitation from S.

   (2) **Minority view:** [§357]   However, California and several other states take the position that since M would be liable to a stranger on the street for S' negligent acts, he should be liable to a trespasser or invitee *within* the vehicle as well. Under this approach, M would be liable as long as S' negligence occurs within the scope of employment—whether the injured party's presence was authorized being immaterial. [Meyer v. Blackman, 59 Cal. 2d 668 (1963)]

   (3) **Other courts:** [§358]   Still other courts would hold M liable where injuries to the unauthorized guest were sustained due to the "wanton and willful misconduct" of the employee, S. [Wilson v. Dailey, 62 A.2d 284 (Md. 1948)]

4. **"Fellow Servant" Exception to Respondeat Superior:** [§359]   An important exception to the doctrine of respondeat superior is the "fellow servant rule"—*i.e.*, that a master is not liable for the injuries inflicted by one servant upon a fellow servant while engaged in the same general enterprise. [Williams v. Dade County, 237 So. 2d 776 (Fla. 1970)]

   a. **Definition:** [§360]   A "fellow servant" is any other employee who serves and is controlled by the same master, *and* is engaged in the "same general enterprise." Both requirements must be met for the rule to apply. [McTaggart v. Eastman's Co., 58 N.Y.S. 1118 (1899)]

   b. **Rationale for the rule:** [§361]   The traditional theories advanced for the "fellow servant rule" are that each servant "assumes the risk" that he might be injured by another servant with whom he is employed, and that the servant is as able as his employer to know of and protect himself against any such danger or risk. [Farwell v. Boston & Worcester Railroad, 45 Mass. (4 Metc.) 49 (1842)]

      (1) **Criticism:** [§362]   Neither of these theories makes sense in large companies with thousands of fellow servants, making it impossible to know which are likely to be careless and which are not.

   c. **Exception for employer's negligence in hiring:** [§363]   Note that the fellow servant rule does *not* apply where the employer has failed to exercise reasonable care in the *selection* of employees. For example, if M hires S to drive a truck, knowing of S' record of careless driving, and S negligently injures a fellow servant, M could be held liable.

   d. **Exception for acts by superior servant:** [§364]   Likewise, the rule does not apply if the servant is injured by a *superior* servant acting within his authority in supervising the inferior servant's conduct or protecting the master's property. [8 A.L.R. 1432]

e. **Effect of Workers' Compensation Acts:** [§365]   Workers' Compensation Acts—in effect in most states today—provide for a fixed compensation to insured workers or their dependents in case of industrial accidents. Where such Acts apply, no legal action is allowed against an employer for injuries sustained on the job and there is no need for the "fellow-servant rule."

(1) **Impact of "fellow servant rule":** [§366]   However, some Workers' Compensation statutes cover only major industrial occupations (excluding domestic workers or laborers); while others exclude employees in shops employing less than a specific number of workers, or injuries caused by wilful misconduct of the employer or fellow servants. In such cases the "fellow-servant rule" is still significant.

(2) **Compare:** [§367]   Workers' Compensation statutes are usually limited to injuries sustained "in the scope of employment." However, this is construed much more liberally than in the case of respondeat superior (*supra,* §§327-358)—so that many accidents which would be *outside* the scope of employment for respondeat superior purposes will be covered. [Zenith National Insurance Co. v. Workmen's Compensation Appeal Board, 66 Cal. 2d 944 (1967)]

(a) And since Workers' Compensation statutes only cover injuries to "employees," and not "independent contractors," courts are more inclined to find an injured worker to be an "employee" for workers' compensation purposes than for purposes of respondeat superior. [147 A.L.R. 828]

5. **Liability of Principal for Personal Breach of Duty—Cases Outside Respondeat Superior:** [§368]   Entirely aside from vicarious liability under the doctrine of respondeat superior, an employer is liable for the tortious acts of a person in her employ where the employer was directly responsible therefor. In these cases, the employer herself is at fault, and her *own* wrongdoing is the proximate cause of the injury (even though inflicted through the employee).

a. **Wrongful act directed or authorized by employer:** [§369]   If the employer directs, authorizes or permits the employee to perform a tortious act, the employer is liable just as if she had committed the tort herself—the act being considered that of the employer done through the employee. [Kalb v. Luce, 291 N.W. 841 (Wis. 1940); Rest. 2d §212]

(1) **Example:** M directs S to destroy machinery belonging to a competitor, T. If S does so, M is liable to T without regard to respondeat superior.

(2) **Example:** The same result follows where the employer knows that the employee is acting recklessly and *permits* him to do so. Thus, if M observes S smoking around inflammable liquids and fails to direct him to cease, M is liable for consequences (*see supra,* §342).

(3) **Compare—liability of agent or employee:** [§370]   In most cases the agent or employee who commits a tortious act upon another is *also* personally liable to the injured party—even though he acted under the directions of his employer, he did not benefit personally, and he did not personally intend to injure anyone. [Rest. 2d §349]

(a) **Example:** M directs S to take possession of certain property. The property in fact belongs to another, and S' act constitutes a conversion. S, as well as M, may be held personally liable for the value of the property—it being immaterial that S believed M to be the rightful owner. [Swim v. Wilson, 90 Cal. 126 (1891)]

(b) **Exception—fraud or duress:** [§371]   However, an otherwise innocent agent or employee is *not liable* for false information supplied by his employer which he relays to third persons at the direction of the employer, provided he had *no knowledge* of the falsity of the information, *i.e.,* the knowledge of a fraudulent principal is not imputed to the agent. [Rest. 2d §348]

    1) **Example:** P authorizes A to sell P's apartment house, and gives A a falsely inflated statement regarding income therefrom. A makes representations to prospective purchaser, T, in reliance thereon. If A had no reason to doubt the information given him by P, he is not liable to T for the misrepresentation. [Seckel v. Allen, 67 Cal. App. 2d 146 (1944)]

b. **Employer ratification of tortious conduct:** [§372]   Similarly, an employer or principal may be liable in tort for the acts of someone not in her employ, or for the acts of an employee outside the scope of employment, if she *ratifies* the conduct in question. By her ratification, the principal becomes liable for such acts *as if they had been authorized by her* at the time they were committed. [Rest. 2d §218]

(1) **Rationale** [§373]

    (a) Technically, a tort *cannot* be ratified. For example, if A negligently injures X, and B voluntarily tells X, "Don't worry...I'll take care of your damages and will be responsible for everything," this is *not* a ratification of A's conduct. B does not become a party to the tort and cannot be held in tort for the damages inflicted by A. (If anything, he may be liable in contract to the extent X relies on his statement, or to the extent he has otherwise agreed to indemnify A.)

    (b) However where the employer *accepts benefits or advantages* obtained from the acts of another, who was otherwise not authorized to act for her, she is deemed to have authorized such acts from their inception—and thereby becomes liable for any torts incident thereto under the theory of respondeat superior. [Colonial Stores, Inc. v. Holt, 166 S.E.2d 30 (Ga. 1968)]

(2) **What acts may be ratified:** [§374]   Any act committed by an employee or agent (or one purporting to act as such) which could have been authorized in the first place, can be ratified. It is essential, however, that in committing the act, the employee or agent *intended to act on behalf of the employer*, rather than on behalf of himself or someone else.

    (a) **Example:** A trades his private auto in on a new car, misrepresenting the condition of the car to the dealer. A's employer, P, subsequently decides that A should use the new car on the job, and it is agreed that P will buy the new car for A's use and will be responsible for any statements made by A in connection with its purchase. There is *no ratification*, since at the time of purchase A was not intending to act on P's behalf.

(3) **What constitutes a ratification:** [§375]   In order to find a ratification, the employer must have *accepted or retained benefits* which were obtained for her through the wrongful act of the employee or agent, *with knowledge* of all relevant facts. [*See* O'Connor v. Central National Bank & Trust Co., 28 N.E.2d 755 (Ill. 1940)]

    (a) **Example:** P authorizes A to sell her house. A shows the house to several prospective purchasers, and in the course of so doing, falsely identifies certain paintings therein as "Picassos." If one of the prospective purchasers offers to buy the paintings, and P accepts the offer knowing of A's misrepresentations, she is deemed to ratify the previously unauthorized representation.

(b) **Failure to fire employee who commits tort:** [§376]   The courts have split on whether the employer's retaining an employee who commits a tort upon another is a ratification of the employee's act. The prevailing view is that this constitutes "slight" evidence that the employer affirms or ratifies the wrongful act, but is by no means conclusive. [Edmunds v. Atchison, Topeka & Santa Fe Railway, 174 Cal. 246 (1917)]

(4) **Employer must know all relevant facts:** [§377]   There can be no effective ratification unless the employer had knowledge of *all* relevant facts surrounding the tortious conduct, *i.e.,* unless the employer knows (or is chargeable with knowledge) that the employee committed a tort incident to the acts in question, her affirmation of the transaction may be rescinded when she discovers the true facts. [Hirzel Funeral Homes v. Equitable Trust Co., 83 A.2d 700 (Del. 1951)]

    (a) **Example:** Without authority from P, A purports to sell P's property to T. In making the sale, A misrepresents the income and expenses attributable to the property. Unless P knew about the misrepresentations when she accepted the purchase price from T, she cannot be deemed to have authorized A's misrepresentations. Therefore, if P only discovers A's misrepresentations *after* consummating the sale to T, she can avoid liability to T by rescinding the transaction and returning the purchase price.

    (b) **No duty to investigate facts:** [§378]   P is generally under no duty to investigate whether A made any representations—*i.e.,* a ratification *cannot* be based upon P's *negligence* or failure to exercise reasonable care to ascertain what may have been said to the other party. [Gallagher v. California Pacific Title & Trust, 13 Cal. App. 2d 482 (1936)]

        1)   On the other hand, P cannot "close her eyes" to apparent fraud by an agent. *Example:* Suppose A brings P an unsolicited offer by T to purchase one of P's paintings for $50,000. If P *knows* the painting is not worth anywhere near this amount, she may be under a duty to inquire into the circumstances by which A obtained the offer. If P fails to do so, she "assumes the risk" and may be held to have ratified any misstatement made by A to obtain the offer. [Wilder v. Beede, 119 Cal. 646 (1898)]

(5) **Effect on contractual liability:** [§379]   Ratification has already been discussed *supra* (§§172-205), in connection with the *contractual* liability of a principal for previously unauthorized acts by the agent.

c. **Independent duty owed to injured party**

(1) **Employer negligence in hiring:** [§380]   Wherever it appears that the employer cannot be held under respondeat superior, consider whether he may be liable for breach of his independent duty of due care in *hiring* the person whose act caused the injury. If it appears that the employer knew or should have known that the person in his employ (servant, agent *or* independent contractor) was not qualified to perform the duties assigned to him, or was likely to perform in a negligent or otherwise dangerous manner, the employer is probably liable for the consequences.

    (a) **Compare:** As noted previously, an employer is generally not liable for torts committed by employees outside the scope of their employment. But where the employer knows or should have known that the employee was likely to commit such torts, he is chargeable nonetheless. *Example:* An employer who continues to use a bartender with known vicious tendencies would be liable for an unprovoked battery inflicted on a patron, which was otherwise outside the scope of employment.

(2) **Employer charged with care of third persons:** [§381]   Wherever the employer is charged with care of the injured person (*e.g.,* common carrier charged with care of its passengers), he is directly liable for any injuries they sustain as a result of the tortious acts of his employee—even though clearly outside the scope of employment. (*See* discussion *supra,* §§338-340.)

(3) **Notice of dangerous condition imputed to employer:** [§382]   As discussed *supra* (§144), an employer is charged with knowledge of all facts which his employee discovers in the course of his employment, and which pertain to the employment. [Rest. 2d §283]

   (a) **Effect:** [§383]   Wherever an employee, S, acquires knowledge of some fact or condition which would require employer, M, to exercise a duty of care to third persons, knowledge of that fact is imputed to M so that he owes a duty of care to third persons—just as if he had actual knowledge of the fact or condition involved.

   (b) **Example:** M employs S as a maintenance man in M's apartment house. S discovers that a stair railing is loose, but neglects to fix same or notify M of the danger. M is *charged* with knowledge of the condition, and will be liable to any third person injured thereby just as if he had actual knowledge thereof.

   (c) **Limitation:** [§384]   It is essential, however, that the facts to be imputed are *within the scope of employment.* Thus, for example, a railroad is not charged with notice of a defective condition on its tracks where the notice was given to a baggage room employee rather than a member of the "line department" charged with repairs. [Comer v. Los Angeles Railway, 66 Cal. App. 219 (1924)]

B. TORT LIABILITY OF PRINCIPAL FOR REPRESENTATIONS BY AGENT [§385]

One of the most frequent problems involving vicarious tort liability of one person for the acts of another concerns the circumstances under which one person will be held liable for the misrepresentations of another. This problem generally arises where representations have been made by an *agent*, rather than merely a servant or independent contractor; and liability turns more on the *authority* than the status of the party making the representations.

1. **General Rule:** [§386]   An employer or principal is subject to tort liability for any loss sustained by third persons as a result of misrepresentations made by one in his employ, *wherever the making of such representations by such person was expressly or impliedly authorized.* [Weise v. Red Owl Stores, Inc., 175 N.W.2d 184 (Minn. 1970)]

   a. **Nature of tort liability:** [§387]   The tort of misrepresentation requires the showing of a false statement of material fact; scienter; intent to deceive; justifiable reliance; and damages. (*See* Torts Summary.)

      (1) The agent's representations may *also* constitute defamation, trade libel, unfair competition, etc.—in effect, *any* tort in which the wrongful act consists of statements or representations.

   b. **Analysis:** [§388]   In analyzing liability for representations, the crucial factor is whether the person making the statements was *actually or apparently authorized* to make any statement at all by the person who is sought to be held liable.

   c. **Status of person making misrepresentation:** [§389]   While the capacity of the person making the representations is not controlling (*e.g.,* agent, servant, independent contractor), that person's capacity may reflect on whether the person had the authority to make representations, *i.e.,* authority to make representations is most frequently found when dealing with *agents*, the creation of the agency relationship often implying certain authority to make representations (*see* below). However, a servant or independent contractor may be found to have authority to make representations as well.

(1) **Example:** M employs S to demonstrate M's wares in a trade show and to answer any questions from potential customers. S recognizes a long-time enemy, X, in the audience, and falsely represents to X that M's product is safe for human consumption. X subsequently purchases and consumes the product in reliance on S' statements, suffering injury. Even though S was acting entirely for her own purposes in deceiving X, and was therefore outside the scope of her employment, she had been given authority by M to make statements about the product. M is thus liable to X. [Rest. 2d §249]

(2) **Example:** E employs independent contractor IC to develop and publish advertising copy for E's products. Since authority has been given IC to publish statements regarding E's products, E will be responsible for any misrepresentations made by the advertiser.

d. **Remedies:** [§390]   The foregoing examples concern representations which exposed the principal solely to tort liability. Frequently, however, an agent's misrepresentations are made in connection with a *contract* between the principal and a third party. *Example:* P authorizes A to sell his car for him. A turns back the mileage on the car from 50,000 miles to 500 miles, and sells the car to an innocent buyer, X, as a "low mileage" special. In such a case—and assuming the agent's representations were authorized (*see* below)—X has a choice of remedies:

(1) X can sue A for damages for fraud (the difference in value between what he actually received and what he would have gotten had the agent's statements been true); and/or

(2) X can sue P for fraud (same measure of recovery); and/or

(3) X can sue to *rescind the contract* with P, on the ground of fraud or mistake. [Holland Furnace Co. v. Williams, 295 P.2d 672 (Kan. 1956)]

2. **Authority to Make Representations:** [§391]   Obviously, false statements by an agent are rarely authorized by the principal, and it is not necessary to show that they were. The injured party need only establish that the agent had authority to make *statements concerning the subject matter involved*. Such authority may be *express*, or *implied* from the circumstances of the case. (The types of authority have already been discussed *supra,* §§70-97, in connection with contractual liability.)

a. **Express authority:** [§392]   An agent or employee may be expressly directed by the principal or employer to disseminate certain information to third parties. Where this is the case, any misrepresentations made by the agent or employee in the course of disseminating such information are deemed to have been "expressly authorized" by the principal.

(1) **Example:** P engages auctioneer A to sell P's apartment house at a public auction. P provides A with detailed information regarding the income and expenses from the property, and directs A to provide this information to all potential bidders. In order to get higher bids (and hence a higher commission for himself), A gives prospective purchaser X a figure for rental income that is falsely inflated. Because A was expressly authorized to disseminate information regarding rental income, his misrepresentation is deemed expressly authorized by P. Thus, upon discovery of the true facts, X can sue P (or A) for damages, or rescind the purchase.

b. **Implied authority—"incidental representations":** [§393]   When the principal authorizes another to deal on his behalf in transactions where representations about the subject matter are customarily made, he is deemed to have impliedly authorized all such representations unless that authority was specifically withheld, *i.e.,* the making of representations by the agent is considered "incidental" to his authority to deal in the transaction, and the principal will be liable therefor unless the third party knows (or should know) that the representations are unauthorized. [Boehm v. Friedman, 1 So. 2d 508 (Miss. 1941)]

(1) **Attorneys:** [§394]   Attorneys are generally regarded as agents of their clients concerning all matters on which they are retained to represent them, and are deemed to have implied authority to make representations as to all such matters, even though the client never specifically authorized the attorney to make any statements at all on his behalf. [Associated Indemnity Corp. v. Industrial Accident Commission, 56 Cal. App. 2d 804 (1943)]

(2) **Brokers and factors:** [§395]   A typical example of implied authority is the employment of a broker or factor to sell property. Whether the broker is considered the agent of the seller or an independent contractor (*see* below), he is deemed to have implied authority *to make representations concerning the property involved*—this being "incidental" to his authority to sell same—and the seller is therefore liable for any misrepresentations made by the broker whether or not express authority to make statements was given. [Speck v. Wylie, 1 Cal. 2d 625 (1934)]

(a) **Definitions** [§396]

1) A "broker" is one employed by the owner of property *to obtain a sale* of the property (although a broker may also be employed by a potential purchaser *to find property to purchase*).

2) Where the broker is given possession of property with the authority to sell same and receive the proceeds on behalf of the owner, he is a *"factor"* or *"commission merchant."*

(b) **Misrepresentations by broker:** [§397]   Under the prevailing view, a broker is an *agent* of the person by whom he is engaged, since he is hired to perform a "legal act"—*i.e.,* to bind his principal in the purchase or sale of property to a third person. Hence, any misstatement by a broker or factor is imputed to the principal, so that any person relying on the broker's *misrepresentation* may rescind the transaction or sue the principal for fraud.

1) A minority view holds that the broker or factor is an *independent contractor*—bargaining with the employer for a result (the sale of property), having his own organization, employing his own personnel, etc. Even under this view, however, the employer is *still* liable for the broker's representations. [Connecticut Mutual Life Insurance Co. v. Carson, 172 S.W. 69 (Mo. 1915)]

(c) **Compare:** [§398]   The result may be different where the owner has *not* conferred the *power to sell* upon the agent (even if the agent is called a "broker" or "factor"). For example, if the only authority conferred was to advertise the property (*e.g.,* by listing it in a catalog or newspaper), there may be no authority to make representations as above. Under such circumstances, misstatements of pertinent information by the broker would not be chargeable to the owner.

1) Thus, the defrauded purchaser could sue the *agent* for fraud, but he could not rescind the purchase or sue the owner for damages.

(d) **Effect of contractual provision limiting P's responsibility for A's representations:** [§399]   To avoid liability for misstatements made by brokers, factors, etc., owners sometimes insist on "exculpatory" provisions in their contracts—*e.g.,* "Representations not contained herein are not part of our agreement, and shall be given no effect." Such provisions will normally absolve the principal from liability for *damages* for fraudulent statements made by his agent. [Fogel Refrigerator Co. v. Di Tulio, 8 Bucks 3 (Pa. Com. Pl.)]

   1) However, *rescission* of the contract is usually still available to protect the purchaser. [Owen v. Schwartz, 177 F.2d 641 (D.C. Cir. 1949)]

   2) And, of course, if the principal *knew* of the agent's misstatements at the time the contract was executed, he may be liable for damages as well. *Rationale:* One cannot exculpate himself from the consequences of his own fraud. [Herzog v. Capital Co., 27 Cal. 2d 349 (1945)]

c. **Agent placed in position to deceive:** [§400]   Where the employer places the servant or agent in a *position* to defraud, and third persons rely upon his apparent authority to make representations, the principal is liable even though the agent is acting for his own purposes and no express or implied authority can be found. The theory is that the agent's *position* facilitates the fraud—*i.e., from the point of view of the third person, the agent appears to be acting in the ordinary course of authority confided to him. In these situations, the principal may be held liable for the agent's false representations even though he receives no benefits from the transaction. [Rutherford v. Rideout Bank, 11 Cal. 2d 479 (1938)]

   (1) **Example:** P employs A as manager of P's bank, and places him in a position to know the affairs of all borrowers at the bank. A falsely tells X, one of these borrowers, that the bank will not renew his note unless he sells certain property to Y (a friend of A) at a certain price less than its reasonable value. P would be liable to X for the loss sustained on his sale to Y.

   (2) **Compare:** [§401]   However, the result would probably be contra if A were only a teller or clerical employee in the bank...since a reasonable person in X's position would not conclude that A was acting within the ordinary scope of his authority in making such representations and any reliance would therefore not be justified.

3. **Effect of Innocent Misrepresentations by Agent:** [§402]   Where the agent or employee makes a misstatement innocently—believing it to be true, and with no intent to deceive—the principal is generally not liable in tort for any damages flowing therefrom. Tort liability requires scienter (knowledge of falsity) and intent to deceive, and in the absence of these elements, neither the agent nor the principal can be held liable. [Rest. 2d §256]

a. **Exception—principal's scienter:** [§403]   Of course, where the principal knows that the agent is not aware of the true facts, but puts him in a position to innocently misrepresent same, and then fails to advise the third party of the error, the principal is deemed *directly* responsible for any damages sustained by the third person in reliance thereon.

b. **Exception—negligent misrepresentations:** [§404]   And, where the agent knows that third persons may rely on his statements (*e.g.,* accountant preparing financial statements knowing that third persons as well as employer may rely thereon), many courts hold that the employer would be held responsible for negligence by the agent in the preparation of such statements. (*See* Torts Summary.)

c. **Effect on contract liability:** [§405] Where the representation is made in connection with a contract involving the principal and a third party, or as part of a warranty therein, the third party may sue to *rescind* on the ground of mistake—even though the misrepresentations were innocent. [116 A.L.R. 1401; *and see* discussion *supra,* §§122-139]

PARTNERSHIP

I. IN GENERAL

Partnership law is akin to the law of Agency in many respects. As discussed below, a partner is considered the agent of co-partners for certain purposes; the acts of a partner within the scope of the partnership relation may be imputed to the other partners; and the agency concept of imputed notice likewise applies to partnerships.

The body of common law dealing with partnerships has been replaced—and in many instances, substantially changed—by the Uniform Partnership Act (UPA), which has been adopted in almost all jurisdictions. [*See, e.g.,* Cal. Corp. Code §§15001 *et seq.*]

A. BASIC NATURE OF PARTNERSHIP [§406]

According to the UPA, "a partnership is *an association of two or more persons to carry on as co-owners a business for profit.*" [UPA §6] It follows that the two essential elements of a partnership are (i) a *community of interest* in the business; and (ii) a *sharing* of profits. [Doan v. Dyer, 286 F. 339 (9th Cir. 1923)]

1. **Distinguish from Agency:** [§407]   The primary distinction between a partnership and an agency is that a partnership consists of *co-owners*. While an agent may sometimes receive a share of the profits of the principal's business as compensation for services, the agent is not an owner thereof.

2. **Distinguish from Unincorporated Association:** [§408] The UPA specifically recognizes other types of unincorporated associations, and provides that such associations shall not be considered partnerships unless they would have been so deemed prior to adoption of the UPA. [UPA §6(2)]

    a. **Thus, the usual "Massachusetts" or business trust** (*see* Corporations Summary) is *not* a partnership. [*See* Goldwater v. Oltman, 210 Cal. 408 (1930)]

        (1) The result would be contra, however, if the shareholders take over management and control from the trustees. [Stitzinger v. Truitt, 81 Cal. App. 502 (1927)]

    b. **Nonprofit purpose:** Whereas other types of unincorporated associations may be formed for nonprofit as well as profit-making purposes, a partnership is an association of co-owners for *profit* and hence cannot be formed for nonprofit purposes.

3. **Distinguish from Joint Venture:** [§409]   A joint venture resembles a partnership in that its members associate together as co-owners of a business enterprise, agreeing to share profits and losses. However, a partnership ordinarily engages in a continuing business for an indefinite or fixed period of time (*see* below), whereas a joint venture is formed for a *single transaction* or series of transactions—thus being more limited in scope and duration. [138 A.L.R. 968]

    a. **Note:** It is often difficult to distinguish between a joint venture and a partnership. What starts out as a joint venture (a single business transaction) turns into more continuous activity and at some point becomes a partnership. However, this difficulty of classification generally has no serious legal consequence, since *the rights and liabilities of partners and joint venturers are the same in all important respects.* Hence, the courts usually apply the provisions of the UPA to joint ventures, wherever appropriate. [*See* Zeibak v. Nasser, 12 Cal. 2d 1 (1938)]

B. ENTITY VS. AGGREGATE CHARACTERISTICS OF PARTNERSHIP

1. **Common Law Theory:** [§410]   At common law, a partnership was never regarded as a separate entity in itself. Rather, it was treated as an *aggregate* of the individual partners.

   a. **Lawsuits:** [§411]   Thus, for example, an action at common law could not be brought against the firm in its firm name; each individual partner had to be sued. [Dunham v. Schindler & Co., 20 P. 326 (Or. 1889)]

   b. **Real estate title:** [§412]   Similarly, title to real estate could not be held in the partnership name. Partnership assets were deemed to be owned by the individual partners as "tenants in partnership," rather than by the partnership as a distinct entity.

2. **The UPA Generally Follows the Aggregate Theory:** [§413]   Under the Act, the most significant aggregate characteristics of a partnership are the joint, or joint and several liability of the partners [UPA §15] and limitations on the transfer of specific partnership property [UPA §25].

   a. **Federal income tax law likewise retains the aggregate theory of partnerships:** [§414]   For tax purposes, the income or losses incurred by a partnership are attributed to the partners individually. The partnership itself is not a *taxpaying* entity. [Int. Rev. C. §701]

      (1) But the partnership *is* a *tax-reporting* entity. It must file an "informational return" to establish the amount of income or loss which partners must include on their individual tax return. [Int. Rev. C. §6031]

3. **Entity Characteristics:** [§415]   For certain purposes, however, the UPA and other statutes treat a partnership as an *entity*, apart from its several members.

   a. **Capacity to sue or to be sued:** [§416]   Modern procedureal statutes vary as to whether a partnership can sue or be sued as an entity.

      (1) **In federal courts**, a partnership can sue or be sued in the firm name if the litigation involves a "federal question" (*see* Civil Procedure Summary). In all other cases (*e.g.,* diversity of citizenship actions), the partnership's capacity to sue or be sued is determined by the law of the state in which the federal court is located. [Fed. R. Civ. P. 17(b)]

      (2) **A number of states** hold that a partnership can *be sued* as an entity (to facilitate jurisdiction and service in action against it), but that it *cannot sue* in the firm name—*i.e.,* partnership claims must be sued upon in the names of the individual partners.

      (3) **Other states**, however, permit a partnership *to sue or be sued* in the firm name. [*See, e.g.,* Cal. Civ. Proc. Code §388]

      (4) **Effect of judgment against partnership only:** [§417]   Even where a suit against the partnership is permitted, good practice generally dictates the joinder of all partners individually, since in most states a judgment recovered against the partnership alone can be enforced only against the partnership assets, *i.e.,* the judgment is not enforceable against the personal (nonpartnership) assets of the individual partners who are not named and served as defendants in the lawsuit.

         (a) Of course, where the plaintiff sues both the firm and its members, any judgment rendered must be consistent—*i.e.,* the firm cannot be held liable if the individual partners are not. *Example:* Plaintiff sues both the individual members and the partnership on an alleged partnership debt. The firm fails to respond, and Plaintiff thus obtains a default judgment against it. However, if the individual partners answer and successfully defend at trial, simultaneously disproving Plaintiff's claim against the partnership, the default judgment against the partnership would have to be vacated. The "entity theory" could not justify the inconsistent judgments. [*See* Nicholls v. Anders, 13 Cal. App. 2d 440 (1936)]

b. **Bankruptcy of partnership vs. partners individually:** [§418] Under federal bankrupcy law, the partnership is likewise treated as an entity, so that the adjudication of the partnership as a bankrupt does not constitute an adjudication that the partners are bankrupt. Nor does an adjudication of a partner as a bankrupt bring the partnership or its assets into bankruptcy. [11 U.S.C. §23]

c. **Capacity to convey property:** [§419] And, a partnership can hold and convey title to *real or personal property* as entity (*i.e.,* in the firm name), without all partners joining in the conveyance [UPA §8]

C. PROPERTY RIGHTS OF PARTNER VS. PARTNERSHIP [§420]

It is frequently necessary to distinguish between property belonging to the firm and property belonging to the individual partners. In the absence of an agreement, there is no limitation or restriction on what can become the property of the partnership. The chief criterion is whether partners *intended* to devote it to partnership purposes. Where the partners' intentions are in doubt, the courts rely on other factors, discussed below.

1. **What Constitutes Partnership Property:** [§421] Under the UPA, "all property originally brought into the partnership stock or subsequently acquired, by purchase or otherwise, *on account of the partnership*, is partnership property." [UPA §8(1)]

   a. **Intention of firm ownership:** [§422] As indicated, it must appear that the property was acquired with the intention that it be a partnership asset—*i.e.,* on account of the partnership."

   b. **Evidence of intention:** [§423] Where there is no clear expression of the partners' intention re ownership of the asset in question, the courts consider the facts and circumstances surrounding acquisition and ownership of the asset:

      (1) **Title:** [§424] The fact that the asset is acquired or held in the name of partnership, rather than in the name of one of the partners, is *not* conclusive as to its ownership. The name in which property is held may be entirely a matter of convenience. Thus, although the status of title will be taken into account, the courts generally consider other factors as being more indicative of the partners' intentions. [Clark v. Lewis, 289 S.W.775 (Ark. 1927)]

      (2) **Purchase with partnership funds:** [§425] This factor alone may justify a conclusion that the asset belongs to the partnership. Indeed, the UPA provides that "*unless the contrary intention appears,* property acquired with partnership funds is partnership property." [UPA §8(2)]

      (3) **Improvements by firm:** [§426] The fact that partnership funds have been used to improve the asset in question is entitled to some weight, but is usually not determinative—particularly where the improvements are severable from the asset.

      (4) **Partnership purpose:** [§427] The more closely the asset is associated with the business operations of the partnership, the more likely it will be held to be a partnership asset. This is particularly true where the dispute is between a partner

and the firm, the courts viewing the partner as a *trustee* for the firm who owes an obligation to purchase assets related to its operation on behalf of the partnership (rather than acquiring them for himself). [Secrest v. Nobles, 223 P. 863 (Okla. 1924)]

(5) **Use of property:** [§428]   Use of an asset in the partnership business is not enough in itself to establish an intent that the partnership own the asset—*e.g.,* it may merely be a loan of the asset to the partnership. However, such use may be relevant in conjunction with other factors tending to show partnership ownership (*e.g.,* purchase with partnership funds). [*See* Bumb v. Bennett, 51 Cal. 2d 294 (1958)]

(a) **Insurance policies:** [§429]   Very frequently, partners purchase "cross life insurance policies" on each other's lives. *Example:* By agreement between the partners, an insurance policy is taken out on the life of partner A, on which B is shown to be the owner and beneficiary; a similar policy is taken out on B's life, with A as owner and beneficiary. Premiums are customarily paid out of the partnership funds, but are usually charged to the draws of each partner. The problem arises when a partner dies, and the benefits are paid to the survivor. Are these benefits partnership assets, which must be used to pay off the debts of the partnership, or are they the sole property of the surviving partner to be used as he pleases?

1) Frequently, the problem is covered by an agreement between the partners—*e.g.,* a provision that insurance benefits paid on the death of one partner *must* be used by the other partner to *buy out* the interest of the decedent partner in the firm.

2) In the absence of an agreement or other clear expression of intent, many courts hold that the benefits belong outright to the surviving partner who is shown as "owner" and "beneficiary." Thus, the fact that the premiums were paid with partnership funds, or that the partnership itself may be in need of funds to pay creditors, is disregarded. [83 A.L.R.2d 1347]

(6) **Status in partnership books:** [§430]   The fact that property is listed as a firm asset on the books and records of the partnership is given considerable weight, especially where all parties are shown to have knowledge of this fact. [Robinson Bank v. Miller, 38 N.E. 1078 (Ill. 1894)]

c. **Real property**

(1) **Common law:** [§431]   As noted previously, a partnership at common law was deemed to be merely an aggregate of individuals, and hence incapable of taking title to real property. A grant of such property to a partnership was ineffective to pass title, and only an equitable interest passed to the partners. [Donohoe v. Rogers, 168 Cal. 700 (1914)]

(2) **UPA view:** [§432]   However, the UPA clearly provides that *any estate in real property may be acquired and held in the partnership name.* [UPA §8(3)]

(a) *Note:* Any estate so acquired must thereafter be conveyed in the partnership name, not in the names of the partners. [Barton v. Ludy, 11 Cal. 2d 1 (1938)]

(b) Practical difficulties are sometimes encountered in determining the validity of conveyances in the partnership name. Since no public record as to members of the partnership is generally required, it may be impossible to tell from a mere conveyance in the firm name whether the party executing same is in fact a partner and/or has authority to convey.

1) To overcome this difficulty, a number of states have enacted special legislation authorizing partners to file a "statement of partnership" listing the members of the partnership. Thereafter, any conveyance executed on behalf of the firm by one of the listed members is conclusively valid as to a bona fide purchaser (unless some other person claiming to be a partner records a different statement of partnership). [*See, e.g.,* Cal. Corp. Code §15010.5]

2. **Rights of Partner:** [§433]   The property rights of a partner are (i) the rights in specific partnership property, (ii) an interest in the partnership, and (iii) the right to participate in the management of the partnership.'' [UPA §24]

a. **Rights in specific partnership property:** [§434]   A partner is a *tenant in partnership* with co-partners as to each asset of the partnership. [UPA §25(1)] The incidents of this tenancy are as follows:

(1) Each partner has an *equal right to possession* for partnership purposes;

(2) The right to possession is *not assignable*, except together with that of the other partners;

(3) The right is *not subject to attachment or execution* except on a claim against the partnership (*i.e.,* entity theory);

(4) The right is *not community property* and hence is not subject to family allowances, dower, curtesy, etc. [Estate of Grivel, 10 Cal. 2d 454 (1937)];

(5) Upon the death of a partner, the right vests in the *surviving partners* (or in the executor or administrator of the last surviving partner).

(a) *Effect:* Partnership property is not a part of the estate of a deceased partner's estate for the value of decedent's interest in the partnership (*see* below; *and see* discussion *infra,* §532).

b. **Interest in the partnership:** [§435]   Under the UPA, "a partner's interest in the partnership is his share of the profits and surplus, and the same is *personal* property." [UPA §26]

(1) **Importance of classification:** [§436]   The classification of a partner's interest as personal property could be important for *inheritance* purposes. For example, if any distinction is made in a partner's will (or under the laws of intestate succession) as to inheritance of his "personal" as opposed to "real" property, his interest in the firm is treated as personalty. And, this is true even where all of the firm's asets are real property. [Comstock v. Fiorella, 260 Cal. App. 2d 262 (1968)]

(a) **Equitable conversions:** [§437]   This is an application of the doctrine of equitable conversion (*see* Equity Summary); *i.e.,* a partner's rights in specific partnership property are *equitable* in nature, and the partnership itself holds full legal title thereto.

(2) **Assignment of interest:** [§438]   A partner's interest in the partnership is assignable unless there is an agreement to the contrary. And, such an assignment will not itself dissolve the partnership. [UPA §27(1)]

(a) **The assignee is merely entitled to receive the profits and capital** to which the assigning partner would have been entitled. The assignee does *not* become a partner; and he is not entitled to interfere with management of the partnership or to exercise any rights with respect to its affairs. [75 A.L.R.2d 1036]

(b) **The assignor-partner remains liable** on all partnership debts.

(3) **Rights of creditors of individual partner:** [§439]   A creditor of an individual partner has no right to execute or attach partnership assets or property; and hence any such attachment or exection is void and ineffective. [Taylor v. S & M Lamp Co., 190 Cal. App. 2d 700 (1961)]

(a) **The creditor's sole remedy** is to prosecute her claim to *judgment* against the debtor-partner, and thereafter to obtain a *charging order* against the debtor-partner's interest in the partnership. The partnership is thereby impressed with a lien in favor of the creditor, who is entitled to all future distributions of surplus or assets otherwise flowing to the debtor-partner until the judgment is satisfied. (The debtor's partnership interest may also be sold under court order, in appropriate cases.) [UPA §28]

(4) **Family rights:** [§440]   The partner's interest in the partnership *is* subject to family allowance, and is generally treated as community property in community property jurisdictions. [*Cf.* Wood v. Gunther, 89 Cal. App. 2d 718 (1949)]

c. **Right to partcipate in management:** [§441]   *See* discussion *infra,* §466.

II. FORMATION OF PARTNERSHIP

A. PARTNERSHIP BY CONTRACT [§442]

It is implicit in the definition of a partnership (*supra*, §407), that it is a *voluntary* association of two or more persons. As such, a partnership must generally be based upon the agreement of the partners; and hence a contract (express or implied) is ordinarily essential to the formation of a partnership.

1. **Formalities:** [§443] A written agreement is *not* ordinarily necessary to create a partnership. However, certain partnership agreements *are* required to be in writing in order to be effective:

    a. **An agreement which provides for mandatory continuance of the partnership for a period in excess of one year** is within the Statute of Frauds (as a "contract which by its terms is not to be performed within a year"), and must be evidenced by a sufficient writing if sought to be enforced for more than one year.

    b. **An agreement authorizing partners to deal in real property** (or otherwise to enter into contracts within the Statute of Frauds) need not be in writing insofar as the rights of the partners *inter se* are concerned. However, when a third person attempts to bind the partnership to such a contract, some courts hold that the authority of the partner executing the same must be evidenced by a sufficient writing.

        (1) Other courts are contra, holding that such authority is inherent in the partnership relation (*see* discussion *infra*, §§490-493).

2. **Duration of Partnership**

    a. **At will:** [§444] Where no time is fixed for the duration of the partnership, it is a "partnership at will," and it can be dissolved at any time by any partner without violating the partnership agreement (*see* discussion *infra*, §§506-507). [Page v. Page, 55 Cal. 2d 192 (1961)]

    b. **For term:** [§445] However, if a fixed term is specified, or if the object of the partnership is the completion of a particular project, it is a "partnership for term." In that case, the partnership agreement is deemed an agreement by the partners to continue their relationship until the expiration of the specified term (or completion of the project), and any prior dissolution of the partnership will constitute a breach of the agreement (*see infra*, §508).

3. **Capacity to Become a Partner:** [§446] Any person having the capacity to contract has the capacity to become a partner.

    a. **Minors:** [§447] A partnership contract in which a minor is one of the partners is voidable and subject to disaffirmance by the minor. [Latrobe v. Dietrich, 78 A. 983 (Md. 1910)]

    b. **Corporations:** [§448] There is some disagreement as to whether a corporation has the implied power to become a partner with an individual or another corporation. The prevailing view is that it does *not* have such power, so that—unless this specific power is provided in the articles of incorporation—entering into a partnership would be ultra vires. (*See* Corporations Summary.)

4. **Consent of Co-Partners:** [§449] As a voluntary association of co-owners, it is essential that each and all of the co-owners agree on who shall be a partner. Thus the UPA provides that "no person shall become a member of a partnership without the consent of *all* the partners." [UPA §18(g)]

5. **Rules for Determining Existence of Partnership:** [§450]   In many cases, there may be a dispute or uncertainty as to whether or not there is a partnership agreement, or whether or not the relationship between the parties is in fact a partnership. In such cases, the courts attempt to ascertain the intent of the parties as expressed by their acts or agreements. The following rules of construction are usually applied in this task:

   a. **Joint ownership of property:** [§451]   A partnership is *not* established merely by the joint ownership of property (*i.e.,* joint tenancies, etc.). The fact that the profits from the use of such property are shared betweeen the owners is significant (*see* below), but likewise is not conclusive. [UPA §7(2); 150 A.L.R. 1003]

   b. **Contribution of capital:** [§452]   The mere contribution of capital to an enterprise does not establish a partnership. And, conversely, it is not essential to the existence of a partnership that all parties contribute capital thereto. [Whitley v. Bradley, 13 Cal. App. 720 (1910)]

   c. **Sharing of gross income:** [§453]   Similarly, the sharing of *gross* income does not itself establish a partnership. This is true whether or not there is a joint interest in the property from which the income is derived. [UPA §7(3)]

   d. **Sharing profits of business:** [§454]   However, the sharing of *profits* from a business *is* prima facie evidence that a partnership exists—except where it appears that such profits are distributed as a bonus or wages to an employee, as rent to a landlord, as an annuity to a widow, as interest on a loan, or as consideration for sale of the goodwill of a business or other property. [UPA §7(4)]

      (1) The effect of the exceptions in UPA section 7(4) is that the sharing of profits will indicate a partnership relationship only when *no other business reason exists* for the sharing. [*See* Martin v. Peyton 246 N.Y. 213 (1927)]

   e. **Parties' designation:** [§455]   While the parties' characterization of their relationship as a "partnership" or some other business form is entitled to some weight, it is not conclusive. *And note:* The parties cannot avoid partnership liability even by an express stipulation negativing the relation, if the evidence establishes the essential elements of a partnership. [Streeter & Riddell, Inc. v. Bacon, 49 Cal. App. 327 (1920)]

B. PARTNERSHIP BY ESTOPPEL [§456]

As between the persons alleged to be partners, a true partnership relation depends upon a contract, express or implied, between the parties. However, parties who are *not* partners in that sense may—in certain circumstances—be held bound as if they were partners in their dealings with third parties.

1. **Liability of Alleged Partner:** [§457]   One who holds herself out to be a partner in an actual or apparent partnership or who expressly or impliedly consents to representations that she is such a partner, is liable to any third person who extends credit in good-faith reliance on such representations. [UPA §16]

   a. **Example:** A owns a retail business as sole proprieter. For the purpose of obtaining credit from C, she represents to C that B, a wealthy businesswoman, is a partner in A's business. B knows about A's statements and fails to advise C to the contrary, although she could easily do so. C relies on B's credit and status in the community and extends credit to A, which he otherwise would not have done. Insofar as this credit is concerned, B is estopped from denying that she is a partner and may be held liable as if she were in fact a partner in A's business.

   b. **Rationale:** [§458]   The rule is one of *equitable estoppel*: One who knowingly permits another to believe that she is a partner and extend credit in reliance thereon cannot later be permitted to deny that she is a partner and escape liability.

    c. **Note:** Even though B is held liable to C as if she were A's partner, this does *not* establish an actual partnership relation between A and B. Thus, B would not be authorized to engage in A's business or to assert any rights with respect thereto.

2. **Liability of Partners Who Represent Third Person to be a Partner:** [§459]   Where an actual partner represents a nonpartner to be a member of the partnership, she thereby constitutes that person as her agent with the power to bind her as though the person were in fact a partner. However, any resultant liability binds *only those partners who made or consented to the representation.* [UPA §16(2)]

    a. **Example:** A represents to the public that T is a partner in A's firm, even though the only partners are A and B. If T enters into a contract on behalf of the firm, the contract is binding on A, but *not* on B, unless B authorized or consented to A's representations.

    b. **Note:** No actual partnership has been created. Thus, for example, T would have no right to manage the business, inspect the partnership books, etc.

III. EFFECT OF THE PARTNERSHIP RELATION

A. RELATIONS BETWEEN PARTNERS

1. **Fiduciary Duty:** [§460]   As between themselves, partners are fiduciaries and owe each other the same duties and obligations as a trustee owes to the beneficiary. (*See* Trusts Summary.)

   a. **Accounting:** [§461]   Thus, a partner must account to the partnership for any profits derived personally from transactions connected with the formation, conduct, or liquidation of the partnership; or from any use of its property, unless with the consent of all the other partners. [UPA §21]

   b. **Competing with partnership:** [§462]   Similarly, a partner does not have the right to engage in any competitive business without the consent of all other partners. If he does so, he must likewise account to the partnership for all profits derived therefrom. [Neilsen v. Holmes, 82 Cal. App. 2d 315 (1947)]

      (1) **Exclusive service:** [§463]   And, if a partner has promised to devote his *full time* and exclusive services to the partnership business, his time is considered to be a partnership asset. Hence, he may not render services to any other employer (even one which does not compete with the partnership) without the consent of all other partners; and if he does so, the salary obtained may be considered partnership income. [*See* Weller v. Simenstad, 127 N.W.2d 794 (Wis. 1964)]

   c. **Assets:** [§464]   A partner who purchases or holds partnership assets in his own name does so as trustee for the partnership, and can be compelled to account to the firm for the assets or their value. It is immaterial that the partner used his own funds in purchasing the property, if it was the partners' intention that the assets would belong to the partnership. [44 A.L.R.2d 519; *and see* discussion *supra,* §§421-430]

2. **Other Rights and Duties of Partners to Each Other:** [§465]   The rights and obligations of the partners are largely governed by the partnership agreement. However, in the absence of provisions to the contrary in the agreement, the law imposes the following rights and duties:

   a. **Management:** [§466]   "All partners have equal rights in the management and conduct of partnership business." [UPA §18(c)]

      (1) **Equality of rights:** [§467]   Note that in the absence of an agreement to the contrary, the partners' management rights are equal, even though some may be entitled to a larger percentage of profits.

      (2) **Majority vs. unanimous vote:** [§468]   "Any difference arising as to *ordinary* matters connected with the partnership business may be decided by a *majority* of the partners; but no act in contravention of any agreement between the partners may be done without the consent of *all* the partners." [UPA §18(h)]

      (3) **Managing partner:** [§469]   By agreement, one or more partners may assume a greater share of the management authority, or may even become the "managing partner" or "general manager" of the partnership. Such assumption of authority carries with it the obligation to deal fairly on behalf of all partners—so that secret dealings by which some partners are favored and others prejudiced by the managing partner's acts will be held invalid as to the nonconsenting partners. [Application of Lester, 87 Misc. 2d 717 (1976)—managing partner of law firm purported to bind firm to purchase interest of retiring partner on terms basically unfair to other partners, and of which they had no knowledge or opportunity to object]

b. **Books and records:** [§470]   Partners must, on demand, present full and complete information on all things affecting the partnership business. [UPA §20] Each partner is entitled to access to the partnership books and records at all times, and the records must be kept at the principal business office of the partnership business. [UPA §19]

   (1) Upon the death of a partner, her personal representative has the same rights with respect to access and inspection of partnership books as the partner would have had. (*See infra,* §532.)

c. **Profits and losses:** [§471]   Each partner is entitled to such share of the profits of the partnership as is specified in the agreement; and she must contribute toward partnership losses in proportion to her share of the profits. Again, in the absence of agreement to the contrary, the partners are deemed to share profits and losses equally. [UPA §18(a)]

d. **Distributions from partnership**

   (1) **Capital account:** [§472]   A partner is entitled to repayment of capital or other advances made by her to the partnership, together with interest, at such time as the partners may agree or, if there is no agreement, upon demand. [UPA §18(a),(d)]

   (2) **Expenses:** [§473]   And, a partner must be reimbursed for all expenses paid or incurred by her in the ordinary conduct of partnership business, together with interest. [UPA §18(b),(c)]

   (3) **Salaries:** [§474]   However, *no partner is entitled to remuneration for her services on behalf of the partnership, except with the consent of all partners.* [UPA §18(f)]

      (a) The only exception to this rule is that, upon *dissolution*, the surviving partner is entitled to reasonable compensation for her services in *winding up* the partnership affairs (*see infra,* §532).

      (b) Otherwise, unless there has been some agreement between the partners for compensation for services, no partner has any right to a greater share of the partnership profits. The mere fact that her services may have been the major factor in creating those profits is not enough to imply an agreement to pay a salary. [*See* Security First National Bank v. Lutz, 322 F.2d 348 (9th Cir. 1963)]

      (c) *Note:* The result may be contra in states where the UPA is not in effect. [*See* Luff v. Luff, 158 F. Supp. 311 (D.C. Cir. 1958)—in exercise of its equitable powers, court in partnership dissolution proceedings could allocate substantial sum to partner whose efforts secured fund for partnership]

3. **Actions Between Partners**

   a. **Dissolution:** [§475]   The principal remedy of a partner against co-partners is a suit in equity for dissolution of the partnership and an accounting of its assets. (*See* further discussion *infra,* §§517-526.)

   b. **Accounting:** [§476]   In addition to the accounting in connection with dissolution proceedings, a partner has the right to obtain an accounting from co-partners as to the affairs of the partnership, whenever (i) he has been wrongfully excluded from the business; (ii) the agreement gives him that right; (iii) any other partner is withholding any benefit or profits belonging to the partnership; or (iv) other circumstances "render it just and reasonable." [UPA §22]

c. **No action at law for damages:** [§477]   Since disputes between partners invariably involve conflicting claims requiring an accounting, there can generally be no action at law by one partner against another. A partner's sole remedy is an equitable suit for dissolution and/or an accounting.

(1) **Exceptions:** [§478]   In a few situations, however, an action at law *is* permitted:

(a) Where there is no complex account involving a variety of partnership transactions (as where the dispute arises at the outset of the partnership). [Van Fleet-Durkee, Inc. v. Oyster, 110 Cal. App. 2d 286 (1952)]

(b) Where the suit is not related to the partnership business (*e.g.,* action on a loan from one partner to another). [Estes v. Delpech, 73 Cal. App. 643 (1925)]

(c) Where the wrongful acts of one partner constitute fraud or a conversion of the partnership assets (since these are not really partnership transactions). [Prince v. Harting, 177 Cal. App. 2d 720 (1960)]

(d) Where one partner is wrongfully excluded and the remaining partner converts the partnership assets (the wronged party may elect to seek damages rather than assert his partnership rights). [Gherman v. Colburn, 72 Cal. App. 3d 544 (1977)]

B. RELATIONS AS TO THIRD PERSONS

1. **Authority of Partner to Bind Partnership:** [§479]   "Every partner is an *agent* of the partnership for the purpose of its business, and the act of every partner, including the execution in the partnership name of *any instrument*, for apparently carrying on in the usual way the business of the partnership, binds the partnership, unless the partner so acting has in fact no authority to act for the partnership in the particular matter, and the person with whom he is dealing has knowledge of the fact that he has no such authority." [UPA §9(1)]

a. **Authority in general:** [§480]   The rules of Agency apply in determining whether the partnership is bound by the dealings of one of the partners with a third person. [Rice v. Jackson, 171 Pa. 89 (1895)]

(1) **Apparent authority:** [§481]   Any contracts made by a partner on behalf of the partnership and related to its business are deemed to be within his apparent authority, and hence binding on the partnership, notwithstanding some secret limitation between the partners of which the third party had no notice. [Stitziner v. Truitt, 81 Cal. App. 502 (1927)]

(a) But an act which is not apparently related to the partnership business is not within his apparent authority, and does not bind his co-partners, unless, of course, it has been actually authorized by them. [UPA §9(2)]

(b) And, of course, if the third party had notice that the partner's acts were in violation of the partnership agreement, the other partners are not liable thereon. [Matanuska Valley Bank v. Arnold, 223 F.2d 778 (9th Cir. 1955)—partner obtained loan from bank on behalf of partnership, but bank manager *knew* that partner had no authority to obtain the loan]

(2) **Limitations on authority:** [§482]   The UPA provides certain inherent limitations on a partner's authority. Unless the partnership business has been abandoned, or all partners have so agreed, *no* partner has authority:

(a) To make an assignment of the partnership property for the benefit of creditors;

(b) To dispose of the partnership good will;

(c) To do any other act which would make it impossible to carry on the ordinary business of the partnership;

(d) To confess judgment against the partnership; or

(e) To submit a partnership claim or liability to arbitration. [UPA §9(3)]

(3) **Termination of authority:** [§483]   It is doubtful that any single partner can terminate the authority of co-partners, short of dissolving the partnership—as where partner A (*without* dissolving his partnership with B) notifies Bank that he will not be liable on any partnership debts, in an effort to exempt himself and the partnership from further liability on B's borrowings in the name of the partnership.

(a) **Two partners:** [§484]   Some cases have held such notice effective—at least where only two partners are involved. [Bank of Bellbuckle v. Mason, 202 S.W. 931 (Tenn. 1918); *but see contra* National Biscuit Co. v. Stroud, 106 S.E.2d 692 (N.C. 1959)]

(b) **More than two partners:** [§485]   But where more than two partners are involved, the "majority rules" on all matters within the scope of the partnership business (1918) so that *the minority cannot refuse to be bound* unless they *dissolve* the partnership *before* the act is done. [UPA §18(h)]

1) **Exception:** [§486]   If the act done is contrary to an *agreement* among the partners, then no partner is bound unless *all* consent. [UPA §18(h)]

(c) **Dissolution:** [§487]   The requirements for an effective dissolution are discussed *infra,* §§503-526.

b. **Admissions and representations:** [§488]   The rules of Agency also apply to charge the partnership with the admissions and representations of any partner concerning partnership affairs, within the scope of her actual or apparent authority. [UPA §11]

c. **Imputed notice:** [§489]   Similarly, knowledge or notice to any one partner of matters pertaining to the regular partnership business is imputed to the partnership; *i.e.,* knowledge by any one partner of matters pertaining to the partnership affairs is binding on all the partners. [UPA §12]

(1) **But there is no imputation** to the partnership where the partner acquiring the knowledge or notice is acting fraudulently or adversely to the partnership. [UPA §12]

(2) **Knowledge acquired by a partner prior to her admission** to the partnership is generally *not* imputed to the partnership, but exceptions are recognized under the same circumstances as in Agency (*e.g.,* where partner is shown to have had facts in mind when she acted for partnership even though knowledge acquired before her admission to partnership; *see supra,* §145).

d. **Conveyance of real property:** [§490]   Any partner has the authority to make a conveyance of partnership real property in the ordinary course of partnership business. [UPA §9(1)]

(1) **Authority to convey:** [§491]   The partner has "inherent" authority to convey partnership realty only where such conveyances are part of the ordinary routine of partnership business. In all other instances, the partner's authority must affirmatively appear; it will *not* be implied. An unauthorized conveyance is not binding on the partnership.

    (a) If a partner exceeds her authority in making a conveyance of partnership real property, the partnership can recover the property from the grantee, unless the grantee is a bona fide purchaser—*i.e.,* one who paid value without knowledge that the partner had exceeded her authority. [UPA §10(1)]

    (b) But in many jurisdictions, an innocent purchaser is protected against any claim of lack of authority when provision is made for the filing of a "statement of partnership" (*supra,* §431).

(2) **Formalities:** [§492]   The cases are split on whether a partner's authority to convey other than in the ordinary course of business must be in writing. The prevailing view is that a writing is *not required*, the authority being inherent in the partnership relation. [McGahan v. Bank of Rondout, 156 U.S. 218 (1895)]

(3) **Compare—effect of partner's conveyance:** [§493]   If title is in the name of the partnership, a conveyance by one of the partners in her own name does not, of course, pass legal title. But if the conveyance was within the partner's authority, *equitable* title is thereby transferred to the purchaser (*i.e.,* treated as a contract *to convey* by the partnership). [UPA §10(2)]

2. **Liability to Creditors**

    a. **Liability on contracts:** [§494]   The partners are *jointly (but not severally)* liable on all partnership debts and contracts. [UPA §15(b)]

    (1) **Dormant partner:** [§495]   Thus, one who is in fact a partner, but whose existence has been kept secret (*i.e.,* a "silent partner") is jointly liable to creditors of the firm, along with all of the known partners.

        (a) It is immaterial that the creditor dealt with the firm without relying upon the "silent partner." [Nelson, Inc. v. Tarman, 163 Cal. App. 2d 714 (1958)]

        (b) Such a partner is bound by the authorized acts of her co-partners exactly as an undisclosed principal is bound by the authorized acts of her agent (*see supra,* §§230-241).

    (2) **Incoming partner:** [§496]   A new partner is jointly liable with the other partners for *all* debts of the partnership, whether incurred before or after his admission to the partnership. He is deemed to assume his share of the liabilities upon admission; and this cannot be avoided by agreement among the partners to the contrary. However, the UPA does provide that his liability must be satisfied only out of the partnership assets. [UPA §17]

    (3) **Effect of joint liability:** [§497]   Since the partners have only a joint liability to creditors, a contract creditor may not proceed against any single partner. If he does so, the partner sued can generally force the joinder of all other partners—*i.e.,* they are "necessary parties" within the rules of compulsory joinder. (*See* Civil Procedure Summary.)

        (a) If the creditor obtains judgment for less than the amount sought, satisfaction of that judgment is a *bar* to any further action against other partners or against the firm. [170 A.L.R. 1180]

(b) Of course, a creditor can always proceed against the partnership as an *entity* by filing suit against the partnership in the firm name, without the necessity of joining all the partners (*see supra,* §§415-418).

    1) In this case, however, any judgment obtained binds only the partnership assets (together with the individual assets of each partner actually served with summons). [*See* Cal. Civ. Proc. Code §388]

(c) In most states, a release of *one* partner operates to release *all* partners, since their liability is joint rather than several. [Blodgett v. Inglis, 115 P. 1043 (Wash. 1911)]

    1) The rule is contra by statute in some jurisdictions. [*See, e.g.,* Cal. Civ. Code §1543]

(4) **Remedies:** [§498] Partnership assets are subject to attachment and execution only upon *partnership* debts. Thus, an attachment or execution against partnership assets is void if the claim at issue is the debt of an individual partner. "A partner's right in specific partnership property is not subject to attachment." [UPA §25(2)]

(a) The creditor's remedy in the latter situation is to obtain a *charging order* against the debtor-partner's interest [UPA §28; discussed *supra,* §439]

b. **Liability in tort:** [§499] The partners are *jointly and severally* liable for torts and breaches of trust injuring third parties. [UPA §15(a)]

(1) **Since the liability is both joint and several,** an action may be brought against any single partner *without* joining the others.

(a) Moreover, if an action is brought against only one of the partners, any judgment obtained against him is *not* res judicata against the other partners in subsequent suits against them. The fact of a partnership relation does not establish the requisite privity to invoke res judicata, since the liability is several. [Dillard v. McKnight, 34 Cal. 2d 209 (1949)]

(2) **The liability of partners** for the torts of their co-partners is analogous to the rules of Agency. Instead of a respondeat superior theory, however, each partner is deemed to assume liability for any tortious act committed by a co-partner. [Madsen v. Cawthorne, 30 Cal. App. 2d 124 (1938)—partnership liable for injuries to guest caused by intoxication of partner-driver]

(a) However, where the tort involved requires a showing of malice or wrongful *intent, it must appear that each* partner sought to be held liable possessed such intent. [88 A.L.R.2d 474]

(3) **Any partner may be held liable to a co-partner** for any torts inflicted by him on the co-partner—*i.e.,* the "fellow servant" rule does not apply. [Campbell v. Campbell, 104 Vt. 468 (1932)]

3. **Third Person's Liability to Partnership for Injuries to Partner:** [§500] A partnership generally has *no* right to recover damages from a third party because of injuries inflicted on a member of the partnership; *i.e.,* a partner is not considered a "servant" or employee of the partnership. [Sharfman v. State, 253 Cal. App. 2d 333 (1967)]

a. **Compare:** [§501] A corporation generally *is* permitted to recover damages for a negligent injury to one of its employees (*see supra,* §292). And, in many states, a husband may recover for loss of the services of his wife or child. (*See* Torts Summary.) But these relationships are deemed more protectible than the relationship between business partners.

IV. DISSOLUTION AND WINDING UP OF PARTNERSHIP

A. IN GENERAL

"The dissolution of a partnership is the change in the relation of the partners caused by any partner ceasing to be associated in the carrying on, as distinguished from the winding up, of the business." [UPA§29]

1. **A Dissolution Does Not Terminate the Partnership Immediately:** [§502] Rather, the partnership continues until the winding up of partnership affairs is completed. [UPA §30] Thus, even after a dissolution has occurred (*e.g.,* by mutual agreement to dissolve, *see* below), the partnership relation continues.

    a. **Example:** In an action against the partnership after dissolution but before the final winding up of affairs, service on one partner is sufficient to obtain jurisdiction over the partnership. [136 A.L.R. 1071]

B. CAUSES OF DISSOLUTION [§503]

Unless otherwise provided by agreement of the parties, the following acts or events will cause a dissolution of the partnership, with the consequences noted. (Remember that these acts or events do *not* instantly terminate the partnership relation, which continues for the purpose of winding up partnership affairs.)

1. **Expiration of Partnership Term:** [§504] If the partnership agreement provides that the partnership is to last for a specific period of time (*e.g.,* one year), or until a certain project is accomplished (*e.g.,* until certain property is sold), the expiration of the period or accomplishment of the objective dissolves the partnership. [UPA §31(1)(a)]

    a. **Note:** Even where the partnership is for a fixed term, either partner can effectively terminate the partnership relationship *prior* to the expiration of the partnership term (*see* discussion below).

    b. **Compare:** Conversely, the partners *can*—at the expiration of the partnership term—continue the partnership business, in which case they become partners at will. In this situation, the rights and duties of the partners remain the same as they were at the expiration of the partnership term, to the extent this is consistent with a partnership at will. [UPA §23]

2. **Express Choice of Partner:** [§505] The partnership relation is personal and cannot be specifically enforced in equity; *i.e.,* a person cannot be forced to become a partner, or to remain a partner, when he does not wish to do so. Thus, any or all of the partners can effect a dissolution of the partnership at any time, merely by expressing their will to dissolve the relationship. [Zeibak v. Nasser, 12 Cal. 2d 1 (1938)]

    a. **Partnership at will—no violation of agreement:** [§506] If the partnership is at will (*i.e.,* no definite term or particular undertaking specified), the partner's election to dissolve is not in violation of the agreement. His right to dissolve at any time is deemed implicit in a partnership at will, and he cannot be held responsible even though his dissolving the firm results in a loss to the other partners. [UPA §31(1)(b)]

        (1) **Limitation:** [§507] However, this assumes that the right to dissolve is exercised in good faith. If a partner acts in bad faith—as by attempting to appropriate personally some special advantage or opportunity that was coming to the partnership—this would be treated as a *wrongful* dissolution, and his rights on dissolution would be affected accordingly (*see* below). In other words, a partner cannot use his right to dissolve to exclude his co-partners from a

business opportunity that rightfully belongs to the partnership. [*Page v. Page,* 55 Cal. 2d 192 (1961)]

b. **Partnership for fixed term—violation of agreement:** [§508] Where the partnership is for a fixed term, dissolving the partnership prior to the expiration thereof *is* a violation of the agreement. A partner still has the power (albeit not the right) to dissolve in this situation, but he may be liable for any losses caused by the dissolution (*see infra,* §529).

c. **What constitutes intent to dissolve:** [§509] In order for a partnership to be dissolved at the will of a partner, the partner must have evidenced his intention to discontinue the partnership *relation*.

(1) **Assignment of partnership interests:** [§510] A partner's transfer to a stranger of his interest in the partnership is some evidence of his intention to dissolve, but is not conclusive (*see supra,* §350). "A conveyance by a partner of his interest in the partnership does not of itself dissolve the partnership." [UPA §27]

(2) **Levy of charging order:** [§511] Similarly, the levy of a charging order on the interest of a debtor-partner [UPA §28; *and see supra,* §439] does not of itself dissolve the partnership.

(3) **Right of assignee to obtain dissolution:** [§512] The *assignee* of the partnership interest (or holder of the charging order) can obtain a *judicial* dissolution of the partnership after expiration of the term or, in a partnership at will, whenever he acquires the interest or the charging order is levied. [UPA §32(2)]

3. **Expulsion of Partner:** [§513] The expulsion of a member from the business will also cause a dissolution. If the expulsion is bona fide and pursuant to a power reserved in the partnership agreement, there is no violation of the agreement and the expelling partners are not liable for any losses caused thereby. (The result would be contra, however, if the expulsion were made in bad faith, or without any right to expel reserved in the agreement.) [UPA §31(1)(d)]

4. **Withdrawal or Admission of Partner:** [§514] Similarly, the withdrawal of a partner, or the admission of a new partner, results in a dissolution of the partnership (unless the partnership agreement otherwise provides—and most do). A newly-admitted partner may become party to any pre-existing agreement by signing it upon his admission. [UPA §31(7)]

5. **Illegality:** [§515] Dissolution of partnership will also result upon the occurrence of any event making it unlawful for the partnership to continue in business.

a. **Note:** Even though the illegality of the partnership business may be a ground for dissolution, the partners may thereafter decide to change their business and continue the partnership relation.

6. **Death or Bankruptcy:** [§516] A partner's credit and services are deemed an integral part of his contribution to the partnership. Thus, in the absence of an agreement to the contrary, the partnership is dissolved upon the death or bankruptcy of any partner. [UPA §31(4),(5)] In this situation, the surviving (or nonbankrupt) partner has the right to wind up the partnership affairs (*see* below).

7. **Decree of Court:** [§517] Any of the acts or events enumerated above is sufficient in itself to dissolve the partnership. However, certain other acts or events may also lead to a dissolution, provided there is an appropriate *judicial* declaration.

a. **Grounds for judicial dissolution:** [§518] UPA section 32 provides that a court "shall decree" a dissolution of the partnership in the following situations:

    (1) **Insanity:** [§519]   Where a partner has been declared insane in any judicial proceeding, or otherwise shown to be of unsound mind.

    (2) **Partner incapable of performing:** [§520]   Where a partner is or has become incapable of performing his part of the partnership contract.

        (a) Illness or incapacity does not in itself justify a dissolution, but where it appears that the incapacity is permanent and will materially affect the partner's ability to discharge the duties assumed by him under the partnership agreement, a court decree of dissolution is proper. [Raymond v. Vaughn, 128 Ill. 256 (1889)]

    (3) **Improper conduct:** [§521]   Where a partner has been guilty of conduct tending to prejudice the carrying on of business, or otherwise constituting a breach of the partnership agreement.

        (a) Where it appears that the partner is acting to further his own interests rather than those of the partnership, or is wrongfully excluding his co-partners from the business, a judicial decree of dissolution is proper. [Vangel v. Vangel, 116 Cal. App. 2d 615 (1953)]

    (4) **Loss inevitable:** [§522]   Where the business can be carried on only at a loss.

    (5) **Dissolution equitable:** [§523]   Where there are other circumstances "rendering a dissolution equitable."

  b. **Nature of proceeding:** [§524]   A suit for dissolution is equitable in nature, and the court therefore generally considers all the facts and circumstances in granting or withholding relief. [Bates v. McTammany, 10 Cal. 2d 697 (1938)—court could refuse decree of dissolution where it would result in substantial loss to innocent partner]

  c. **Accounting:** [§525]   The judicial action is generally for dissolution and an accounting, since the court has to determine the credits and debits to each partner in order to provide for distribution of the partnership assets (*see* discussion *supra,* §476).

  d. **Distribution of assets:** [§526]   Usually the court orders partnership assets sold and the proceeds applied to payment of all partnership debts. The balance remaining is then applied (i) to repayment of each partner's capital account (his contributions plus accumulated earnings), and (ii) to payment of current earnings in accordance with each partner's share of the partnership profits. (Detailed rules for distribution are contained in UPA section 40.)

    (1) **Where there are no partnership debts,** the court may order distribution of the partnership assets *in kind.* [Hooper v. Barranti, 81 Cal. App. 2d 570 (1947)]

    (2) **Where there are losses** (*i.e.,* partnership liabilities exceeding assets available for distribution), each partner must contribute according to his share of the profits. [UPA §18(a)]

        (a) If any partner has not contributed the full share of capital which he agreed to contribute, he must pay this before other partners are required to make up any losses sustained.

        (b) If one of the partners is insolvent or refuses to contribute his share of the losses, the remaining partners must make up his share proportionately. They will then have a right of action against the defaulting partner to enforce his contribution (which can also be enforced by an assignee for the benefit of creditors or by bankruptcy trustee, if the partnership has become insolvent). [UPA §40(d)-(f)]

C. RIGHTS OF PARTNERS IN DISSOLUTION

1. **Where Dissolution Does Not Violate Partnership Agreement:** [§527]   Where the cause of dissolution is *not* a violation of the partnership agreement (*e.g.*, a dissolution upon expiration of partnership term), no partner has a claim or cause of action against any other partner for any loss sustained in the dissolution. Each partner has the right to have the partnership assets applied to the discharge of its liabilities, and the balance distributed to the partners in accordance with their respective interests. [UPA §38(1)]

   a. **Compare:** In this situation, no partner can appropriate the partnership assets for herself, nor can one partner be forced to pay the other the appraised value of any asset (as is the case where dissolution violates the agreement; *see* below). [Pluth v. Smith, 205 Cal. App. 2d 818 (1962)]

2. **Where Dissolution Violates Partnership Agreement:** [§528]   Where the dissolution is caused by an act in violation of the partnership agreement (*e.g.*, a partner's electing to dissolve a partnership for a fixed term prior to the expiration thereof), the other ("innocent") partners are accorded certain rights in addition to those listed above:

   a. **Right to damages:** [§529]   The partnership agreement is a contract, and even though a partner may have the power to dissolve, she does not necessarily have the right to do so (*see* discussion *supra,* §508). Therefore, if the dissolution she causes is a violation of the agreement, she is liable for any damages sustained by the innocent partners as a result thereof (*e.g.*, loss of profits due to interruption of business). [UPA §38(2)]

   b. **Right to purchase business:** [§530]   The "innocent" partners also have the right to continue the partnership business in the firm name, provided they pay the partner causing dissolution the value of her interest in the partnership (less any damages recoverable).

      (1) Alternatively, the partners wishing to continue the business may post a bond in an amount approved by the court and institute appropriate proceedings for a determination of the dissolving partner's interests and any damages to be charged against same. [UPA §38(2)(b)]

      (2) If the partners fail to pay or post bond within a reasonable time, the partner causing dissolution is entitled to compensation for the use of her partnership assets in the continuing business measured in the same way as if she had died or retired. [*See* UPA §42; *and see infra,* §532]

         (a) Should the dissolving partner be requested by the remaining partners to continue any services for the partnership, she is entitled to reasonable compensation for such services. [Vangel v. Vangel, 45 Cal. 2d 804 (1955)]

   c. **Right to wind up partnership affairs:** [§531]   If they decide not to purchase the wrongdoer's interest, the innocent partners have the right to wind up the partnership affairs and arrange for distribution of assets. [UPA §37]

3. **Rights and Duties of Surviving Partner(s):** [§532]   Upon the death of a partner, the surviving partners are entitled to possession of the partnership assets, and are charged with the winding up of partnership affairs. [UPA §37]

   a. **The surviving partner acts as a fiduciary** in liquidating the partnership, and he must account to the estate of the deceased partner for the value of the decedent's interest in the partnership. [Sibert v. Shaver, 111 Cal. App. 2d 833 (1952)]

(1) The surviving partner is under a duty to settle the partnership affairs without delay. If he continues the business *without the consent* of the deceased partner's estate, the surviving partner is liable for interest on the amount which he is found to owe the decedent's estate, *or* an appropriate share of any profits earned by the surviving partner through use of partnership property following the decedent's death, whichever is greater. [UPA§42; 55 A.L.R.2d 1391]

(2) And if an unjustified delay *diminishes* the value of the partnership business, the surviving partner may be held accountable for the value of the deceased partner's interest *at the date of death*, rather than the value at date of ultimate liquidation. [Sibert v. Shaver, *supra*]

b. **However, the surviving partner is entitled to compensation** for his services in winding up the partnership, as well as reimbursement for any costs incurred or expended in doing so. [UPA §18(f)]

D. EFFECTS OF DISSOLUTION

1. **Liability for Existing Partnership Debts:** [§533]   A dissolution in no way affects each partner's liability for the partnership debts. The partners' joint liability *remains* until the debts are discharged. [Faricy v. J. F. Brown Mercantile Co., 288 P. 639 (Colo. 1930)]

   a. **Novation:** [§534]   However, there may be a *novation* whereby creditors agree to look only to certain of the partners for payment, thereby releasing the others. [UPA §36(3)]

2. **Liability of Partners Continuing Business:** [§535]   Where, after a dissolution, there is a change in the composition of the partnership (*e.g.,* death or retirement of a partner, or admission of new partner) and the business continues, the new partnership remains liable for all the debts of the previous partnership. The creditors of the first or dissolved partnership are also creditors of the partnership continuing the business. [UPA §41; *and see*, Blumer Brewing Corp. v. Mayer, 269 N.W. 693 (Wis. 1936)]

   a. **Incoming partners:** Note, however, that an incoming partner's liability is limited to her interest in the partnership. [UPA §17; *see* discussion *supra,* §496]

3. **Retiring Partner's Liability for Debt Incurred by Partners Continuing Business:** [§536] A dissolution ends the power and authority of a partner to bind the partnership, except to the extent necessary to wind up its affairs and complete transactions begun but not yet finished at the time of dissolution. [UPA §33] Hence he is no longer liable for debts incurred after the dissolution.

   a. **Exceptions:** [§537]   Even after dissolution, contracts with third persons are binding on the partnership and all partners if the third person knew of the partnership prior to the dissolution, had no knowledge of the dissolution, and the fact of dissolution was not advertised in a newspaper of general circulation. [UPA §35(1)]

      (1) **Notice of withdrawal:** [§538]   For this reason, and as part of any dissolution, a retiring partner generally publishes notice of his withdrawal from the firm—to protect against future debts incurred by the partners continuing the business.

   b. **Knowledge requirement:** [§539]   Note that a partner's authority to bind the partnership terminates only if and when he acquires knowledge of the dissolution. Thus, in an A-B-C partnership, if A notifies B of his election to dissolve, and before this information is communicated to C, C enters into a contract with a third party, the contract is binding on all partners. [UPA §34]

V. LIMITED PARTNERSHIPS

A. IN GENERAL

1. **Background:** [§540]   Limited partnerships did not exist at common law. They are entities created by modern statutes. They were developed to facilitiate commercial investments by those who want a financial interest in a business but do not want all the responsibilities and liabilities of partners.

   a. **Uniform act:** [§541]   In recent years, most states have adopted the Uniform Limited Partnership Act (ULPA). [*See, e.g.,* Cal. Corp. Code §§15501 *et seq.*]

   b. **Revised uniform act:** [§542]   The ULPA was completely revised by the National Conference of Commissioners on Uniform State Laws in 1976. As of 1981, the Revised Uniform Limited Partnership Act has been adopted by nine states.

2. **Definition:** [§543]   A limited partnership is a partnership formed by two or more persons, having as its members one or more general partners and one or more limited partners.

   a. **General partner:** [§544]   The *general partner* is a partner who assumes the management responsibilities of the partnership, and full personal liability for the debts of the partnership.

   b. **Limited partner:** [§545]   The *limited partner* is a partner who makes a contribution of cash or other property to the partnership and obtains an interest in the partnership in return—but who is not active in management, and whose liability for partnership debts is limited.

   c. **Dual status:** [§546]   A person may be *both* a general partner and a limited partner in the same partnership at the same time. In such a case, the partner has, in respect to her contribution as a limited partner, all the rights which she would have if she were not also a general partner. [ULPA §12; ULPA (1976) §404]

3. **Purposes:** [§547]   A limited partnership may carry on any business which a partnership could carry on. [ULPA §3; ULPA (1976) §106]

   a. **Contemporary uses of limited partnership:** [§548]   Although section 7 of the UPA allows one to loan money to an ordinary partnership and take profits instead of interest (thus providing limited liability and responsibility advantages similar to that of a limited partnership), there has been a resurgence in use of the limited partnership form. Limited partnerships are often set up to provide tax shelters for persons in higher income tax brackets. (*See* Income Tax Summary.)

4. **Liability:** [§549]   The general partner is personally liable for all obligations of the partnership. A limited partner has *no personal liability* for partnership debts, and her maximum loss is the amount of her investment in the limited partnership. [ULPA §1; ULPA (1976) §§303, 403; *and see* Silvola v. Rowlett, 272 P.2d 287 (Colo. 1954)]

   a. **Limited partner as manager:** [§550]   However, where a limited partner takes part in the *management and control* of the business, she becomes liable as a general partner. [ULPA §7; *and see* Holzman v. De Escamilla, 86 Cal. App. 2d 858 (1948)]

   b. **Creditors:** [§551]   The revised ULPA requires that a creditor must have actual knowledge of a limited partner's participation unless his "participation in the control of the business is...substantially the same" as that of the general partner. In addition certain "safe" acts of participation are enumerated. [ULPA (1976) §303]

5. **Rights of Limited Partners:** [§552]   The rights of a limited partner are substantially the same as those of a partner in an ordinary partnership, except that he has no rights in regard to management. Hence, he has rights of access to the partnership books, to an accounting as to the partnership business, and to a dissolution and winding up by decree of court. [ULPA §10; ULPA (1976) §305]

   a. **Transacting business with partnership:** [§553]   A limited partner may lend money to, or transact business with, the partnership. [ULPA §13; ULPA (1976) §107]

   b. **As creditors:** [§554]   Claims of limited partners against the partnership are subordinated only to the rights of general creditors. [Krellberg v. Gregory, 31 Misc. 2d 1093 (1961)]

   c. **Assignment:** [§555]   A limited partner's interest is assignable. The assignment vests in the assignee all rights to income or distribution of assets of the partnership, but unless and until the certificate of limited partnership is amended with the consent of all other partners, the assignee is *not* entitled to inspect partnership books, obtain an accounting, etc. [ULPA §19; ULPA (1976) §702]

B. FORMATION OF LIMITED PARTNERSHIP [§556]

While formalities are usually not required to create a partnership, there are certain requirements for the formation of a limited partnership: (i) The partners must execute a certificate setting forth the name of the partnership, the character of the business and the location of the principal office, the name and address of each partner and his capital contributions, a designation of which partners are "general" and "limited," and the respective rights and priorities (if any) of the partner. (ii) One copy of the certificate must be filed (usually with the County Clerk). (iii) A copy of the certificate must be recorded in the county of the principal place of business as well. [ULPA §2] The revised ULPA requires central filing with the Secretary of State. [ULPA (1976) §203] The certificate may be amended or cancelled by following similar formalities. [ULPA §25] The revised ULPA places an affirmative duty upon general partners to amend when certain specified events occur. [ULPA (1976) §202]

1. **If the Certificate Contains False Statements:** [§557]   Anyone who suffers a loss by reliance thereon can hold all of the partners (general and limited) liable. [ULPA §6; *and see* Walraven v. Ramsay, 55 N.W.2d 853 (Mich. 1953) *and* Giles v. Vette, 263 U.S. 553 (1924)] The revised ULPA extends this liability to all persons signing a certificate as agent. [ULPA (1976) §207]

2. **Purpose of Certificate:** [§558]   The purpose of the certificate is to give all potential creditors notice of the limited liability of the limited partners.

3. **Minimum Compliance:** [§559]   The ULPA requires at least "substantial compliance in good faith" with these requirements. Where there has been no substantial compliance, the purported limited partner may be held liable as a general partner.

   a. **Note:** A purported limited partner can escape liability as a general partner if—upon ascertaining the mistake—he "promptly renounces his interest in the profits of the business or other compensation by way of income." [ULPA §11; ULPA (1976) §304]

C. DISSOLUTION OF LIMITED PARTNERSHIP [§560]

A limited partnership may be dissolved in any of the ways provided for dissolution of a partnership (*see* discussion *supra,* §§503-526).

1. Unless otherwise provided in the agreement, the retirement, death or insanity of a general partner dissolves the partnership. [ULPA §20; ULPA (1976) §801]

2. However, the death of a limited partner does *not* dissolve the partnership. Instead, the decedent's executor or administrator is given all the rights of a limited partner for purposes of settling the estate. [ULPA §21; ULPA (1976) §705]

3. Section 802 of the revised ULPA provides for judicial dissolution whenever it is not reasonably practicable to continue the business. [ULPA (1976) §802]

D. REVISED ULPA (1976) [§561]

The 1976 revision of the ULPA has added several new provisions which are intended to fill gaps in the prior law.

1. Section 103 permits a limited partnership to reserve the exclusive right to the use of a name by filing with the Secretary of State. [ULPA (1976) §103]

2. Section 503 provides a basis for determining the sharing of profits and losses absent express agreement. [ULPA (1976) §503]

3. Section 606 grants creditor status to partners entitled to distribution without requiring the partner to seek dissolution. [ULPA (1976) §606]

REVIEW QUESTIONS

FILL IN
ANSWER

1. Indicate whether each of the following statements is true or false:

    a. As a general rule, agents have greater discretion in carrying out the duties of their employment than do servants. _____

    b. One person cannot be employed simultaneously as an agent and a servant by the same employer. _____

    c. An employer is not liable for tortious acts committed by an independent contractor. _____

    d. The relationship between principal and agent must be supported by consideration in order for the agent's acts to bind the principal. _____

2. Jackie meets Truman at a party where she offers to find a publisher for Truman's new book "solely as a friend." Jackie promptly forgets the matter, and makes no attempt to find a buyer for the manuscript. Is Jackie liable to Truman for breach of contract? _____

3. Manufacturer hires O as a sales representative in California. May O properly handle sales for Manufacturer's competitors as well? _____

    a. As part of the job, O is authorized to rent warehouse space on Manufacturer's account. O rents space from landlord W, who agrees in return therefor to give O a reduced rental on O's apartment. Has O breached his fiduciary duty to Manufacturer? _____

4. A is engaged to find and purchase "suitable farming property" for her principal, P. While searching for such property, A discovers a small apple orchard for sale and purchases the orchard for herself. Has A breached her fiduciary duty to P? _____

    a. A's uncle R is attempting to sell his farm Greenacre, and promises A a commission if she can find a buyer. A then arranges for P to purchase the farm from R. Assuming that the sales price represents the fair market value of the property, can P rescind the sale? _____

5. An agent is responsible to the principal for acts by subagents hired by him, whether or not such hiring was authorized by the principal. True or false? _____

6. Bob hires Cathy as an engineer to maintain Bob's automated assembly line. While repairing a portion of the line, Cathy discovers a new method of lubricating certain moving parts which would not work for Bob's plant but would have wide applicability in other industries. Is Cathy entitled to patent this discovery in her own name? _____

7. A principal has a right to indemnification for any loss sustained as a result of his agent's improper acts, but an employer has no similar right against his employee. True or false? _____

8. P hires A on commission to sell P's boat, "Res Ipsa." A in turn engages S on the same basis to help him find a buyer. S induces B to purchase the boat. Is P liable for S' commission on the sale? _____

9. Marvin hires Bill as his exclusive sales agent to sell Marvin's new line of widgets. After Bill has developed a substantial market for the product, Marvin enters the field to sell

directly to customers. Does Bill have an action against Marvin for the profits on Marvin's sales?

    a.   Would the result be different if Marvin had subsequently retained Carol as a sales agent to compete with Bill?

10.   Principal hires Agent to transport a load of steel ingots across the state, and Agent (with Principal's consent) engages Trucker to help him on the trip. En route, the ingots slide off Trucker's truck and injure Driver, the driver of a passing car.

    a.   If Driver obtains a judgment against Agent for his damages, is Agent entitled to indemnification from Principal?

    b.   Assuming Driver's judgment is against Trucker rather than Agent, would Trucker be equally entitled to indemnification from Principal or Agent?

    c.   Suppose instead that Principal changes his mind for no apparent reason and engages another agent to haul his steel. If Agent has turned down an alternative job to make the trip, can he obtain specific performance of his agreement with Principal?

11.   An agency agreement must be based upon the mutual consent of the purported agent and principal. True or false?

12.   A minor can appoint an agent, but generally lacks the capacity to serve as an agent. True or false?

13.   At a local bar, Leslie overhears Yolanda say, "I certainly would like to find a good Picasso for my study." Unbeknownst to Yolanda, Leslie contacts collector Pierre and purchases one of his Picasso paintings "as Yolanda's agent." Can Yolanda refuse to pay for the painting?

    a.   If Pierre has relied upon Leslie's statements to his detriment, can he allege an agency by estoppel against Yolanda?

14.   P tells A, "Please try to collect this overdue account from T. You may have 20% of what you collect as your fee." Does A have authority to settle with T for less than the full amount owed?

15.   Rancher telephones Agent and asks her to sell Rancher's Brownacre Ranch "for any price more than $200,000" and deposit the proceeds in Rancher's account. Agent signs a purchase agreement with Buyer, whereby the latter contracts to buy the ranch for $250,000. Can Buyer enforce the contract against Rancher?

    a.   Would the result be different if Rancher had negotiated the sale with Buyer and instructed Agent by telephone to sign his name to the agreement?

16.   Louise gives Stephen her power of attorney to purchase for her certain pieces of sculpture upon Stephen's representation that he is an art expert with considerable experience. Stephen then contracts with Dealer for several expensive items on Louise's account. If Louise subsequently discovers that Stephen has no art experience whatever, can she rescind the sale?

    a.   Would the result be different if Louise discovered Stephen's misrepresentations prior to the sale by Dealer?

17. Elmer writes to Graham, authorizing Graham to act as his agent for the sale of Elmer's automobile. Elmer then mails a copy of the letter to Hector whom Elmer believes to be a prospective buyer. Does Graham have apparent authority to sell the car to Hector? _____

    a.   Would the result be different if Hector instead had spotted a notation on Elmer's desk, "Contact Graham regarding the sale of the car"? _____

    b.   Assuming Elmer mailed to Hector a copy of the above letter to Graham, can Elmer avoid liability to Hector by expressly revoking Graham's authority in writing, prior to any agreement with Hector? _____

18. Suppose Elmer tells Graham, "You are authorized to sell my car, but *only* during the next thirty days." At the same time, Elmer—who is leaving the country for several months—signs over the "pink slip" on the car to Graham, it being clearly understood that this is solely for purposes of the agency. If Graham sells the car to Francine ninety days later, can Francine enforce the sale against Elmer? _____

19. Claudia borrows Don's lawnmower, and then offers to sell the mower to Ned. Ned mentions the offer to Don, who merely says, "I think it's a good mower, alright." Ned pays Claudia for the mower, and Claudia moves to another town after returning the mower to Don. Can Ned obtain the mower from Don? _____

20. As a general rule, courts will construe the powers of an authorized agent broadly, in order to protect the interests of third parties dealing with the agent. True or false? _____

21. P authorizes A to sell her boat for $5,000. C offers to pay $50 for a right of first refusal on the boat. Does A have the power to accept C's offer? _____

22. P engages A, a real estate broker, to sell his house. Does A have the power to negotiate and conclude a sale with D, a prospective buyer? _____

    a.   Suppose A appoints fellow broker E her agent to help secure a buyer for P's house. E produces the highest bidder on the house, who signs a purchase contract with P. If the appointment of brokers as subagents is customary in the area, can E recover compensation from P for his services? _____

    b.   In describing P's house to a potential buyer, A represents that it has "copper plumbing throughout." In fact, P told A that there are only two small sections of exposed copper pipe and that she should make no statements about it. Are A's representations binding on P? _____

    c.   Does A have the power to warrant the structure of P's house "sound against any and all defects"? _____

    d.   If the sales contract used by P contains a disclaimer as to "any warranties not contained herein," will P be relieved of liability for customary warranties made by A but not contained in the contract? _____

23. Owner decides to open a store and hires Max as his general manager. Before leaving on a sailing trip, Owner tells Max not to spend more than $2,000 on "noninventory items" while he is away. Shortly after Owner's departure, Max receives a call from a city official indicating that certain rewiring in the store must be completed within twenty-four hours in order to avoid losing its business permit. If the rewiring will cost $3,000 to complete in that period, does Max have authority to have it done? _____

a. While Owner is away, someone tells Max that several people have been living on Owner's remote mountain property for some time. Max neglects to mention this fact to Owner, and thereafter the "squatters" claim title to the land by adverse possession. Is Max's knowledge imputed to Owner in resolving the claim? _____

b. Shortly before his employment by Owner, Max managed a similar store and became familiar with Fair Employment Act hiring requirements. If such requirements are significant in his present position, will Max's knowledge thereof be imputed to Owner? _____

24. P engages broker A to purchase a summer home for her in Woodland Glen. Five years elapse without further communication between P and A, whereupon A discovers a prospective property. Is A authorized to proceed with a purchase? _____

a. Shortly after she is hired by P, A learns that Woodland Glen is being rezoned to permit logging and heavy industry. Can A proceed to purchase a home there on P's behalf? _____

25. O engages A to sell his collection of antique guns. Thereafter, he enters a purchase agreement with S and receives payment for the collection. Unbeknownst to A or S, O has died in the interim. Can S enforce the sales contract against O's estate? _____

a. Would the result be different if O had hired A to sell the guns as a means of discharging a loan from A to O? _____

26. Brandon hires Chuck as exclusive agent to sell his estate for a period of six months, the agreement between the two providing that the agency is irrevocable during that period. Two weeks later, Brandon writes Chuck a "letter of termination" and engages Daphne to sell the property. Can Chuck obtain specific enforcement of the agreement against Brandon? _____

a. Would the result be different if Chuck's employment was a means of discharging a debt owed by Brandon to Chuck? _____

27. The apparent authority of an agent can never terminate until proper notification of the termination is given to third parties. True or false? _____

28. Purporting to act on L's behalf (but without authority), M agrees to purchase O's skis and bindings for $200. N then give M $10 for an assignment of rights under the agreement and tenders the $200 contract price to O. Is O free to rescind? _____

29. Thief steals Owner's television set and, posing as Owner, purports to sell it to X. Feeling guilty about the theft, Thief informs Owner, who decides that the sale would be advantageous and affirms it. Can Owner enforce the purchase agreement against X? _____

a. Suppose instead that Thief forges Owner's name to a gambling wager, intending that the proceeds will go to Owner if he wins. Can Owner later affirm and enforce the wager? _____

30. Without authority, A hires T to install a new roof on P's house. T arrives and, informing P of the agreement, installs the roof. Does T have an action against P for the price agreed upon by A? _____

a. Would the result be different if P were out of town when T arrived to install the roof? _____

31. Without authority, A purports to sell P's rare Stradivarius violin to T. When informed of this, P says, "I was thinking of selling it anyway, and A would certainly be the one to

handle it for me. Fine.'' If the agreed price were $25, can T enforce the contract by tendering that amount to P? _____

32. Acting without authority, Jack purports to sell Lucy's farm, Blackacre, to Paul. If Lucy later telephones Paul to say that she affirms the sale, can Paul enforce the purchase agreement against her? _____

    a.   Suppose that the agreed sales price between Jack and Paul is $200,000. Subsequently, and without knowledge of the above agreement, Lucy contracts to sell the farm to her neighbor for $150,000. When Lucy learns of Jack's agreement, she promptly ratifies it in writing. Can Paul then enforce the contract? _____

33. Without authority, R purports to sell T's collection of antique automobiles to S. Before T learns of the agreement, S dies. Can T subsequently affirm the sale? _____

34. Although he has no authority to do so, A agrees to sell P's house to T ''as agent for P.'' A believes in good faith that he is authorized to sell the house; but P does not ratify the sale. Is A liable to T? _____

    a.   Suppose instead that P authorized A to sell the house. In negotiating with T, A (without authority) contracts to sell the house *and* an adjoining shop in a ''package deal.'' T makes the agreed down payment, whereupon P learns of the unauthorized additional terms and repudiates the contract. Does T have any rights against P? _____

35. Smith Company authorizes Jones to purchase a new generator for the company plant. Jones enters an agreement to purchase a generator from O and executes the agreement, ''Smith Company, by its agent, Jones.'' Can O enforce the agreement against both Smith and Jones? _____

    a.   Is extrinsic evidence admissible to show who the parties actually intended would be liable on the contract? _____

36. P authorizes A to purchase a mountain cabin for him. A discovers that T has a cabin for sale and signs a purchase agreement with T, in his own name and without mention of his agent's role.

    a.   T conveys title to the cabin to A, but P does not pay as required in the agreement. Can T sue A to enforce the contract? _____

    b.   After signing the purchase agreement, T learns that A was actually an agent for P. Can T sue both P and A on the contract? _____

    c.   Suppose instead that A pays the purchase price to T, but the latter refuses to convey title to the cabin. Can P sue T on the contract? _____

    d.   Would the result in the preceding hypothetical be different if P knew that T would never sell the cabin to him? _____

    e.   Assume that P gives A sufficient funds to purchase the cabin, but A absconds with the money to Brazil. Can T sue P for the purchase price? _____

37. Nelson engages agent Kristin to hire a tutor to teach him French. Kristin contracts with Marie for this purpose, failing to inform Marie that Nelson will be her student. Can Nelson enforce the agreement against Marie? _____

38. B authorizes C to sell an inventory of his spare parts. C enters an agreement with D to purchase the parts, which C signs "as agent." B's identity is not revealed; D pays C for the parts. If the goods are not delivered, can D sue C on the contract? _____

    a. Would the result be different if D knew that C was B's agent, even though C had never mentioned his identity? _____

39. Indicate whether each of the following statements is true or false:

    a. Under the doctrine of respondeat superior, the employer alone is liable for the tortious acts of her servant-employee. _____

    b. An employer may avoid vicarious liability if she expressly contracts that the employee assumes full responsibility for his actions. _____

    c. A master may be liable for the acts of her servant even though the servant is exonerated from liability. _____

    d. An employer is not vicariously liable for an employee's torts if she has no right of control over the physical acts of the employee. _____

    e. A minor who hires a servant and has the right of control over the acts of the servant can be held vicariously liable therefor. _____

40. Tim is walking through Mac's warehouse to meet a friend when he sees several workers trying to lift a large box. Although not an employee, Tim offers to assist them, and negligently upsets the box on Mac's customer, injuring him. Could Mac be held vicariously liable for Tim's acts? _____

    a. Suppose instead that the box falls on one of Mac's employees. Can Mac recover for injuries to his employee? _____

41. Mario's sporting goods store advertises that Kermit, a noted gymnast, will formulate personalized exercise programs at the store. During a demonstration, Kermit negligently injures Lincoln, a customer at the store, while adjusting an exercise device on Lincoln's arms. The agreement between Mario and Kermit gives Mario no right to control Kermit's actions during demonstrations. Could Mario be held vicariously liable to Lincoln? _____

    a. Would the result be different if Lincoln had entered the store to purchase some ski wax and, while waiting at the sales counter for his purchase, was injured by Kermit's negligently thrown barbell? _____

42. P hires A to drive a truckload of wheat from Kansas to Los Angeles. A in turn hires S to help him as a relief driver. While S is driving en route, she negligently collides with an auto, injuring its driver. Is P vicariously liable to the injured driver? _____

43. M, a heavy equipment contractor, leases a scoop-shovel tractor and a skilled operator, S, to T to excavate a standard sewer line at T's home. In the process of digging, S negligently severs an electric line which falls on and injures T's neighbor, R. Can M be held vicariously liable to R? _____

    a. Would the result be different if the power line was severed while S was making a special excavation ordered by T? _____

44. X is a truck driver hired by Y to transport construction materials. In determining whether X is a servant or an independent contractor, would it be helpful to know

whether X drives one of Y's trucks?   _____

45. Alex falls and injures himself while staying at Bessie's resort. Bessie calls Doctor, a physician employed by the resort, to treat Alex. Doctor negligently wrenches Alex's back, aggravating the injury. Is Bessie liable to Alex for the aggravation?   _____

    a. Would the result be different if the aggravation were due to the fact that Doctor was intoxicated at the time he treated Alex?   _____

46. P hires independent contractor IC to spray his alfalfa crop. IC uses all reasonable care in spraying, but a certain amount of gas is blown onto Q's land, killing two of his sheep. Is P liable to Q?   _____

47. Delilah, a department store owner, hires Samson as a sales clerk in the book department. Although he is instructed never to wait on customers in the adjoining sporting goods department, Samson nevertheless does so and injures a customer while demonstrating how to fire a spear gun. Is Delilah liable to the customer?   _____

    a. Would the result be different if Samson had been employed in the sporting goods department, but instructed never to demonstrate spear guns?   _____

48. Ace Bar & Grill employs W as a dishwasher. Shortly thereafter, W hears Z, a customer in the establishment, whistling off key and asks him to stop. When Z refuses, W takes a baseball bat from under the bar and hits Z over the head, severely injuring him. Is Ace vicariously liable to Z?   _____

    a. Would the result be different if W had been employed in a railroad dining car and the same incident had ensued?   _____

    b. Suppose instead that W is taking a smoke break when he carelessly flips his cigarette into a corner. A fire ensues, which injures two customers in the Bar & Grill. Is Ace liable to the injured patrons?   _____

    c. During a lull in business, W decides to clean his bicycle chain in the Ace dishwasher. This causes the washer to explode, injuring customer N. Is Ace vicariously liable to N?   _____

    d. W is asked to clean grease off a stove top in the Ace kitchen. W uses gasoline to cut the grease, which promptly ignites and burns a patron. Is Ace vicariously liable to the injured customer?   _____

49. Where a servant acts partly on his own behalf and partly for his employer, the employer is vicariously liable only for that conduct designed to further the employer's business. True or false?   _____

50. A is hired by P to deliver newspapers in P's truck. While on the delivery route, A (without authority) invites a friend T to ride along. A then negligently collides with a car, injuring T. Is P liable to T?   _____

    a. Would the result be different if T were an employee of P hired to unload papers from the truck?   _____

51. Usury Loan Company hires Acme Collection Agency to collect a debt owed by Debtor and instructs Acme to "repossess the car" if Debtor refuses to pay. Acme takes possession of the car in Debtor's garage, which turns out to be the property of S. Can S hold both Usury and Acme liable?   _____

a. Suppose that Usury merely tells Acme to collect Debtor's debt, but Acme (without authority) takes the car which actually belongs to S and delivers it to Usury. Can S hold Usury liable if he discovers the car in its possession?   _____

b. Would the result be different if Acme took the car for its own purposes, but inadvertently delivered it to Usury?   _____

52. P employs A as manager of her apartment building. A notices a loose step on the stairwell of the building, makes a note to repair same, but does not mention it to P. Z, a tenant in the building, falls through the step and breaks her leg. Can Z hold P liable?   _____

a. Would the result be different if A were P's bookkeeper instead of her manager?   _____

53. Unless all of the essential elements for misrepresentation are proved, an employer (or principal) cannot be held liable in tort for the statements of his employee. True or false?   _____

54. While an employer can be liable for false statements made by servants or agents, he cannot be held for the statements of an independent contractor. True or false?   _____

55. Burns hires Allen to sell his art collection and provides Allen with recent appraisal information for prospective buyers. To induce a higher sales price, Allen actually gives Purchaser an inflated appraisal figure, and Purchaser buys the collection. Can Purchaser hold Burns liable for Allen's false statements?   _____

a. Would the result be different if Burns had given no appraisal information to Allen?   _____

b. Would the result be different if Burns had engaged Allen merely to advertise his collection?   _____

56. Lester engages Vanessa to sell his car, and tells Vanessa that the car has been driven 50,000 miles (the present setting on its odometer). In fact, Lester knows the car has been driven 150,000 miles. Upon Vanessa's representation of the lower mileage, a buyer purchases the car. Can the buyer sue Lester?   _____

a. Would the result be different if neither Lester nor Vanessa were aware of the true mileage on the car?   _____

57. A partnership must always consist of co-owners carrying on a business for profit. True or false?   _____

58. For purposes of determining rights and liabilities, a partnership is always treated as an aggregate of the individual partners. True or false?   _____

59. Partner X purchases a warehouse with his own money but puts title to the building in the name of the partnership. Does the warehouse thereby become partnership property?   _____

a. Would the result be different if X had purchased the warehouse with partnership funds?   _____

b. Assume X purchases the warehouse with his own funds, but records title in the partnership name. Later, in a dispute with the partnership, X alleges that he never intended that the building be partnership property. If the partnership shows that it urgently needed this type of warehouse, is it likely to prevail?   _____

60. P, one of several partners in a fast-food restaurant, incurs heavy personal debts which she is unable to pay. Can P's creditors attach her interest in the restaurant premises to satisfy their claims against her? _____

    a. Can P's creditors proceed against P's interest in the partnership? _____

61. Indicate whether each of the following statements is true or false:

    a. A partnership is equally effective whether formed by oral or written agreement of the partners. _____

    b. A corporation is presumed to have the power to become a partner with individuals in other corporations. _____

    c. No person may become a member of a partnership unless all partners consent thereto. _____

    d. The sharing of gross income is more likely to establish a partnership relation than the sharing of profits from the business. _____

    e. If an actual partner represents that a nonpartner is a member of the partnership, the "nonpartner" can bind the partnership as though he were a partner. _____

    f. In the absence of a contrary agreement, the management rights of a partner in the partnership are proportional to his agreed share in partnership profits. _____

    g. As a general rule, a partner cannot be reimbursed for his services to the partnership unless all partners agree thereto. _____

    h. Any action by one partner against another involving partnership business must be brought in equity rather than at law. _____

62. Partner A signs a loan agreement with Bank to borrow $500,000 for the partnership. Unbeknownst to Bank, the partnership agreement provides that no single partner may borrow for the partnership without the written consent of all partners. Is the agreement enforceable against the partnership? _____

    a. After hearing about the loan, partner C notifies Bank that she will not be liable on any subsequent partnership debts. Is this notice effective to relieve C of further liability? _____

    b. Shortly after obtaining the loan, A purports to convey a partnership storage building in his own name to W. If A was authorized to sell the building, does W take legal title thereto? _____

63. Marcus joins the business partnership of Steele and Wool as a new partner. Shortly thereafter, Acme, a creditor of the partnership, commences suit for partnership debts incurred before Marcus became a member. Does Marcus have any liability for the debts? _____

    a. Can Acme sue Steele directly on the claim? _____

    b. On a business trip for the partnership, Marcus negligently runs his car onto a sidewalk, injuring Plaintiff. Can Plaintiff recover from Wool alone for Marcus' tortious conduct? _____

c.   Suppose instead that Steele is the person injured by Marcus' negligence. Can Marcus be held liable to Steele? _____

64.   Indicate whether each of the following statements is true or false:

a.   If a partnership is one for a specified period of time (*e.g.,* two years), the partners cannot continue the relation beyond that period without a new agreement. _____

b.   Any partnership may be dissolved at any time at the express choice of any partner. _____

c.   The withdrawal or admission of a partner results in an automatic dissolution of the partnership. _____

d.   The fact that the partnership business can only be carried on at a loss is sufficient per se to dissolve the partnership. _____

e.   Where there are net partnership losses upon dissolution, these are divided equally among all partners. _____

65.   A, B and C form a partnership for a three year period to produce widgets. Six months later, B elects to dissolve the partnership.

a.   Is B liable to A and C for any damages resulting from the dissolution? _____

b.   After B's election, A and C continue to operate the business in the firm name. Can B sue A and C for compensation accruing after he withdrew from the partnership? _____

c.   Would the result in the preceding situation be different if B had died six months after formation of the partnership? _____

d.   If A and C continue the business after B withdraws, can B be held liable for subsequent partnership debts? _____

66.   X, Y and Z decide to form a limited partnership, with X as general partner and Y and Z as limited partners.

a.   Can Y and Z contribute services to the partnership? _____

b.   Are Y and Z personally liable for the debts of the partnership? _____

c.   If Z dies, will this dissolve the partnership? _____

d.   Would the result be different if X had died? _____

e.   Can Y assign his rights in the partnership to W without the approval of X or Z? _____

REVIEW ANSWERS

1.a. **TRUE**   The servant is under the control of his master and has much less discretion than an agent. [§§3, 5]

b. **FALSE**   The employee may be a servant as to certain duties, and an agent as to others. [§5]

c. **FALSE**   While the doctrine of respondeat superior does not apply to independent contractors (since the employer has no right of control of their actions), the employer may still be liable for their acts in certain situations (*e.g.,* highly dangerous activity). [§§8, 321-326]

d. **FALSE**   A gratuitous agency can also impose liability on the principal. [§10]

2. **DEPENDS**   Assuming Jackie was a gratuitous agent, she is probably not liable for her failure to act at all. However, if Truman detrimentally relied on Jackie's promise (*e.g.,* did not arrange for another agent), some courts might permit Truman to recover any damages suffered by Jackie's failure to act. [§14]

3. **PROBABLY**   In general, manufacturers' representatives often handle competing lines, and absent some agreement to the contrary with this manufacturer, O could properly do so. [§18]

a. **PROBABLY**   Assuming Manufacturer did not know of or consent to the arrangement, this probably represents a breach of O's fiduciary duty—since the reduced apartment rental is in effect a "rebate" to O on the commercial rent paid by Manufacturer. [§21]

4. **DEPENDS**   If A knows that P would be interested in acquiring the orchard for himself (as "suitable property"), she owes P the right of first refusal before purchasing same on her own account. [§22]

a. **YES**   A is acting as a "dual agent" for both R and P, and the same is therefore voidable by P (unless P knew of the arrangement in advance and consented thereto). The fairness of the price paid is immaterial (though it might reduce any damages against A were P to sue for fraud). [§24]

5. **TRUE**   Authority to hire a subagent will affect the principal's liability to third persons (and the subagent's liability to the principal), but the agent remains responsible to the principal in either case. [§§26-27]

6. **PROBABLY NOT**   While this is a close situation, Bob could probably argue that he is entitled to Cathy's discovery under the "shop right" doctrine—since it was developed on the job and as a result of Bob's business (although not specifically applicable thereto). [§31]

7. **FALSE**   Both the principal and the employer have a right to indemnification. [§32]

8. **DEPENDS**   P is not liable unless A was authorized to hire *additional* personnel on the same commission basis. If A was not, S must look solely to A for his compensation. [§36]

9. **SPLIT OF AUTHORITY**   Some courts would allow Bill to recover against Marvin, on the ground of Marvin's prevention of performance by Bill. Others, however, hold that Marvin *can* compete with his own agent. [§38]

a.	**YES**	Assuming this was done without Bill's consent, all courts would allow Bill an action against Marvin for prevention of performance in hiring a competing *agent*. [§38]
10.a.	**DEPENDS**	Agent cannot be indemnified for unauthorized acts which do not benefit Principal, or acts which are the result of his own negligence. Thus, for example, if Agent *or Trucker* negligently loaded the truck, Agent may not be entitled to indemnification. [§§42-44]
b.	**YES**	Assuming indemnification is otherwise proper (*i.e.,* no unauthorized or negligent act), Trucker—as an authorized subagent—can recover against *either* Principal or Agent. [§45]
c.	**NO**	While Agent may be entitled to damages against Principal for breach of contract, the agency agreement *cannot* be specifically enforced. [§50]
11.	**TRUE**	Such consent may be either express or implied from the conduct of the parties. [§§53-55]
12.	**FALSE**	Minors generally have *no* capacity to appoint an agent, but they *can* be appointed as the agent of another. [§57]
13.	**DEPENDS**	If Yolanda has *ratified* Leslie's acts—either expressly, or by accepting delivery of the painting—she may be bound to the purchase agreement entered into by Leslie. [§§63-64]
a.	**NO**	An ostensible agency (or agency by estoppel) must be based upon statements by the alleged *principal*—not the agent—which create the appearance of an agency. [§67]
14.	**PROBABLY**	Ordinarily, authority "to collect" a debt would not authorize an agent to compromise same. But P's additional reference to a fee based on "what you collect" probably *implies* authority in A to settle the debt for a lesser amount. [§73]
15.	**NO**	Since a contract for the sale of land is involved, Agent's authority to sell must be in *writing* to make the contract enforceable against Rancher. (Note, however, that the agreement could be enforced *by* Rancher, if he so chooses.) [§§77-79]
a.	**YES**	The "equal dignity" rule does not apply to purely *mechanical* acts by the agent (such as signing the principal's name). [§80]
16.	**NO**	Louise clearly intended to authorize Stephen's purchase of sculpture for her—even though this was induced by Stephen's fraudulent misrepresentations about his qualifications. Hence Louise is bound by the contract with Dealer. [§§81-82]
a.	**YES**	Louise can rescind Stephen's authority (even if otherwise irrevocable) because of the fraud—*provided* she does so prior to any agreement effected by Stephen. [§82]
17.	**YES**	Graham has actual authority to sell the car to anyone (because of Elmer's letter to him), but Elmer's manifestations *to Hector* give Graham apparent authority as to him, as well. [§§84-85]
a.	**PROBABLY**	Apparent authority also requires *reasonable reliance* by the third party upon manifestations by the principal. It is doubtful that a reasonable person would in-

terpret Elmer's note as authorizing Graham to sell the car on Elmer's behalf. [§87]

b.	**NOT NECESSARILY**	The revocation will terminate Graham's *actual* authority, but *unless communicated to Hector*, Graham's apparent authority continues and is binding on Elmer. [§88]
18.	**YES**	Elmer has clothed Graham with both possession *and* apparent ownership of the car, and hence Elmer will be estopped to assert the invalidity of Graham's dealings against an innocent purchaser. [§89]
19.	**PROBABLY**	Don's statement to Ned could be interpreted to mean that Claudia had authority to sell the mower, and hence Claudia would have *authority by estoppel*—so that Don could not prevent Ned from obtaining what he paid for (even though Don never received payment). [§96]
20.	**FALSE**	The agent's powers are *strictly* construed, in order to protect the principal from liability. A third party who knows he is dealing with an agent has the duty of ascertaining the scope of the agent's authority. [§§99-101]
21.	**YES**	Barring an unusual set of circumstances, C's terms are not inconsistent with A's authority from P (and actually represent a "gift" of $50 to P, since C has merely purchased the right to match any other offer made); they are thus within A's incidental powers. [§§103-110]
22.	**PROBABLY NOT**	A mere authority "to sell," without specification of terms, generally does *not* give a real estate broker the power to conclude a sale (even if the broker has an exclusive agency). [§110]
a.	**SPLIT OF AUTHORITY**	Even if A had the *power* to delegate her authority to a subagent, E is not a party to the P-A agreement and cannot sue P thereon. However, some courts would allow E to recover from P in quasi-contract for the reasonable value of his services. [§§116-117]
b.	**YES**	An agent is deemed to have an *inherent* power to make representations about the subject matter of the agency—even when specifically instructed *not* to do so by the principal. Thus P could be liable for A's misrepresentations despite P's express instructions. [§§119, 122]
c.	**PROBABLY NOT**	An agent has the inherent power to make all warranties implied by law or customary in the community as to the property she is selling. However, this power to warrant is *narrowly* construed by the courts, and a warranty of "absolute structural soundness" is probably outside the scope of A's inherent powers. [§§123, 132, 137]
d.	**PROBABLY**	This should be sufficient notice to a purchaser of the limits on A's power to warrant, and hence P would not be bound by A's warranties outside those specified in the contract. (The same result could probably be achieved with a "waiver" clause in the sales contract.) [§§138-139]
23.	**PROBABLY**	Despite Owner's statements, it may be assumed that he would have intended that such an emergency expenditure be made (particularly where it appears to be in his best interests). [§§118, 140]
a.	**PROBABLY NOT**	As Owner's store manager, Max probably had no authority to receive notice of facts concerning Owner's personal affairs, and the facts are not within the scope or subject matter of his position as manager. [§§145-146]

b.	**PROBABLY**	Generally, knowledge gained by the agent *prior* to his employment is not imputed to the principal, but an exception is made where there is a close connection between the two situations. (The Restatement imputes *any* knowledge of the agent, if he had it in mind when it became relevant to his present work.) [§145]
24.	**PROBABLY NOT**	Even though no time is specified for A's agency, a reasonable time period is implied—and five years is probably beyond that period (considering the lack of communication between P and A, possible change in P's purposes, etc.). [§151]
a.	**PROBABLY NOT**	The change in zoning represents a sufficient change in circumstances to terminate A's authority (unless P knew of the proposed change when she engaged A). [§§154-155]
25.	**SPLIT OF AUTHORITY**	Under common law, the death or incapacity of the principal *automatically* terminates the agent's authority—whether or not the agent or third parties have knowledge of the death or incapacity. However, some states have statutes permitting a third party without knowledge to enforce a bona fide agreement with the agent despite death or incapacity of the principal. [§§156-158]
a.	**YES**	In this case, A's agency is "coupled with an interest" (*i.e.*, the guns secure the loan to O), and even under common law, S can enforce the agreement against O's estate. [§159]
26.	**NO**	Either party can terminate an agency relationship at will—despite a specified time period and a provision asserting that it is irrevocable for that period. However, Brandon may be liable in damages to Chuck for breach of contract. [§§160, 162-163]
a.	**YES**	In this case, Chuck holds an agency coupled with an interest; and he *can* obtain specific enforcement of his agreement with Brandon. (This is the only exception to the general power to terminate an agency.) [§§164, 167]
27.	**FALSE**	While the third party must generally receive notice of the termination of authority, the termination is *automatic* in the case of death or incapacity of the principal. [§§170-171]
28.	**SPLIT OF AUTHORITY**	Most courts would say that O was free to rescind, on the ground that an "offer" rather than a contract existed until ratified by the purported principal, L. However, a minority would not excuse O from performing, where he receives the contract price and incurs no additional burdens. [§§172-176, 178-179]
29.	**NO**	Thief was not intending to act on Owner's behalf when he agreed to sell the set to X, and thus Owner cannot subsequently ratify the act. [§§180-181]
a.	**DEPENDS**	Affirmation of the forgery is proper, since Owner would have authorized Thief to sign his name. The ratification will therefore turn on whether the wager itself was a legal act (and therefore capable of being authorized). [§182]
30.	**YES**	P will be deemed to have ratified A's acts, both because of her retention of benefits from T and her failure to repudiate the unauthorized agreement. [§§188, 191]
a.	**YES**	Unless P knew of the agreement and failed to repudiate it, her "retention" of the benefits is involuntary and could not be deemed a ratification. [§189]
31.	**PROBABLY**	As a general matter, a ratification is not effective unless the principal knows all material facts concerning the transaction. However, P assumes the risk of lack of

knowledge when she affirms without inquiring about the terms; and hence T could probably enforce the contract. [§§192-193]

| 32. | **PROBABLY NOT** | A ratification must be in the same form required for an original authorization, and an oral affirmation of a sale of real property would therefore be insufficient under the "equal dignity" rule. [§194] |

a. **NO** The neighbor has acquired *intervening rights* in Blackacre, and Lucy's subsequent ratification of the contract between Jack and Paul thus does not "relate back." The neighbor can compel specific performance of his agreement with Lucy, and Paul may also be able to recover damages from her. [§199]

33. **NO** The death or incapacity of the third party terminates the power to ratify. [§201]

34. **PROBABLY** Unless T knew that A had no authority (and hence could not be said to have relied thereon), A is liable to T for breach of warranty regardless of his good faith belief. [§§207-210]

a. **YES** Although T cannot enforce the contract without P's ratification, he can sue in quasi-contract for the value of benefits conferred (*i.e.*, the down payment). [§216]

35. **NO** Jones' signature clearly indicates that he signed the contract only as Smith's agent; and hence the Company alone is liable thereon. [§218]

a. **PROBABLY NOT** Such evidence is generally admissible only to resolve an *ambiguity* in the contract; and here the agreement on its face indicates that Jones acted solely as Smith's agent. [§223]

36.a. **YES** Under the objective theory of contracts, the agent of an undisclosed principal is liable to a third party contracting with him. (Of course, A would also have a *right of indemnification* against P for any amounts collected by T.) [§§225-229]

b. **SPLIT OF AUTHORITY** Once P's identity is known, T has a right to sue him and most courts permit T to sue *both* P and A (requiring an election only prior to judgment). However, some courts require T to make an election *before* filing suit—*i.e.*, to sue *either* P or A, but not both. [§§236-239]

c. **YES** Even though the principal is undisclosed, he is deemed the assignee of all rights in contracts entered into by his agent—and hence may sue a third party to enforce the contract. [§§242-243]

d. **DEPENDS** This may amount to fraudulent concealment, giving T a right to rescind the agreement. However, T is generally allowed to rescind only if A made an *affirmative representation* that he was acting only for himself. Mere purchase in his own name may not give T a right to rescind—in which case P could still enforce the contract. [§244]

e. **PROBABLY** The weight of authority holds an undisclosed (but subsequently discovered) principal liable on the agent's contract in this situation—on the ground that since P created A's authority, he must assume the risk of a dereliction of duty. (One state statute is contra, but is distinctly a minority view.) [§230]

37. **PROBABLY NOT** This would probably be considered a personal services contract, allowing Marie to rescind. (This would certainly be true if the positions were reversed and Marie

had contracted with Kristin to *receive* French lessons.) [§246]

38.	**PROBABLY**	Unless the parties had agreed that C would not be bound (as to which parol evidence is admissible), D *can* hold C on the contract. [§257]
a.	**YES**	Where the principal's identity is known to the third party, the principal is "disclosed" even if his name does not appear in the contract—and the agent is no longer considered a party thereto. [§261]
39.a.	**FALSE**	An injured person can proceed against *both* the employee (who is directly liable) and the employer (who is vicariously liable). [§264]
b.	**FALSE**	Respondeat superior imposes strict liability on the employer; this cannot be "contracted away." [§208]
c.	**TRUE**	If the employer was herself guilty of negligence or other breach of duty toward the injured party (or where the employee is *immune* from liability), the employer may be liable even though the employee is not. (Generally, however, exoneration of the employee relieves the employer of liability as well.) [§269]
d.	**TRUE**	Respondeat superior depends upon this right of control—which means that the employer generally is not liable for the physical torts of agents or independent contractors. [§280]
e.	**FALSE**	A master must have the *capacity to contract*, and hence a minor cannot assume that position (although he can certainly be hired as an employee-servant). [§286]
40.	**DEPENDS**	The master-servant relation is consensual, but mutual consent can be implied from the circumstances. If Mac had no knowledge of Tim's actions, he could not be held vicariously liable; but if he *knew* Tim was assisting the employees and did not intervene, he would probably be deemed to have consented (and hence be subject to vicarious liability). [§288]
a.	**NO**	Even assuming that Mac knew nothing of Tim's attempts to assist (and hence cannot be said to have consented thereto), he cannot recover for *negligent* (as opposed to intentional) injuries to his servant by third persons. [§292]
41.	**PROBABLY**	If the advertising gave the impression that Kermit was Mario's employee, and if Lincoln relied on the ads in requesting an exercise program, there is an *employment by estoppel*—and Mario would be vicariously liable despite his lack of control over Kermit's acts. [§294]
a.	**YES**	Here, Lincoln's injury was not sustained in reliance on Kermit's purported employment, and hence there is no ostensible employment. [§297]
42.	**DEPENDS**	If P had authorized A to hire a relief driver, he may be liable (assuming a right to control, etc.). If P had not authorized such employment, he would be liable only if S had been hired in an *emergency* (*e.g.,* A's illness en route, perishability of load, etc.). [§§299, 301, 303]
43.	**PROBABLY**	A lessor renting equipment with an operator is presumed to retain control over the operator and would—absent a showing that the operator was required to take orders from the lessee—be liable to persons injured by the operator's tortious acts. [§305]
a.	**YES**	In this case, T will be liable for S' acts even if M retained a primary right of control. [§305]

44.	**YES**	Truckers who drive their own vehicles on specific jobs are usually independent contractors, whereas those driving their employers' trucks are more likely to be servants (*i.e.,* greater control by employer over their conduct). [§311]
45.	**PROBABLY NOT**	Most courts hold that physicians or lawyers are independent contractors, even when employed on a retainer basis. Hence, Doctor alone would be liable for the negligent acts. [§314]
a.	**DEPENDS**	If Bessie were aware of Doctor's drinking habits, she might be found negligent in her retainer of Doctor—in which case she would be *directly liable* to Alex even though Doctor remained an independent contractor. [§318]
46.	**YES**	Crop-spraying is considered a highly dangerous act imposing *strict liability* on the party contracting for the work—irrespective of whether the actor is an independent contractor *or* whether his conduct was negligent. [§322]
47.	**PROBABLY NOT**	Although it is a matter of degree in each case, Samson's forbidden act appears to deviate sufficiently from his assigned duties of book salesman that it is outside the scope of employment—and hence relieves Delilah of liability. [§§330-333]
a.	**PROBABLY**	Here, Samson's act—even though forbidden—appears to be related to his assigned duties (selling, *e.g.,* spear guns) and thus within the scope of employment. [§330]
48.	**PROBABLY NOT**	Control of patrons was probably not related to W's duties, and his action appears to have been personally motivated. Hence, Ace would not be liable to Z under respondeat superior. [§§334-335]
a.	**YES**	A common carrier is held to a higher standard of care and thus is liable for *any* tortious acts inflicted by employees on passengers—whether or not within the scope of their employment. (Note, however, that this is *direct* liability, not an application of respondeat superior.) [§§338-339]
b.	**PROBABLY**	Under the weight of modern authority, employee carelessness while on lunch or other "breaks" is still within the scope of employment, thus imposing vicarious liability on the employer. [§§342-344]
c.	**NO**	Washing the bicycle chain is outside the scope of W's employment and does nothing to further the interests of Ace. Hence the fact that W was permitted to use the dishwasher in his job will not impose vicarious liability on Ace. (*Note:* In each of these examples, Ace might be liable for negligence in *hiring* W.)[§345]
d.	**PROBABLY**	If W were given no instructions on what solvent to use, Ace is probably liable for W's negligent use of gasoline. [§347]
49.	**FALSE**	If *any* substantial part of the servant's act was done for the employer, the latter is liable for *all* the consequences of the act. [§§351-353]
50.	**SPLIT OF AUTHORITY**	Under the general rule, P would *not* be liable to an unauthorized invitee of her employee, the invitation being outside the scope of employment. However, some courts would hold P liable if A's misconduct were "wanton and wilful"; others would hold P liable so long as A's *negligent acts* (as distinguished from the unauthorized invitation) were within the scope of employment. [§§355-358]
a.	**PROBABLY**	Unless P was shown to have been negligent in *hiring* A, the "fellow servant" rule would relieve P of any liability to T for A's conduct. [§§359-363]

51.	**YES**	Usury ordered Acme to "repossess the car"—the tortious act—and hence is directly liable to S. Likewise, Acme is liable even though acting under Usury's direction and without an intent to convert S' car. [§§369-370]
a.	**DEPENDS**	Usury can become liable if it "ratifies" Acme's unauthorized conduct—*i.e.,* by accepting benefits therefrom *with knowledge of the relevant facts*. In this situation, liability may turn on the number of accounts Acme was handling for Usury: If only Debtor's debt was involved, Usury would probably be held to know the car was improperly obtained and thus be accountable to S. [§§372, 375]
b.	**YES**	Usury cannot "ratify" this act, since it was not done on behalf of the loan company. [§374]
52.	**YES**	P is charged with an employee's knowledge of dangerous conditions in the scope of employment, and thus is liable to Z just as if she had personally observed the defective stairstep. [§382]
a.	**PROBABLY**	Only those facts known to the employee *and* within the scope of employment are imputed to the employer. It is unlikely that a bookkeeper would be involved with building maintenance, and hence A's knowledge of the defective stair would not bind P. [§§382-384]
53.	**FALSE**	While misrepresentation is one type of tortious statement, an employer would *also* be liable if the employee's statements constituted defamation, trade libel, etc. [§387]
54.	**FALSE**	The statements of an independent contractor can also make the employer liable, provided the former had the requisite authority. [§389]
55.	**YES**	Allen had *express* authority to disseminate appraisal data to buyers, and any misrepresentations by her in the course of such dissemination are binding on P. [§392]
a.	**PROBABLY NOT**	An agent has *implied* authority to make customary statements about the subject matter, and the appraisal value of an art collection would certainly appear to be such a statement (*i.e.,* "incidental" to her authority to sell the collection). [§393]
b.	**PROBABLY**	Under these circumstances, Allen would probably have no authority to make statements concerning the appraisal value (unless Burns had specifically given her such information for use in the advertisements). [§398]
56.	**YES**	Although Vanessa's misrepresentation may have been innocent, Lester had the necessary scienter and thus would be liable to the buyer. [§403]
a.	**NOT NECESSARILY**	Lester could be liable for negligent misrepresentation, and in any case, the buyer could seek rescission of the sale based on *mistake*. [§§404-405]
57.	**TRUE**	These characteristics distinguish a partnership from an agency (not co-owners) and unincorporated associations (which can be organized for nonprofit purposes). [§§407-409]
58.	**FALSE**	This was true at common law; even under the UPA, a partnership is viewed as an aggregate for most purposes. However, for certain purposes—*e.g.,* capacity to sue or be sued, conveyance of title, etc.—a partnership is considered an *entity*. [§§411-419]

59.	**NO**	X must have acquired the property *on account* of the partnership, and while record title is relevant, it is by no means determinative. [§§421-424]
a.	**YES**	This factor alone will establish that an asset is partnership property, absent evidence of a contrary intention. [§425]
b.	**YES**	The fact that the building is closely associated with a partnership purpose is likely to mean a finding that it is partnership property, since X will be deemed to have purchased it as *trustee* for the partnership. [§427]
60.	**NO**	As to each partnership asset, P is a tenant in partnership with her co-partners, and her rights therein are *not* subject to attachment for her personal debts. [§§433, 439]
a.	**YES**	P's interest in the partnership—*i.e.,* her right to a share in the profits or surplus thereof—is her *personal* property. Thus, a judgment creditor can lien against this interest (the effect being that P's share in the profits, or some portion thereof, goes to the creditor). [§439]
61.a.	**FALSE**	Certain partnership agreements—*e.g.,* those for a mandatory period of one year—*must* be in writing to be effective. [§443]
b.	**FALSE**	Unless this power is specifically provided in its Articles, a corporation's entering a partnership is usually considered ultra vires. [§448]
c.	**TRUE**	Each and all partners must agree on whom will be a partner, since the partnership is a voluntary association of co-owners. [§449]
d.	**FALSE**	While neither factor is conclusive (the business purpose of the undertaking being the crucial test), a sharing of profits *will* establish a prima facie partnership (unless other business reasons exist for the profit sharing). Income sharing, however, is not prima facie evidence of a partnership. [§§453-454]
e.	**FALSE**	The nonpartners can bind only those partners who *made or consented* to the representations that he was a partner. [§459]
f.	**FALSE**	All partners have *equal* management rights (regardless of their agreed share of the profits), unless there is a provision to the contrary. [§466]
g.	**TRUE**	The UPA recognizes only one exception to the rule—remuneration to a surviving partner for winding up the partnership affairs. [§474]
h.	**TRUE**	The few exceptions where an action at law is permitted (*e.g.,* personal disputes between partners, fraud or conversion of partnership assets) do not really involve partnership transactions. [§§477-478]
62.	**PROBABLY**	A partner has apparent authority to sign contracts on behalf of the partnership and related to its business. Thus unless the loan would make it impossible to carry on business, the agreement is binding on the partnership. [§§481-482]
a.	**DEPENDS**	If A and C are the only partners, some cases would hold this notice effective. In any other situation, however, C will be bound unless she *dissolves* the partnership before the debts are incurred. [§483]
b.	**NO**	However, the transfer does give W *equitable* title to the building. [§493]

63.	YES	Marcus is jointly liable for the debts, whenever they were incurred (and irrespective of any agreement with Steele and Wool "relieving" him of liability). [§496]
a.	NO	The partners have only a *joint* contract liability; and Acme must therefore proceed against all partners or against the partnership itself. [§§494, 497]
b.	YES	Tort liability is joint *and* several; and hence Plaintiff can proceed against *any* of the partners for X's tortious acts. [§499]
c.	YES	The "fellow servant" rule does not apply to injuries negligently inflicted by one partner upon another. [§499]
64.a.	FALSE	If the partners continue the partnership business beyond the period, they are deemed *partners at will* with the same general rights and duties. [§504]
b.	TRUE	Unless a partnership at will is involved, however, the termination may violate the partnership agreement and subject the partner to liability (since a *power*, rather than a *right*, is involved). [§§505-508]
c.	FALSE	The partnership agreement can (and usually does) provide that the partnership will continue despite a withdrawal or admission. [§514]
d.	FALSE	This situation will, however, support a *judicial decree of dissolution*. [§522]
e.	FALSE	Each partner must contribute to the loss according to his or her share of the profits, once all have contributed their agreed capital shares. [§526]
65.a.	YES	The termination violates the agreement, and hence the "innocent" partners (A and C) have a right to any damages sustained as a result. [§529]
b.	PROBABLY	If A and C fail to pay B for his partnership interest (or post a bond for same), B is entitled to compensation for the use of his partnership assets in the continuing business. [§530]
c.	NO	The estate of a deceased partner is likewise entitled to compensation for the decedent's interest in the partnership, and if there is undue delay in paying the estate, the surviving partners are liable for an appropriate share of any profits earned, or interest on the value at death (whichever is greater). [§532]
d.	DEPENDS	If the fact of dissolution was not advertised in a newspaper of general circulation, B could be liable to third persons dealing with the business without knowledge of B's withdrawal therefrom. [§538]
66.a.	NO	Limited partners *cannot* contribute services to the partnership. [§545]
b.	NO	The liability of Y and Z is limited to their respective investments in the partnership. [§549]
c.	NO	The death of a limited partner does not dissolve the partnership. Instead, the decedent's executor is given the rights of the limited partner. [§557]
d.	YES	Unless the agreement otherwise provides, the death of a general partner *does* dissolve a limited partnership. [§557]
e.	YES	W is thereby entitled to all of Y's rights to income or distribution or partnership assets. However, W is *not* entitled to inspect the books or obtain an accounting until the certificate of limited partnership has been amended with the consent of all other partners. [§552]

SAMPLE EXAM QUESTION I

Hannigan owned and operated a route for the sale and delivery of bakery products. In July 1981, Hannigan, desiring to take a vacation, made a contract with Rest, whereby Rest was to take over the bakery route during Hannigan's absence. Hannigan took Rest over the route for two days' training and on September 1, 1981, Rest assumed the operation of the route for six weeks. Since Rest did not have a truck, Hannigan allowed Rest to use his truck without charge for the six-week period. During this time, Rest purchased and paid for the bakery products which she sold on the route. She retained the entire proceeds from the sales she made.

On September 26, 1981, Rest was involved in a collision with an auto being driven by Jonathan. As a result of the collision, Jonathan was severely injured. Subsequently, Jonathan brought an appropriate action against Hannigan to recover for damages suffered as a result of the collision.

What decision? Give reasons.

SAMPLE EXAM QUESTION II

Milton, a meat processor, in 1976 employed Sylvester to purchase livestock for him. Sylvester, from the beginning of his employment by Milton, purchased beef cattle from Thomas, who operated a stockyard. Thomas would bill Milton, who then forwarded his check in full payment. Milton had instructed Sylvester that he was not to purchase any sheep from Thomas. Between 1976 and 1980, Sylvester bought over 5,000 head of cattle for Milton's account. On February 12, 1981, Milton discharged Sylvester, refusing to pay severance pay, to which Sylvester thought he was entitled. Sylvester, upset over his discharge, told Thomas, on February 14, to forward 100 sheep to Milton. Milton refused delivery of the sheep and refused to pay on the grounds (a) he had expressly ordered Sylvester never to purchase sheep from Thomas and (b) he had discharged Sylvester on February 12.

What decision? Give reasons.

SAMPLE EXAM QUESTION III

Carlton, a contractor, was building a multi-story building. Carlton had ordered materials for the construction, to be shipped by rail. The carrier was the Diamond Railway Company. This railroad owned a large crane which was used for loading and unloading heavy articles from cars.

Heracles, the crane operator, was a regular employee of the railroad. Peters, an employee of Carlton, was helping with the unloading of the materials. The railroad permitted Carlton to use the crane without cost to assist in unloading. During the unloading, Heracles followed instructions and suggestions given him by Carlton.

Because of Heracles' negligent operation of the crane, Peters was injured. Peters subsequently brought an action against the Railway Company to recover damages for his injury. At trial, it was shown that the Railway Company might have called Heracles to some other job and also could have told him exactly how to use the crane.

May Peters recover for his injuries from the railroad? Give reasons.

SAMPLE EXAM QUESTION IV

Roberta Rich was the owner of a racehorse named "Herald," which had won more than $100,000 from races run prior to being retired to stud. Rich, wishing to sell "Herald," executed and delivered to Terry Siegel, a broker of horses, the following power of attorney:

"May 1, 1981

I hereby authorize Terry Siegel to act as my agent with authority to sell my horse "Herald," for the price of $150,000, all cash. Siegel shall not be entitled to receive from me a commission for making the sale, but is authorized to retain from the purchaser any sum paid by the latter in excess of the price herein named. The authority to Siegel shall in no event expire until November 1, 1981.

/s/ Roberta Rich"

On October 15, 1981, Siegel met with Arthur Champion, praised the qualities of "Herald," and on showing Champion the written power of attorney, Champion agreed to buy "Herald" for $160,000 to be paid on the following day on delivery of the horse. On October 16, when Champion and Siegel were on their way to deliver the purchase price and turn over the horse, they learned, to their surprise, that on September 20, by proper judicial proceedings, Rich had been adjudicated insane and that her cousin Bill had been duly appointed guardian of her person and property. When Champion and Siegel asked Bill to accept payment on behalf of Rich and to authorize delivery of "Herald," Bill refused, saying that he thought the horse could be sold for more than the $160,000 tendered. Champion now consults you and inquires what rights of action, if any, he has against Bill in his capacity for Rich.

How should you advise Champion?

SAMPLE EXAM QUESTION V

Ardmore sold goods to Bobolink, in good faith believing him to be a principal. Bobolink, in fact, was acting as agent of Casper, within the scope of his authority. The goods were charged to Bobolink, and on his refusal to pay, he was sued by Ardmore for the purchase price. While this action was pending, Ardmore learned of Bobolink's relationship with Casper. Nevertheless, thirty days after learning of that relationship, Ardmore secured judgment against Bobolink and had an execution issued which was never satisfied. Three months after securing that judgment, Ardmore sued Casper for the purchase price of the goods.

Is Ardmore entitled to collect from Casper?

SAMPLE EXAM QUESTION VI

Price and Wells had a partnership agreement of twenty years' standing. The agreement required each partner to devote her entire time to the partnership business. For a period of eighteen months, Price performed no services for the partnership. The value of the services which she failed to perform was $500 per month. At the end of the eighteen months, Price brought an appropriate action to dissolve the partnership. A dissolution was ordered and an accounting rendered. In the accounting, Price was debited $9,000, and Price and Wells were each credited with $4,500.

Price appeals. What decision, and why?

SAMPLE EXAM QUESTION VII

Albatross, Barnwell and Collins were equal partners in the operation of a department store in Baltimore. In June 1980, Moroni, the promotion manager of the store, threatened to go into business for himself unless he received greater compensation for his services. Albatross, Barnwell and Collins thereupon entered into a written contract with Moroni which provided that he would continue to work at his current salary of $15,000 a year, and in addition, would receive ten percent of the profits of the firm each year commencing immediately. The contract also provided that Albatross, Barnwell and Collins would continue in full charge of the business, make all contracts and be liable for all debts. Thereafter, Moroni told his family and many of his friends that he had been made a partner in the business, but he made no such statement to any of the partnership's suppliers.

In March 1981, Collins went to New York City where he purchased $2,500 worth of dresses from Silvers, who knew nothing about the agreement with Moroni, and $4,000 worth of men's suits from Thompson, who had heard rumors that Moroni had some interest in the business but had no actual knowledge of Moroni's agreement. Both purchases were made by Collins on partnership credit, as he had done on many prior occasions.

In July 1981, the store was destroyed by fire. The partnership does not have available assets sufficient to pay its obligations.

What are the rights of Silvers and Thompson, if any, against Moroni?

SAMPLE EXAM QUESTION VIII

Cornelius and Robert were partners in a fairly large widget business. The assets of their business had a market value of $200,000. Lacking in business experience, Cornelius and Robert allowed the business to become overextended, so that the partnership had obligations of $300,000. Realizing the desperate nature of their situation, Cornelius and Robert persuaded Veronica to invest $50,000 in the capital of the partnership and to become a full partner, assuring her that her financial contribution would be instrumental in allowing the partnership to overcome its difficulties.

One year after Veronica became a partner, the financial situation of the partnership remained in the same woeful state. In fact, the partnership was now further in debt. This lead to a suit to wind up the partnership affairs.

In regard to this suit, answer the following questions:

(a) Is Veronica's $50,000 contribution available for payment of creditors who had claims against the partnership prior to her entry into the partnership?

(b) Would the answer to (a) be different if Veronica, upon her entry into the partnership, had agreed with Cornelius and Robert that the $50,000 would be exempt from such debts?

(c) Is Veronica personally liable for the partnership debts that existed prior to the time she became a partner?

SAMPLE EXAM QUESTION IX

Ron and Al decided to open a gun-manufacturing business as partners. The written partnership agreement provided that the partnership would only be dissolved by death or by mutual agreement of the partners.

Ron and Al became involved in a disagreement regarding the running of the business, as a result of which Ron left the partnership premises, moved to a new location, and indicated to Al that he no longer wished to be associated with him. At the new location, Ron commenced to do business on his own account.

Consequently, Al brought an action against Ron to recover profits made by Ron after his departure from the company. Al contended that the partnership relation continued since the agreement concerning dissolution had not been complied with, and that he was entitled to his share of the profits.

What decision? Give reasons.

SAMPLE EXAM QUESTION X

Phil, Bob, and Louise form a partnership, executing a certificate setting forth, among other things, a designation that Phil and Bob are general partners and Louise is a limited partner. Their business, which consists of manufacturing widgets, prospers beyond their wildest expectations. Eventually, they reach a point where Louise, due to her extensive past managerial experience, is required to devote extensive time to the actual management of the business.

However, after two years' time, a recession hits, particularly affecting the widget market. As a result, the partnership falters, and incurs massive debts.

In determining liability for the partnership debts, is Louise personally liable?

ANSWER TO SAMPLE EXAM QUESTION I

Hannigan should win. Rest should be deemed to be an independent contractor, rather than a servant. Therefore, Hannigan is probably not liable for the injuries caused by Rest's actions. Factors contributing to the determination that Rest is an independent contractor include Rest's working without Hannigan's supervision, and the failure of Hannigan to pay Rest a salary for her efforts. In fact, for six weeks, Rest went into the business of operating the bakery route for herself.

It is also necessary to consider whether Rest's use of Hannigan's truck should subject Hannigan to liability. If the truck were to be considered a dangerous instrumentality, then Rest's independent contractor status might not relieve Hannigan of liability. Whether the truck was a dangerous instrumentality is a question of fact, and there appears to be nothing in the statement of facts indicating that the truck was such an instrumentality—*i.e.,* it was not to be used to transport explosives, dangerous chemicals, etc., nor was it apparently in need of repair to make it safe.

Finally, there is nothing to indicate that Hannigan's selection of Rest to operate his bakery route was in any way negligent. There is nothing to indicate that Rest was a known poor driver, drug abuser, etc. Therefore, Hannigan should not be liable for the torts committed by Rest acting as an independent contractor.

ANSWER TO SAMPLE EXAM QUESTION II

Milton prevails. The issue here is whether Sylvester had the authority to bind Milton. Sylvester, having been discharged on February 12, possessed no actual authority. Consequently, it is necessary to examine the question of apparent authority. There is apparent authority if Milton created the impression that Sylvester had authority to enter into such a contract, and Thomas reasonably relied on this holding out by Milton.

Sylvester had been an agent with actual authority for four years and thus would appear to have authority to make this contract. On the facts given, Milton did not take adequate steps to apprise those with whom Sylvester had dealt that Sylvester was no longer in Milton's employ. Thus, the only ground upon which Milton may be able to rely is the fact that Sylvester could not be viewed as having authority to purchase sheep. The fact that Milton had given express orders not to purchase sheep is not persuasive if Thomas could have reasonably believed that Sylvester was also authorized to make such purchases. This is a close fact question, but because, in the four years that he dealt with Thomas, Sylvester had never bought sheep, it seems that such reliance by Thomas would not be reasonable. Thomas should probably have called Milton before relying on Sylvester's order.

ANSWER TO SAMPLE EXAM QUESTION III

Peters should be able to recover damages for his injuries from the Diamond Railway Company.

The main issue is whether Heracles was employed by the Diamond Railway Company or Carlton at the time Peters was injured. The general rule is that a master-servant relationship exists whenever one person has the right to control the manner and method in which a task is performed by another. At issue, however, is whether the railroad has transferred its right of control over Heracles to Carlton.

This question is a borrowed servant situation. In such a situation, the original employer (here, the railroad) remains the master (and hence liable for the torts of its servants) unless there is clear evidence of the transfer of the right to control. There is no question that Heracles is normally a servant of the railroad, and there seems to be insufficient evidence that Diamond, in fact, transferred the right to control Heracles' actions over to Carlton. The mere fact that Heracles followed some of Peters' suggestions, or that the railroad allowed Heracles to use the railroad's crane to unload the construction materials, does not constitute a transfer of the right to control. The railroad was always in a position to tell Heracles exactly how to operate its equipment, and could have pulled him off the Carlton job at any time. Such facts indicate that control over Heracles was not transferred to Carlton, and that as the master, Diamond Railway Company remained liable for the torts of its servant Heracles under the principle of respondeat superior.

The fellow-servant issue may not be raised, as Peters was a servant of Carlton while Heracles remained a servant of Diamond Railway Company. For the foregoing reasons, Peters should recover damages from Diamond for the injuries caused by Heracles' negligence.

ANSWER TO SAMPLE EXAM QUESTION IV

Champion has no rights against Bill. Generally, when either a principal or agent is adjudicated insane or dies, the agent's power is automatically terminated. Notice need not be given to anyone. Therefore, even though neither Siegal nor Champion knew of Rich's incompetency and both were acting in good faith, the contract would not bind Rich because Siegal's authority had ended.

The only exception to the rule that the incapacity of the principal terminates the agent's authority is if the agency is one coupled with an interest, but this is not the case here. An agency coupled with an interest is an agency created for the benefit of the agent (or a third party). It requires that the agent's authority be granted to secure performance of a duty to, or to protect the title of, the agent (or a third party), and that the authority be given, supported by consideration at the time the duty or title was created. If these requirements are met, the agency coupled with an interest will not terminate with the incapacity of the principal.

Here, the authority to sell "Herald" was given not for the benefit of the agent, but for the benefit of the principal. Siegal had no interest in the sale of the horse. He was not given the authority to sell the horse to secure any duty owed to him nor did he give any consideration for the agency. Also, the fact that Champion was willing to pay more than Rich's price does not make this an agency coupled with an interest. Siegal's interest ($10,000) is merely in the proceeds of the sale, and he has no beneficial interest in the subject matter of the agency. Therefore, Siegal had no authority to sell the horse, and Champion has no rights against Bill.

ANSWER TO SAMPLE EXAM QUESTION V

Ardmore is not entitled to collect from Casper. When Ardmore's relationship with Bobolink began, Casper was an undisclosed principal (*i.e.,* both Casper's identity, and the fact that an agency relationship existed were undisclosed). The undisclosed principal situation remained through the filing of suit against Bobolink and existed until thirty days before judgment against Bobolink was rendered. During the existence of an undisclosed principal situation, the remedy of the third party (here, Ardmore) is to bring suit against the agent. (Should a judgment be rendered against the agent, the agent ordinarily has a right to indemnity against the principal.)

Once the principal's identity (and her place in the agency relationship) is disclosed, the third party may elect to sue either the principal or the agent for breach of contract. Here the principal was disclosed thirty days prior to judgment, but Ardmore elected to continue his suit against Bobolink, rather than to sue Casper. Generally, the third party must elect to sue either the principal or the agent, but may not have judgments rendered against both successively. When Ardmore elected to sue Bobolink, and that suit was rendered to judgment, Ardmore's right to sue Casper on the same issue (breach of contract for nonpayment) was cut off.

Therefore, Ardmore's suit against Casper should be dismissed.

ANSWER TO SAMPLE EXAM QUESTION VI

Price should win her appeal. A partner is not entitled to remuneration for her services on behalf of the partnership unless all the partners consent to such remuneration. In the instant case, there is no indication that Wells gave such consent, and the implication is clearly that she did not give such consent. Therefore, the value of Price's services is inappropriately considered in the accounting.

Price's failure to work did, in fact, breach the partnership agreement, and Wells may well be entitled to damages. However, the measure of damages is not the value of Price's services, but rather the damage caused to the partnership as a result of Price's inactivity. If Wells found it necessary to hire and compensate others to perform tasks usually performed by Price, then Price should be charged for those additional costs to the partnership in the accounting. If the firm lost business as a direct result of Price's failure to work, Price may also be held liable for any lost profits resulting therefrom.

However, if Wells simply worked harder, and there was no loss to the partnership, then there were no damages for which Price could be held accountable. If this were the case, Wells should have sought a judicial dissolution of the partnership. (Price's failure to work constituted a breach of the partnership agreement, and the court would almost certainly have dissolved the partnership on this ground.) Had Wells sought a timely dissolution, Price's right to share in partnership assets could have been cut off much sooner.

On a new accounting, partnership assets will be divided equally (absent an agreement otherwise); only damage to the partnership caused by Price's breach will be charged against Price's share.

ANSWER TO SAMPLE EXAM QUESTION VII

Neither Silvers nor Thompson has any viable action against Moroni.

Despite his assertions to the contrary, Moroni was not, in fact, a partner with Albatross, Barnwell and Collins. The fact that Moroni was to receive ten percent of profits does not alter the situation. Although receipt of profits is usually prima facie evidence that the recipient is a partner, there is an exception where the profits are distributed (as in this case) in the form of wages to an employee of the partnership. The facts clearly indicate that the ten percent share of the profits was intended as additional compensation to Moroni, in order to keep him in the partnership's employ.

Even though Moroni was not a partner in fact, he could have acquired the liabilities of a partner by representing to be a partner (or consenting to be represented as a partner). In this manner, Moroni could have become a "partner by estoppel," and be held liable on partnership obligations to any person to whom the representation was made, if such person in good faith extended credit on the faith of such representation. Creditors who can estop the apparent partner include those to whom the representation was made directly and those who come to learn of the representation via a public holding out.

It may be argued here that Moroni did publicly hold himself out to be a partner with Albatross, Barnwell and Collins. Moroni told his family and friends that he was a partner, and some word of this had spread to New York. However, the holding out here was insufficient to attach liability to Moroni for the partnership's debts to either Silvers or Thompson. Moroni never represented to either Silvers or Thompson (or any other supplier) that he was a partner. Silvers had never even heard of the arrangement with Moroni, and could in no way be deemed to have extended credit based upon Moroni's supposed partnership interest. Thompson has a slightly stronger case, but still should be unable to hold Moroni liable. Thompson heard only a vague rumor (that did not even specify that Moroni was a partner) and failed to question Collins about it. Thus, there is no evidence that Thompson extended credit to the partnership based upon Moroni's participation or status.

Therefore, neither Silvers nor Thompson will be able to reach Moroni's assets for satisfaction of their claim against the partnership.

ANSWER TO SAMPLE EXAM QUESTION VIII

(a) Veronica's contribution is available to satisfy claims which arose prior to her participation in the partnership. The essence of a partnership is the sharing of rights and responsibilities. When Veronica entered the partnership, she assumed her share of such rights and responsibilities. A new partner (here, Veronica) is jointly liable with the other partners for all partnership debts. This includes debts which were incurred by the partnership prior to the new partner's admission. Upon admission the partner is deemed to have assumed her share of the partnership liabilities.

As applied to this case, the above-stated principles mean that Veronica's contribution of $50,000 is available for payment of partnership creditors, even though such creditors' claims against the partnership arose prior to Veronica's entry into the partnership.

(b) Since the sharing of responsibilities goes to the essence of the partnership relation, the partners may not exempt one partner from partnership liability by agreement. (The limited partnership form of doing business is an exception to this, but those designated as limited partners do not participate in management of the business.) Thus, Veronica's $50,000 contribution may be reached by prior creditors despite the agreement to the contrary by the partners. Such agreement is voidable by the partnership's creditors and will not be enforced in Veronica's favor against them.

(c) Veronica is not personally liable for the preexisting debts. Although Veronica's partnership property may be reached by preexisting creditors; her personal assets may not. Veronica is only personally liable for partnership debts which accrue after her entry into the partnership. Only partnership property (and the personal assets of Cornelius and Robert) are available to satisfy debts which accrued prior to Veronica's becoming a partner.

ANSWER TO SAMPLE EXAM QUESTION IX

Al can recover damages from Ron for breach of the partnership agreement, but Al should not be able to reach the profits Ron received from operation of his new business.

A partnership agreement, such as the one at issue here, may establish a definite term for the partnership, by specifying the events that will cause a dissolution to occur (here, the events were death or mutual agreement). Dissolution is a change in the relation of the partners caused by any partner ceasing to be associated in the carrying out of the business. While this partnership agreement specified that only death or mutual agreement would dissolve the partnership, a partner may not be held in a partnership relation against his will. Any partner has the power (although not the right) to dissolve the partnership by his express will. Ron has exercised that power, causing a dissolution of the partnership.

However, because Ron's dissolution contravened the partnership agreement, he is liable to Al for damages for breach of the contract setting up the partnership. The partnership itself would continue to exist until Al completed the winding up of the partnership affairs. (Al is entitled to do this, as Ron wrongfully dissolved the partnership.) It is unlikely that Al will be able to reach any profits which Ron earned from his separate business, as there is no indication that Ron held himself out to be a member of the partnership while conducting his business. Had Ron set up his competing business while he remained part of the partnership, he would have breached his fiduciary duty to Al, and been liable to account for profits from the new business. Since a dissolution has taken place Al will be able to recover damages arising from the breach of the partnership agreement, but not the profits earned by Ron in his new business.

ANSWER TO SAMPLE EXAM QUESTION X

Louise may be held personally liable for the partnership obligations as if she were a general partner.

A limited partnership is a partnership formed by two or more persons, having as members one or more general partners and one or more limited partners. One must assume from the facts that the certificate filed to establish the limited partnership met all the formal requirements of the Limited Partnership Act in force in the jurisdiction. Under the provisions of legislation establishing limited partnerships, those designated as limited partners (here, Louise) are normally not personally liable for the obligations of the limited partnership. The liability of a limited partner is usually limited to the amount she has invested in the limited partnership.

Here, however, Louise has forfeited the protection of the Limited Partnership Act. One of the essential characteristics of a limited partner is that she has no right to take part in the management of the limited partnership business. Here, however, Louise has assumed an active role in the management and operation of the limited partnership's business. When Louise ceased to behave as a limited partner, she ceased being protected from personal liability. Since Louise has assumed an active management role, she will be treated as if she were a general partner for liability purposes. Louise will be personally liable for the limited partnership's debts along with Bob and Phil.

TABLE OF CASES

INDEX

partnership, §488
remedies, §390
Respondeat superior, §§264-384
    deeper pocket theory, §268
    entrepreneur theory, §267
    exoneration, §273
    fellow servant rule, §§359-367
        negligent hiring, §363
        superior servants, §364
        workers compensation, §§365-367
    generally, §§264-278
    indemnification, §277
    master-servant relationship, §§279-326
        borrowed servants, §§304-306
        capacity, §286
        control, §§280-283
        creation, §§284-293
        employment by estoppel, §§294-297
        independent contractors, §§283, 307-326. See also Independent contractors
        misrepresentations, §282
        ostensible employment, §§294-297
        servant's injuries, §§291-293
        sub-servants, §§298-303
            emergencies, §303
            unauthorized, §§301-302
            undisclosed principal, §300
        volunteers, §288
    personal breach of duty, §§368-384
        authorization, §§369-371
        independent duty, §§380-384
            care of third persons, §381
            dangerous conditions, §§380-382
            negligent hiring, §380
        ratification, §§372-379
    scope of employment, §§327-358. See also Scope of employment
    servant's immunity, §275
    single recovery, §272
    vicarious liability, §271
    waiver, §270

S

Sales agents
    compensation, §35
    purchases by, §23
Scope of employment, §§327-358. See also Respondeat superior
    acts on servant's own behalf, §§351-354
        mixed motives, §354
        substantial departure, §§352-353
    authorization, §§329-334
    drinking, §§342-344
    forbidden acts, §330
    intentional torts, §§334-340
        common carriers, §339
        criminal liability, §336
        defamation, §340
    omissions, §341
    smoking, §§342-344
    to and from work, §§348-350

special errand rule, §349
        traveling salespersons, §350
    unauthorized guests, §§355-358
    unauthorized instrumentalities, §347
    vehicles, §§345-346
Servant's immunity, §275
Servant's injuries, §§291-293
Shop right doctrine, §31
Single recovery. See Election of remedies; Respondeat superior
Smoking, §§342-344
Special errand rule, §349
Specific performance, §50
Statute of Frauds. See Equal dignities
Subagents
    compensation, §36
    duty owed to principal, §§26-27
    indemnification, §45
    liens, §48
    unauthorized hiring, §27
Sub-servants, §§298-303. See also Respondeat superior
Superior servants, §364

T

Termination of agency, §§150-171. See also Authority of agent
Torts
    partnership, §499
    respondeat superior, §§264-384. See also Respondeat superior
Traveling salespersons, §350
Truck drivers, §311

U

Unauthorized acts. See Authority of agent; Partnership relations; Respondeat superior
Unauthorized guests, §§355-358
Unauthorized instrumentalities, §347
Undisclosed principal. See Contracts of agents
Unincorporated associations, §409

V

Vicarious liability, §271
Volunteers, §288

WXYZ

Warranties
    agent's authority to make, §§123-139. See also Authority of agent
    of authority, §§207-210
    of competence, §213
    of performance, §212
Winding up, §531
Workers' compensation, §§365-367
Working conditions, §410

LAW SUMMARIES

AGENCY &
PARTNERSHIP

1995 PARTNERSHIP
SUPPLEMENT

HARCOURT BRACE LEGAL AND PROFESSIONAL PUBLICATIONS, INC.

EDITORIAL OFFICES: 176 W. Adams, Suite 2100, Chicago, IL 60603

REGIONAL OFFICES: New York, Chicago, Los Angeles, Washington, D.C.

Distributed by: **Harcourt Brace & Company** 6277 Sea Harbor Drive, Orlando, FL 32887 (800)787-8717

SUPPLEMENT TO GILBERT AGENCY & PARTNERSHIP SUMMARY
(Fourth Edition)

August 1995

Page   **Revision**

65   **Delete** the second para. of para. I., before §406; substitute the following and reletter subsequent paras. accordingly:

In 1914, the Commissioners on Uniform State Laws approved the Uniform Partnership Act ("UPA"), which has been adopted by most states as the basis for their partnership law. In 1994, the Commissioners approved a new uniform act: the Revised Partnership Act of 1994 ("RUPA"). The RUPA has clarified some ambiguities contained in the UPA and has attempted to align partnership law with contemporary business practices. This supplement notes the RUPA provisions that differ substantially from the UPA provisions.

67   **Insert** the following after para. c. [§419]:

RUPA: The RUPA treats partnerships as entities distinct from the partners.

68   **Insert** the following after para. 1) of §432; renumber subsequent para. accordingly:

2.   **RUPA Rules:** The RUPA provides four specific presumptions for determining whether property is partnership property.

a.   **Acquired in name of partnership:** The RUPA provides that if property is acquired in the name of the partnership, it is partnership property. [RUPA §204(a)(1)] Property is considered to be in the name of the partnership not only when it is held in the actual name of the partnership, but also when it is held in the name of one or more partners in their capacity as partners and the instrument transferring title indicates the name of the partnership. [RUPA §204(b)]

b.   **Acquired in name of partner with indication of partnership:** Property is also considered to be partnership property if it is acquired in the name of one or more partners and the instrument transferring title indicates the named person's capacity as a partner or the existence of the partnership, but without an indication of the name of the partnership. [RUPA §204(a)(2)]

c.   **Purchased with partnership assets:** Under the RUPA, property is considered to be partnership property if it is purchased with partnership assets. [RUPA §204(c)]

d.   **Separate property presumption:** If property is acquired in the name of one or more partners and the instrument transferring title indicates neither the person's capacity as partner nor the existence of the partnership *and* the property is purchased without use of partnership assets, it is presumed to be separate property even if it is used for partnership purposes.

69   **Insert** the following after para. (5)(a) of §434:

b.   **RUPA approach to partner rights in specific partnership property:** In effect, the RUPA closely follows the UPA's approach to partnership property by providing simply that a partner is not a co-owner of partnership property and has no interest in partnership property that can be transferred. [RUPA §501]

72 **Insert** the following after para. (1) of §454:

    (2) **RUPA:** The RUPA provides that sharing of profits *raises a presumption of partnership* (rather than constitutes prima facie evidence of partnership, as under the UPA) unless the sharing is in payment of wages, as rent, etc. [RUPA §202(c)(3)]

• 72 **Delete** para. 1. [§457]; substitute the following:

    1. **Liability of Alleged Partner:** [§457] One who holds herself out by words or conduct to be a partner in an actual or apparent partnership, or who expressly or impliedly consents to representations that she is such a partner, is liable to any third person to whom the representations are made who extends credit in good faith reliance on the representations. [UPA §16; RUPA §308—purported partner]

73 **Insert** the following before para. 2. [§459]:

    d. **Extent of liability**

      (1) **UPA:** UPA section 16(1) distinguishes cases of public holding out from cases of private holding out by providing:

> When a person . . . represents himself, or consents to another representing him . . . as a partner, . . . he is liable to any such person to whom the representation has been made . . . and if [the representation was] made in a public manner he is liable to such person, whether the representation has or has not been made or communicated to such person so giving credit by or with the knowledge of the apparent partner . . .

Some courts have interpreted this language to mean that the apparent partner is liable to the third party even if the third party did not know of the representation. [*See* Brown & Bigelow v. Roy, 132 N.E.2d 755 (Ohio 1957)] Other courts have held that section 16 always requires reliance on the representation of partnership; the ambiguous language merely means that if the holding out is in a public manner, the plaintiff need not prove that the apparent partner specifically consented to having the communication made to the plaintiff. [*See* Reisen Lumber & Millwork v. Simonelli, 237 A.2d 303 (N.J. 1967)]

      (2) **RUPA:** The RUPA follows the approach of *Reisen Lumber*, by providing that a person who *relies on the representation* of partnership can hold the purported partner liable "even if the purported partner is not aware of being held out as a partner to the claimant." [RUPA §308(a)]

74 **Insert** the following after para. c. [§464]:

    d. **Under RUPA:** The RUPA limits the partners' fiduciary duties to the duty of loyalty, the duty of care, and the duty of good faith and fair dealing.

(1) **Duty of loyalty:** The RUPA generally limits the duty of loyalty to the duties specified above as to accounting, competing, and assets [RUPA §404(b)], and specifically provides that a partner may make loans to or transact other business with the partnership.

(2) **Duty of care:** Under the RUPA, the partners' duty of care is to refrain from gross negligence, reckless conduct, intentional misconduct, or knowing violation of the law in the conduct or winding up of partnership business. [RUPA §404(c)]

(3) **Good faith and fair dealing:** The RUPA imposes on partners the duty to discharge the duties of loyalty and care in good faith and with fair dealing. [RUPA §404(d)]

75 **Insert** the following after para. (1) of §470:

(2) **Note:** RUPA section 403(c) also requires that certain information be given to the partners *without demand*—*i.e.,* any information concerning the partnership reasonably necessary for the exercise for the partners' rights and duties.

75 **Delete** paras. d.(1)-(3) [§§472-474] and all subparas. thereof; substitute the following:

(1) **Agreed upon capital contribution:** [§472] Upon dissolution, partners have a right to the return of the capital that they contributed to the partnership. [UPA §18(a); RUPA §§401(a), 807(b)] No interest is due on account of the contribution until after the contribution should have been repaid. [UPA §18(d)]

(2) **Indemnification for expenses; advancements:** [§473] A partnership must reimburse a partner for expenses the partner reasonably incurs while conducting partnership business. Similarly, a partner has a right to the return of any capital that the partner advances beyond the partner's agreed upon contribution. In either case, the payments made by the partner constitute loans to the partnership and thus accrue interest from the date the payments are made. [UPA §18(b)-(c); RUPA §401(c)-(e)]

(3) **Remuneration:** [§474] A partner generally has no right to remuneration for work performed on behalf of the partnership unless the partners agree otherwise. [UPA §18(f); RUPA §401(h)] Thus, a partner is not entitled to extra money even when her efforts have been the major factor creating the profits of the partnership. [*See* Security First National Bank v. Lutz, 322 F.2d 348 (9th Cir. 1963)]

(a) **Exception for winding up:** A partner who winds up the partnership's affairs upon dissolution is entitled to reasonable compensation for services rendered to wind up. [UPA §18(f); RUPA §401(h)]

76 **Insert** the following after para. (d) of §478:

4. **Actions Between Partners Under RUPA:** RUPA section 405(b) specifically allows partners to maintain actions against other partners for either legal or equitable relief to enforce:

(a) A right *under the partnership agreement*;

(b) A right under *section 401* (relating to sharing profits, participating in management, indemnification, etc.), *section 403* (relating to the right to obtain partnership information), or *section 404* (relating to the standards of conduct);

(c) Rights relating to **dissociation or dissolution and winding up** the business of the partnership; and

(d) **Any other right of the partner**, including rights and interests arising independently of the partnership relationship.

77 **Insert** the following after para. (c) [§487]; reletter subsequent paras. accordingly:

b. **Statement of partnership authority under RUPA:** The RUPA allows a partnership to publicly file a statement of partnership authority which may state the authority, or limitations on the authority, of some or all of the partners to enter into transactions on the partnership's behalf. [RUPA §303(a)(2)]

(1) **Mandatory contents:** The statement of partnership authority must include: (i) the **name of the partnership**; (ii) the **address of the partnership's chief executive office** and of an office within the state; (iii) the **names and addresses of all partners or of an agent who has a list of such information**; and (iv) the names of the **partners authorized to execute an instrument transferring real property** held in the partnership name. [RUPA §303(a)(1)]

(2) **Effect of statement of authority**

(a) **Grants of authority:** When a statement of authority grants authority to enter into transactions on behalf of the partnership, the grant generally is **conclusive** evidence of authority in favor of a person who gives value and who did not have sufficient notice that the transaction exceeded the acting partner's authority.

1) **Example:** Andy, Bob, and Carla are partners in a boat building business. They file a statement of authority granting Carla authority to sell all of the partnership's business equipment from time to time. Subsequently, the partners orally agree that Carla shall not sell any of the partnership's business equipment without first obtaining permission from either Andy or Bob. Three days after the oral agreement was made, Carla sells three of the partnership's desks, at fair market value, to Dan. Dan can use the statement of authority as conclusive proof that Carla had authority to sell the desks.

2) **Real property:** To provide conclusive proof of authority to transfer the partnership's **real property**, a certified copy of the statement of authority must be filed in the office for recording interests in the real property involved.

(b) **Limitations on authority:** A limitation on the authority to enter into transactions on behalf of the partnership may be contained in the statement of authority itself or may be filed separately at any time. However such a limitation generally is **ineffective** against a person **without knowledge** of the limitation, **except:**

(i) To the extent that it **limits à filed grant of authority**; and

(ii) A limitation on authority to transfer *real property* that is filed with the recorder's office for the real property involved is effective even against a nonpartner who does not know of the limitation.

1) **Example:** Same facts as in the example above, but the statement of authority also provides that Carla shall not have authority to sell the partnership's computers. In addition to the three desks, Carla sold Dan one of the partnership's computers. The limitation in the statement of authority is effective to obviate the conclusive effect of the grant of authority to sell the partnership's business equipment with respect to the sale of the computer.

2) **Example:** Same facts as above, but the statement of authority also provides that Andy shall have no power to sell the partnership's boats and Bob shall have no power to sell the partnership's real property. Andy sells one of the partnership's boats to Edna and Bob sells a lot that the partnership had purchased for future expansion to Fred. The statement of authority's limitation on Andy is not effective against Edna if she did not know of the limitation, but the limitation on Bob is effective against Fred, even if he did not know of the limitation, assuming a copy of the statement of authority was filed with the recorder of deeds.

(3) **Statement of denial:** The RUPA also provides that a partner or person named as a partner may file a statement of denial, denying any fact, including denial of the person's authority or status as a partner. [RUPA §304]

77 **Insert** the following after para. (2) of §489:

(3) **RUPA reasonable diligence test:** The RUPA provides that a partnership will be deemed to have notice or knowledge of a fact when the individual conducting the transaction has notice or knowledge or would have had notice or knowledge of the fact had reasonable diligence been exercised. Reasonable diligence can be shown through maintenance and use of reasonable routines for communicating significant information. It does not require an individual to communicate a fact unless the communication is part of the individual's regular duties or the individual has reason to know of the transaction and that the transaction would be materially affected by the information. [RUPA §102(e)]

78 **Insert** the following at the end of para. a. [§494]:

The RUPA makes partners jointly *and severally* liable for *all* obligations, including those arising under contract. [RUPA §306]

78 **Insert** the following at the end of para. (2) [§496]:

Thus, in effect, the incoming partner's personal liability for old debts is limited to his partnership contribution unless the incoming partner agrees otherwise. The RUPA, more straightforwardly, provides that a person admitted into an existing partnership is *not* personally liable for any partnership obligation incurred before admission as a partner. [RUPA §306(b)]

79 **Insert** the following after para. (3) of §499:

c. **RUPA exhaustion requirement:** The RUPA provides that a judgment against the partnership entity is ***not*** a judgment against an individual partner. A judgment may be satisfied from a partner's personal assets only if there is also a judgment against the partner (which may be sought in the same action as the action against the partnership). [RUPA §307(b), (c)] Moreover, the partner's personal assets cannot be reached unless [RUPA §307(d)]:

(1) A judgment on the same claim has been taken against the partnership, which has ***not been fully satisfied*** after execution on the judgment;

(2) The partnership is a ***debtor in bankruptcy***;

(3) The ***partner has agreed that the creditor need not exhaust partnership assets***;

(4) A ***court grants permission*** to levy on the partner's assets because the partnership assets are clearly insufficient to satisfy the judgment, exhaustion of partnership assets would be excessively burdensome, or the grant is otherwise appropriate; or

(5) Liability is imposed on the partner by ***law or contract independent*** of the existence of the partnership.

84   **Insert** the following after para. b. [§539]:

E. RUPA APPROACH

1. **Dissociation:** Whereas the presumption under the UPA is that a partnership ordinarily will terminate after a partner leaves, the RUPA recognizes that in modern partnerships it is common for a partner to leave and the partnership to continue. Thus, the RUPA has substituted the term "***dissociation***" for many of the concepts that are part of the concept of dissolution under the UPA.

   a. **Effect in general:** Dissociation terminates a partner's rights to participate in the business and the partner's duty to refrain from competing. [RUPA §603]

   b. **Events causing dissociation:** RUPA section 601 provides that a partner will become dissociated upon:

      (1) The partnership's receipt of a ***notice to withdraw*** from the partner;

      (2) The ***happening of an event agreed to in the partnership agreement*** as a cause of dissociation;

      (3) The partner's ***expulsion pursuant to the partnership agreement***;

      (4) The partner's ***expulsion pursuant to a unanimous vote of the partners*** where it is unlawful to carry on the business with that partner, substantially all of the partner's interest in the partnership has been transferred, or the expelled partner is a corporate entity that has given up or lost its right to do business in the corporate form or a partnership that has dissolved;

      (5) ***Judicial determination*** on application of another partner or the partnership that the partner engaged in wrongful conduct that adversely

and materially affected the partnership, the partner willfully breached the partnership agreement or statutory standard of conduct, or the partner is engaged in conduct that makes it impracticable to carry on the partnership business with the partner;

(6) The partner's **bankruptcy, assignment of assets for the benefit of creditors, or acquiescence to appointment of a trustee, receiver,** or the like to take **substantially all of the partner's property,** or failure to have an appointment of such person vacated within 90 days;

(7) **Death** of the partner, **appointment of a guardian or conservator** for the partner, or **judicial determination** that the partner has become **incapable of performing his duties to the partnership**;

(8) If the partner is a trust, **distribution of the trust's interest in the partnership** (except merely to substitute a successor trustee);

(9) If the partner is an estate, **distribution of the estate's interest in the partnership** (except merely to substitute a personal representative); or

(10) **Termination of a partner who is not an individual, partnership, corporation, trust, or estate**.

c. **Wrongful dissociation:** A partner who wrongfully dissociates is liable for any damages caused by the wrongful dissociation. Dissociation will be deemed wrongful where it is in **breach of an express provision of the partnership agreement**. This includes most cases of withdrawal or judicial expulsion before the completion of a partnership for a definite term or undertaking. [RUPA §602]

2. Effect Where Business Not Wound Up

a. **Purchase of dissociated partner's interest:** If the dissociation does not result in a dissolution, the partnership must buy the dissociated partner's interest in the partnership. The buyout price is equivalent to the amount that would be distributable to the partner if, on the date of dissociation, partnership assets were sold at the greater of their **liquidation value or their value if the partnership were sold as a going concern** without the dissociated partner. [RUPA §701(a), (b)]

(1) **Liabilities offset:** Damages for wrongful dissociation and all other amounts that the dissociating partner owes must be offset against the buyout price. [RUPA §701(b)]

(2) **Interest:** Interest must be paid from the date of dissociation to the date of payment. [RUPA §701(b)]

(3) **Indemnification:** The partnership must indemnify the dissociated partner against all partnership liabilities, except liabilities incurred by the dissociated partner's acts after dissociation which bind the partnership. [RUPA §701(d)]

(4) **Where partner disputes value:** If an agreement cannot be reached as to value within 120 days after the dissociated partner demands

payment in writing, the partnership must pay based on what the partnership estimates to be the buyout price. [RUPA §701(e)]

    (a) **Action against partnership:** If the dissociated partner disagrees with the buyout price, offsets, etc., the partner may bring an action against the partnership within 120 days after the partnership has tendered payment or an offer to pay, or within one year after the partner's written demand if there has been no payment or tender. The court may assess attorney's fees and costs against a party that the court finds to have acted not in good faith. [RUPA §701(i)]

    (5) **Dissociation before expiration of term:** A partner who dissociates before expiration of the partnership term or completion of an undertaking is not entitled to payment of the buyout price before expiration of the term or completion of the undertaking unless the partner can prove that payment will not harm the partnership. [RUPA §701(h)]

b. **Dissociated partner's power to bind partnership:** Under the RUPA, a partnership will be bound by any act of the dissociated partner done within *two years* after the dissociation if: (i) the *act was within the partner's apparent authority*; (ii) the other party *reasonably believed the dissociated partner was still a partner*; and (iii) the other party *did not have notice or knowledge* of the dissociation. [RUPA §702(a)] Of course, the partnership can hold the dissociated partner liable for losses it incurs as a result of the dissociated partner's conduct. [RUPA §702(b)]

c. **Dissociated partner's liability to others:** The dissociated partner remains liable on partnership obligations incurred before the dissociation. [RUPA §703(a)] The dissociated partner can also be held liable on partnership obligations incurred within *two years* after dissociation if the party dealing with the partnership reasonably believed the dissociated partner was still a partner and did not have notice or knowledge of the partner's dissociation.

    (1) **Release:** Of course, the creditor may agree to release the dissociated partner from liability. [RUPA §703(c)] A release will also occur where the creditor knows of the dissociation and agrees with the partnership to materially alter the nature or time of payment of the obligation without the dissociated partner's consent. [RUPA §703(d)]

d. **Constructive notice through statement of dissociation:** To limit liability after dissociation, the dissociated partner or the partnership may file with the state a statement of dissociation. Nonpartners will be deemed to have notice of the dissociation *90 days* after the statement of dissociation is filed. [RUPA §704]

e. **Continued use of partnership name:** Continued use of the partnership name, even if it includes the dissociated partner's name, does not alter the liabilities discussed above. [RUPA §705]

3. **Dissolution and Winding Up of Partnership:** Under the RUPA, dissolution connotes the process that leads to termination of the partnership.

a. **Events causing dissolution and winding up:** A partnership is dissolved and its affairs must be wound up upon:

   (i) Receipt by a partnership at will of notice from a partner, other than a dissociated partner, of an *express will to withdraw*;

   (ii) In a partnership for a definite term or particular undertaking: (a) the *express will of at least half the partners* to wind up after a partner's wrongful dissociation or dissociation by death or termination of a non-individual partner, (b) the express will of *all* partners to wind up, or (c) the *expiration of the term or accomplishment of the undertaking*;

   (iii) Occurrence of an *event that the partnership agreement states will cause dissolution* unless *all* partners agree to continue the business;

   (iv) Occurrence of an *event that makes it unlawful to carry on the partnership business* (unless cured within 90 days);

   (v) Judicial determination, *on application of a partner*, that the economic purpose of the partnership is likely to be unreasonably frustrated, that another partner has engaged in conduct that makes it unreasonably impracticable to carry on the partnership business, or that it is otherwise not reasonably practicable to carry on the partnership business; or

   (vi) Judicial determination, *on application of a transferee* of a partner's interest, that winding up is equitable (if the partnership was for a definite term or particular undertaking at the time of transfer, the term must have expired or the undertaking must have been accomplished).

[RUPA §801]

b. **Effect:** The partnership continues after dissolution only for purposes of winding up its business. The partnership is terminated when the winding up is completed. [RUPA §802]

c. **Right to wind up:** The rules for winding up under the RUPA are similar to the rules under the UPA: Any partner who has not *wrongfully* dissociated may participate in winding up, or the legal representative of the last surviving partner may wind up. Unlike the UPA, however, the RUPA specifically allows the person winding up to run the business as a going concern for a reasonable time. [RUPA §803] After dissolution, the partnership is bound by any partner's acts appropriate for winding up or, if the other party does not know of the dissolution, any act within the partner's apparent authority. [RUPA §804] However, a partner who binds the partnership to an act not appropriate for winding up is liable to the other partners for any loss caused by the act. [RUPA §806]

d. **Statement of dissolution:** After dissolution, a partner who has not wrongfully dissociated may file a statement of dissolution. The statement is sufficient to cancel any additional authority granted under a filed statement of authority. A nonpartner will be deemed to have notice of the dissolution 90 days after the statement of dissolution is filed. [RUPA §805]

e. **Distribution of assets:** Under the RUPA, when a partnership is formed, an account is established for each partner. The account is credited with the money and the value of property contributed by the partner to the partnership, plus any profits due the partner. The account is charged with any distributions made to the partner and with the partner's share of any losses. [RUPA §401] On dissolution, after all creditors (including partners who are creditors) are paid, positive balances in the partners' accounts are paid to the partners; any partner with a negative balance must contribute that amount to the partnership. [RUPA §808(a), (b)]

   (1) **Where partner fails to contribute to loss:** If a partner fails to contribute his share of the losses, the other partners must pay that share in the proportion in which they share losses, but have a cause of action against the noncontributing partner. [RUPA §808(c)]

   (2) **Deceased partner:** The estate of a deceased partner is liable for the partner's obligation to contribute to the partnership. [RUPA §808(e)]

F. CONVERSIONS AND MERGERS UNDER RUPA

1. **Introduction:** In addition to the provisions for dissociation and dissolution, the RUPA provides rules for converting a partnership into a limited partnership and for merging partnerships.

2. **Conversion to Limited Partnership:** A partnership may be converted to a limited partnership upon the unanimous consent of the partners (or by such vote as is specified in the partnership agreement) by filing a certificate of limited partnership with the state. [RUPA §902(a), (b)]

   a. **Contents of certificate:** In addition to the other mandatory provisions (*see infra*), the certificate must include the partnership's former name, a statement that the partnership was converted to a limited partnership, and the number of votes cast for and against conversion. [RUPA §902(c)]

   b. **Liability:** A general partner who becomes a limited partner as a result of the conversion remains liable as a general partner on obligations incurred before conversion. A limited partner has no liability on obligations incurred after conversion except for obligations incurred within 90 days after conversion if the other party reasonably believed that the limited partner was a general partner. [RUPA §902(e)]

3. **Conversion of Limited Partnership to Partnership:** A limited partnership may be converted to a partnership only upon the consent of **all** partners (notwithstanding a contrary provision in the limited partnership agreement). Conversion is accomplished by canceling the certificate of limited partnership. A limited partner who becomes a general partner remains liable only as a limited partner for obligations incurred by the partnership before conversion, but is liable as a general partner for all post-conversion obligations. [RUPA §903]

4. **Mergers:** A partnership may merge with one or more partnerships or limited partnerships upon approval of a merger plan: (i) where the party is a partnership, by all partners or the number set in the partnership agreement, or (ii) where the party is a limited partnership, by the vote required by statute, or if

there is none, by the consent of *all* partners, notwithstanding a contrary provision in the partnership agreement. [RUPA §905(c)]

    a. **Contents of plan:** The plan must state (i) the name of each partnership or limited partnership that is a party to the merger; (ii) the name of the surviving entity, its status as a partnership or limited partnership, and the status of each partner; (iii) the terms and conditions of the merger; (iv) the basis for converting the interests of each party into interests in the surviving entity; and (iv) the street address of the surviving entity. [RUPA §905(b)]

    b. **Liabilities:** A partner of the surviving partnership is liable for (i) all obligations of the merging entity that the partner was liable for before the merger, (ii) all other obligations of the surviving entity incurred *before* the merger to the extent of partnership property, and (iii) all obligations of the surviving entity incurred *after* the merger takes effect (but such obligations may be satisfied only out of property of the entity if the partner is a limited partner). [RUPA §906(a)-(c)]

85   **Delete** all of Chapter V. [§§540-561]; substitute the following:

V. LIMITED PARTNERSHIPS

A. IN GENERAL

1. **Nature:** [§540] Limited partnerships are hybrid business organizations offering limited partners a structure similar to that of a partnership, but limited liability similar to that of a shareholder in a corporation. They were developed to facilitate commercial investments by those who wanted a financial interest in a business but did not want all of the responsibilities and liabilities of partners. They are becoming increasingly popular under current laws because they allow profits and losses to flow directly to the limited partners—thus avoiding the "double tax" on corporate profits—and, unlike S corporations, they are not limited in size. (*See* Income Tax Summary.)

    a. **Limited liability rationale:** [§541] The limited liability of a limited partner is rationally supported by two attributes of the limited partnership structure. First, at least one person in the limited partnership is personally liable for all partnership debts—the general partner. Second, since it is difficult to justify immunity from debt to persons who actively create the debt, limited partners are not allowed to participate in the management or control of the limited partnership. Both of these topics will be discussed in greater detail below.

2. **Governing Law:** [§542] Limited partnerships did not exist at common law. They are entities created by modern statutes. Almost every state now has a limited partnership statute based on one of the following uniform acts, although many states have varied the uniform provisions.

    a. **Uniform Limited Partnership Act:** [§543] In 1916, the original Uniform Limited Partnership Act ("ULPA") was adopted. A number of states have retained this act.

b. **Revised Uniform Limited Partnership Act:** [§544] The ULPA was completely revised by the National Conference of Commissioners on Uniform State Laws in 1976. This Revised Uniform Limited Partnership Act ("RULPA") was amended in 1985 and is followed by a majority of the states.

c. **Note:** Many of the basic rules under the two acts are similar, either expressly so or by court interpretation. Where there is significant divergence, it will be noted below.

3. **Structure:** [§545] A limited partnership is a partnership formed by two or more persons, having as its members one or more general partners and one or more limited partners. [ULPA §1]

   a. **General partner:** [§546] A general partner is a partner who assumes the management responsibilities of the partnership and full personal liability for the debts of the partnership. [ULPA §9; RULPA §§101, 403] A general partner is similar to a partner in a regular partnership, and may be a natural person or a corporation.

   b. **Limited partner:** [§547] A limited partner is a partner who makes a contribution (*e.g.*, cash) to the partnership and obtains an interest in the partnership's returns, but who is not active in the partnership's management and is not liable for partnership debts beyond her contribution. A limited partner may be a natural person, a partnership, trust, estate, association, or corporation. [RULPA §101(11)]

4. **Permitted Activities:** [§548] Neither limited partnership act contains any limitation on the activities in which a limited partnership may engage, although many jurisdictions forbid certain activities to this type of organization (*e.g.*, banking and insurance).

B. FORMATION OF LIMITED PARTNERSHIP

1. **Certificate of Limited Partnership:** [§549] To form a limited partnership, a certificate of limited partnership must be executed and filed in an appropriate place. The limited partnership comes into existence at the moment of filing if there has been substantial compliance with the requirements regarding content and execution. [ULPA §2(2); RULPA §201(b)] Absent substantial compliance, all partners may be held liable as general partners.

   a. **Where to file:** [§550] Under the *ULPA, filing is local*, in the county where the limited partnership's principal place of business is located. Under the *RULPA, filing is central*, with the secretary of state.

   b. **Contents**

      (1) **ULPA:** [§551] Under the ULPA, the certificate of limited partnership is intended to give creditors notice of the limited liability of the limited partners and the basic finances of the limited partnership. Much detail is required in the certificate, including: (i) the name of the partnership and the general character of its business; (ii) the location of its principal place of business; (iii) the name and address of

each partner (both general and limited); (iv) a description and valuation of the contribution made or to be made by each partner; (v) any rights of the partners to receive property; and (vi) any times or events that will trigger dissolution.

(2) **RULPA:** [§552]   The RULPA recognizes that the document that truly governs the limited partnership is the *partnership agreement*, not the certificate of limited partnership, and that creditors should and do look there for information on the nature and financing of the partnership. Thus, the information required in the certificate of partnership is minimal; it need only include: (i) the name and address of the limited partnership; (ii) the name and address of an agent for service of process; (iii) the name and address of each general partner (*not* the limited partners); and (iv) the latest date upon which the limited partnership is to dissolve. [RULPA §2]

(a) **Partnership agreement:** [§553]   Under the RULPA, additional information is required to be kept in the partnership agreement or other record, including: (i) the amount of cash or agreed value of all property or services contributed (or agreed to be contributed) by each partner; (ii) the times or events upon which future contributions are to be made; (iii) any right of a partner to receive distributions (including a return of the partner's contribution); and (iv) any events that will cause dissolution. [RULPA §105(a)(5)]

c. **Liability for false statements:** [§554]   Under the ULPA, anyone who suffers a loss by relying on a false statement in the certificate of limited partnership may hold liable any party to the certificate (i) who signed it knowing of the falsity or (ii) who subsequently discovered the falsity before the reliance but failed to correct it. [ULPA §6] The RULPA is similar, but extends liability to *anyone* who signs the certificate (including agents) and to any general partner, whether or not she signed. It also limits liability for failure to amend to the general partners.

d. **Amendment of certificate of limited partnership:** [§555]   If there are errors in the certificate or significant changes concerning information required to be kept in the certificate (*e.g.*, change in general partners or time for dissolution), an amendment must be filed. [ULPA §24; RULPA §202] Under the RULPA, no liability can arise from reliance on pre-amendment information if the amendment is filed within 30 days of the event necessitating the amendment.

2. **Records Office (RULPA):** [§556]   The RULPA (but not the ULPA) requires a limited partnership to maintain a records office with records of, inter alia: (i) the names and addresses of all partners; (ii) copies of the firm's tax returns and partnership agreements for the three most recent years; and (iii) the information mentioned in §553, *supra*.

C. NAME OF PARTNERSHIP

1. **General Rule:** [§557]   A limited partner's name cannot be used in the name of the partnership unless: (i) it is also the name of a general partner; or (ii) prior

to the time the limited partner became such, the business had been carried on under a name in which his name appeared. [ULPA §5(1); RULPA §102(2)]

    a. **Additional RULPA requirements:** [§558] The RULPA also requires that the name include the words "limited partnership" and that it not be the same as or deceptively similar to the name of any corporation or limited partnership licensed or registered in the state.

2. **Liability for Use of Limited Partner's Name:** [§559] The ULPA provides that a limited partner whose name appears in the firm's name contrary to the Act's provisions is liable, as a general partner, to creditors who extend credit to the limited partnership without knowledge that he is not a general partner. [ULPA §5(2)] The RULPA imposes such liability only if the limited partner *knowingly permits* his name to be so used. [RULPA §303(d)]

D. CHANGES IN MEMBERSHIP

1. **Admission of Additional General Partners:** [§560] An additional general partner may be admitted upon the *written consent of all partners*. [ULPA §9(1)(e); RULPA §401] The RULPA also permits admission of additional partners in any manner provided by the partnership agreement. An amendment to the certificate of partnership must also be filed. (*See supra*, §555.)

2. **Admission of Additional Limited Partners:** [§561] Under the ULPA, the procedure for admitting limited partners is similar to that for admitting general partners (*see* above). [ULPA §8] The RULPA permits admission of limited partners upon compliance with the applicable provisions of the partnership agreement, or by written consent of the partners if the agreement is silent. [RULPA §301]

3. **Assignment of Partner's Interest:** [§562] A limited partner's interest is assignable, although the RULPA specifically permits the partnership agreement to alter this rule. [ULPA §19(1); RULPA §702] Under the RULPA, a general partner's interest is assignable to the same extent as that of a limited partner [RULPA §702]; although this would be an "event of withdrawal," which causes significant consequences. (*See infra*, §§568, 570.)

    a. **Effect of assignment:** [§563] Unless otherwise provided in the partnership agreement, the assignment by a limited partner of her interest does *not* dissolve the partnership, but under the RULPA a partner ceases to be a partner upon assignment of *all* of her partnership interest. [RULPA §702]

    b. **Assignee's rights:** [§564] An assignee of an interest in a limited partnership, unless she becomes a substitute partner, is entitled to receive only the share of profits or return of contribution to which her assignor would have been entitled. [ULPA §19(3); RULPA §702] The assignee does not have the other rights of a limited partner.

    c. **Creditor's right to charge:** [§565] A creditor of a limited partnership does not have the right to become a limited partner, but may charge the partner's interest. [ULPA §22; RULPA §703] In effect, the creditor becomes an assignee of the partner's interest.

4. **Death, Incompetency, or Withdrawal of a Partner**

    a. **Limited partners:** [§566] The death, incompetency, or withdrawal of a limited partner does *not* dissolve the partnership.

        (1) **Death or incompetency:** [§567] If a limited partner dies or becomes incompetent, his legal representative may exercise all of his rights for the purpose of settling his estate and administering his property. [RULPA §705]

        (2) **Withdrawal:** [§568] A limited partner may withdraw at the time or upon the happening of the events specified in the certificate of limited partnership [ULPA §16(2)] or in the written partnership agreement [RULPA §603]. If no time or event is specified, a limited partner may withdraw on six months' notice to *all* partners under the ULPA or the *general* partners under the RULPA.

    b. **General partners:** [§569] The death, incompetency, or withdrawal of a general partner dissolves the partnership unless the business is carried on by the remaining general partners under a right to do so or on consent of all of the remaining partners. [ULPA §20; RULPA §801]

        (1) **Events of withdrawal:** [§570] The ULPA mentions only death, incompetency, and retirement of the general partners as events that will cause dissolution. Under the RULPA, other events constitute "events of withdrawal" that will cause dissolution, including bankruptcy of the general partner and assignment by the general partner of his partnership interest. [RULPA §402]

E. NATURE OF LIMITED PARTNER'S CONTRIBUTION

1. **In General:** [§571] Under the ULPA, a limited partner's contribution to the partnership may be cash or property, but *not* services. [ULPA §4] The RULPA allows the contribution to be cash, property, or services, or a promise to contribute such in the future. [RULPA §501]

2. **Liability for Unpaid Contribution**

    a. **ULPA:** [§572] Under the ULPA, a limited partner is liable to the partnership for the difference between the contribution he actually made and the contribution stated in the certificate as having been made, and for any unpaid contribution that he agreed in the certificate of limited partnership to make in the future. [ULPA §17(1)]

    b. **RULPA:** [§573] The RULPA is similar to the ULPA, making partners obligated to perform any written promise to contribute cash or property or to perform services. The limited partner is obligated even if he is unable to perform because of death, disability, or other reason. However, because death (or other reason) may make it impossible for the limited partner to perform promised services or contribute specified property, the RULPA gives the partnership the option of holding the partner liable for the cash equivalent of the contribution due. [RULPA §502(a)]

3. **Compromise of Partner's Liability:** [§574]   A partner's obligation to make a contribution may be compromised by the consent of all of the partners. However, even where there has been a compromise, it does not affect a creditor of the partnership who extended credit or whose claim arose after the filing of a certificate of limited partnership (or under the RULPA, after the partner signs a writing) that reflects the obligation and before the amendment thereof to reflect the compromise. [ULPA §17(3); RULPA §502]

4. **Liability for Return of Contribution**

   a. **Rightful returns:** [§575]   As a general rule, a limited partner may not withdraw any part of his capital contribution unless sufficient assets remain to pay the firm's liabilities, excluding liabilities owed to partners on account of their partnership interests (*e.g.*, profits). Thus, even if the withdrawal is rightful (*i.e.*, does not violate any provision of the certificate of partnership, the limited partnership act, or the partnership agreement), the receiving partner may be held liable for the return to the extent necessary to discharge prewithdrawal creditors. [ULPA §17(4)] The RULPA limits such liability, however, to one year. [RULPA §608(a)]

   b. **Wrongful returns:** [§576]   If a return of contribution is wrongful, the limited partner is liable to the partnership for the return. [ULPA §17(b)] The RULPA limits such liability to six years. [RULPA §608(b)]

F. RIGHTS AND LIABILITIES OF A GENERAL PARTNER

1. **General Rule:** [§577]   Except as provided by statute or in the partnership agreement, a general partner of a limited partnership has all of the rights and powers and is subject to all of the restrictions and liabilities of a partner in a partnership without limited partners. [ULPA §9(1); RULPA §403]

2. **Right to Compensation:** [§578]   The limited partnership acts do not specifically address a general partner's right to compensation. Thus, the provisions of the Uniform Partnership Act apply, and under that Act, a general partner is ***not*** entitled to compensation beyond his share of the profits for services rendered to the partnership, unless otherwise agreed.

3. **Restrictions on Powers:** [§579]   The ULPA provides that a general partner may not, without the written consent or ratification of the specific act by all of the limited partners:

   (i)   Do any *act in contravention* of the certificate;

   (ii) Do any act that would *make it impossible to carry on the ordinary business* of the partnership;

   (iii) *Confess a judgment* against the partnership;

   (iv) *Possess partnership property*, or assign the limited partners' rights in specific partnership property, for other than a partnership purpose;

   (v)   *Admit a person as a general partner*;

(vi) ***Admit a person as a limited partner***, unless the right to do so is given in the certificate of limited partnership; or

(vii) ***Continue the business*** with partnership property ***after the death, retirement, or insanity*** of a general partner, unless the right to do so is given in the certificate.

[ULPA §9] The only equivalent provision in the RULPA forbids admitting a general partner without the consent of all partners. [RULPA §401]

G. RIGHTS AND LIABILITIES OF LIMITED PARTNERS

1. Rights

a. Right to share in profits and losses

(1) **Specified share:** [§580]   A limited partner is entitled to the share of the profits and losses specified in the certificate of limited partnership [ULPA §15] or the partnership agreement [RULPA §503].

(2) **If no share specified:** [§581]   If no share is specified, the ULPA is silent on allocation. The RULPA, on the other hand, provides that if the agreement is silent, profits and losses shall be split on a ***pro rata*** basis, according to the ***value of the contribution made by each partner***. [RULPA §503]

(3) **Time for distribution:** [§582]   Beyond providing for sharing of profits and losses and the return of contributions, the ULPA is largely silent on when and how the partnership is to make distributions. The RULPA, on the other hand, specifically addresses this issue.

    (a) **Interim distributions:** [§583]   The ULPA provides for distributions to be made upon dissolution or upon withdrawal of a partner. (*See infra.*) The RULPA goes further and specifically provides that the partnership agreement may set times for interim distributions, *i.e.*, distributions to be made before withdrawal or dissolution. [RULPA §601]

    (b) **Sharing of distributions:** [§584]   The RULPA also provides that the partners may agree to allocate distributions on any basis, including a basis different than the partners' shares of the profits and losses. However, if no provision is made, distributions are made on a pro rata basis, according to the partners' contributions (same as for profits). [RULPA §504] The ULPA is silent on this point.

(4) **Rights of partner entitled to distribution:** [§585]   Under the RULPA, when a limited partner becomes entitled to a distribution, she obtains the status of a creditor with respect to the distribution. [RULPA §606] Thus, she is entitled to any remedy that a nonpartner creditor could obtain. The ULPA does not have a similar provision.

b. Derivative actions: [§586]   The RULPA grants limited partners the right to bring a derivative action to enforce the partnership's rights when the

general partner refuses to do so. The limited partner must have been such when the transaction she is complaining of occurred, or her interest must have devolved upon her from one who was a limited partner at the time of the transaction. [RULPA §§1001, 1002] The ULPA does not have a similar provision, but some courts have implied such a right. [*See* 9 St. Mary's L.J. 443]

    c.   **Right to information:** [§587]   The ULPA gives limited partners the same rights as a general partner to: (i) examine and copy the partnership books and (ii) have full information regarding the affairs of the partnership. [ULPA §10(1)] The RULPA provides similar rights, but is more detailed. It provides that each limited partner has the right to: (i) *inspect and copy any partnership records* required to be maintained (*see supra*, §559); and (ii) obtain from the general partner, upon reasonable demand, *full information regarding the state of the business* and its financial condition, its income tax returns, and other similar information. [RULPA §305]

    d.   **Right to vote:** [§588]   The RULPA gives limited partners the right to vote on *limited issues* by providing that a limited partner shall not be deemed to participate in control of the business (and thus not be liable as a general partner) by voting on certain issues, generally regarding fundamental changes in the partnership. [RULPA §302] The ULPA has no similar provision.

    e.   **Right to transact business with the partnership:** [§589]   Both the ULPA and the RULPA give limited partners the same right to transact business with and make loans to the partnership as one who is not a general partner. Thus, creditor-limited partners can share pro rata with nonpartner-creditors in the assets of the partnership in the event of a claim thereon. The ULPA places some restrictions on this right, while the RULPA expands the right.

        (1)   **ULPA fraudulent conveyance provision:** [§590]   The ULPA takes away from partner-creditors one of the more important rights of a nonpartner-creditor. It provides that limited partner-creditors cannot be paid on claims arising from transaction of business with the partnership if the partnership lacks sufficient funds to pay nonpartner-creditors' claims. Thus, the limited partners' pro rata rights in assets apply only if the partnership is *solvent*. The Act also prohibits partners from holding partnership property as security. [ULPA §13]

        (2)   **RULPA:** [§591]   The RULPA does *not* include restrictions on limited partner-creditors' rights similar to those of the ULPA. In fact, the RULPA extends the right to transact business with the partnership to general partners. [RULPA §107]

    f.   **Right to assign interest:** [§592]   A limited partner has no right to specific partnership property, but rather has an interest in the profits and losses of the partnership. This interest is assignable. [ULPA §19(1); RULPA §702]

    g.   **Right to withdraw:** [§593]   A limited partner has a right to withdraw from the partnership. (*See supra*, §568.)

(1) **ULPA—return of contribution:** [§594]   Under the ULPA, upon withdrawal a limited partner has a right to the return of the cash equivalent of her contribution. [ULPA §16(2)]

(a) **Limitations:** [§595]   A withdrawing limited partner cannot receive back her contribution until: (i) the assets of the partnership are sufficient to *pay all partnership liabilities*, except upon account of the other partners' contributions; and (ii) the *certificate of limited partnership is amended* to reflect the withdrawal. [ULPA §16(1)]

(b) **Dissolution:** [§596]   If the withdrawing partner has rightfully demanded a return of her contribution and the partnership refuses to pay or the return is otherwise due but the partnership legally cannot pay, the withdrawing partner has a right to have the partnership dissolved.

(2) **RULPA—right to distributions:** [§597]   A limited partner's rights upon withdrawal under the RULPA are more expansive than under the ULPA. The limited partner has a right to receive in cash any distribution for which the partnership agreement provides. [RULPA §604]

(a) **If agreement silent:** [§598]   If the partnership agreement does not provide for distribution, the limited partner is entitled to receive the value of her interest in the partnership on the date of withdrawal based on her right to distributions from the partnership. The partnership may make a distribution of property in kind, but it cannot force the withdrawing partner to accept any share of an asset that exceeds her proportional share of the distributions (*e.g.,* a partner entitled to 10% of the distributions cannot be forced to accept more than 10% of any asset.)

(b) **Solvency limitation:** [§599]   The RULPA has a provision similar to the ULPA's solvency restriction. A distribution cannot be paid unless partnership assets are sufficient to satisfy all partnership liabilities, other than those arising on account of the partners' interests in the partnership. [RULPA §607]

2. **Liabilities of Limited Partners:** [§600]   The general rule is that limited partners, as such, are not liable for the debts of the partnership beyond their contributions. [ULPA §7; RULPA §303]

a. **Exceptions to general rule:** [§601]   Several exceptions to the rule of nonliability have been mentioned above, including where a limited partner: (i) *is also a general partner* (*see supra*, §577); (ii) *permits her name to be used* in the partnership name contrary to statute (*see supra*, §557); (iii) *signs the partnership certificate knowing of a falsity* in the certificate (*see supra*, §554); and (iv) *participates in control* of the business. The first three exceptions have been detailed in the sections indicated. The fourth exception will be discussed in greater detail below.

b. **Participates in control:** [§602]   The ULPA provides that a limited partner can be held liable as a general partner if she participates in control of the partnership business. The RULPA contains a similar provision, but limits it.

(1) **RULPA limitations:** [§603]   Under the RULPA, a limited partner can be held liable as a general partner for participating in control of the business only by those who transact business with the partnership *reasonably believing*, based on the limited partner's conduct, that the limited partner is a general partner. [RULPA §303(a)]

    (a) **Note:** Before the 1985 amendments, the RULPA provided that a creditor could hold a limited partner liable as a general partner if he had *actual knowledge* of the limited partner's controlling acts, regardless of whether the third party reasonably believed the limited partner to be a general partner. [RULPA (1976) §303(a)] A number of states have retained this rule.

(2) **"Safe harbors":** [§604]   The ULPA does not define what constitutes "participation in control of the business," but courts and legislatures began filling the gap by setting aside certain acts that a limited partner could perform without fear of being held liable as a general partner. Some of these "safe harbors" were formally adopted by the RULPA, including:

    (i) *Being a contractor* for or an agent or employee of the firm or of a general partner, or being an officer, director, or shareholder of a corporate general partner;

    (ii) *Consulting with and advising a general partner* with respect to the business of the firm;

    (iii) *Acting as surety* for the firm or guaranteeing or assuming one or more specific firm obligations;

    (iv) *Approving or disapproving an amendment* to the partnership agreement or the certificate of limited partnership;

    (v) *Requesting or attending a meeting* of the partners and/or voting on a fundamental change in the partnership (*e.g.*, removing or adding a partner, dissolving the partnership, etc.); and

    (vi) *Winding up* the limited partnership.

[RULPA §303(b)] Note that the statutory list of safe harbors is not exclusive; whether other activities constitute "exercising control" is determined on a case-by-case basis.

H. RIGHTS OF ONE ERRONEOUSLY BELIEVING HERSELF TO BE A LIMITED PARTNER

1. **ULPA:** [§605]   The ULPA provides that a person who makes a contribution to a business and *erroneously* believes that she has thereby become a limited partner can avoid being held liable as a general partner if, on ascertaining the mistake, she immediately *renounces her interest in the profits* or other compensation from the business. [ULPA §11]

2. **RULPA:** [§606]   The RULPA is similar, but specifically requires that the erroneous belief be in *good faith*. Also, the RULPA gives the would-be limited partner a choice. On ascertaining the mistake, the person can either: (i) *cause an appropriate certificate of limited partnership or certificate of amendment to be filed*; or (ii) *withdraw from future equity participation* in the enterprise (thus retaining a right to any then-current interest in the partnership). [RULPA §304(a)]

    a. **Exception:** [§607]   Under the RULPA, the mistaken party is liable as a general partner to third parties who reasonably believe the person to be a general partner *and* transact business with the partnership before the person withdraws or before her true status is reflected in the certificate. [RULPA §304(b)]

I. DISSOLUTION AND DISTRIBUTION

1. **Methods of Dissolution:** [§608]   A limited partnership can be dissolved nonjudicially or judicially.

    a. **Nonjudicial dissolution:** [§609]   A limited partnership will be dissolved whenever any of the following occur:

        (i) The *occurrence of the time for or events of dissolution specified in the certificate* of limited partnership (or partnership agreement);

        (ii) *All of the partners consent in writing* thereto; or

        (iii) *A general partner withdraws* and no provision is made for continuation and the partners do not consent to continue.

    [*See* RULPA §801]

    b. **Judicial dissolution**

        (1) **ULPA:** [§610]   Under the ULPA, a limited partner can have the partnership dissolved when she has rightfully demanded a return of her contribution and the partnership has refused to pay or the return is otherwise due but the partnership cannot legally pay. (*See supra*, §§593-599.)

        (2) **RULPA:** [§611]   The RULPA provides that any partner can have the limited partnership dissolved whenever it is not reasonably practicable to carry on business in conformity with the partnership agreement. [RULPA §802] Dissolution is most commonly granted when the general partner is guilty of misconduct, such as neglect or self-dealing. [*See, e.g.,* Wood v. Holiday Mobile Home Resorts, Inc., 128 Ariz. 274, *cert. denied,* 454 U.S. 826 (1981)] Although not specifically so provided, under the ULPA most courts would grant dissolution under similar circumstances. [*See, e.g.,* Weil v. Diversified Properties, 319 F. Supp. 778 (D.D.C. 1970)]

2. **Winding Up of Partnership Affairs:** [§612]   Once the partnership has been dissolved, its affairs must be wound up. The winding up process is similar to

that of a general partnership. Any general partner who has not wrongfully dissolved the partnership can wind up the partnership's affairs. If no such general partner is available, the limited partners may wind up. The RULPA also provides that upon application of a partner or his assignee, the court may wind up. [RULPA §803]

3. **Distribution of Assets:** [§613] The distribution of assets upon winding up the partnership's affairs varies between the ULPA and the RULPA.

    a. **ULPA:** [§614] ULPA section 23 provides for distribution of assets in the following order:

        (1) *To creditors.* This includes limited partners who are creditors to the extent that assets are sufficient to pay nonpartner creditors, but does *not* include general partners who are creditors (*see* (4), below).

        (2) *To limited partners for their share of profits* and any other compensation for their capital contributions as provided in the partnership agreement. This does not include the return of limited partners' contributions. (*Note:* Even though capital contributions have a lower priority (below), as a practical matter there will be no profits if capital contributions cannot be repaid.)

        (3) *To limited partners for their capital contributions.*

        (4) *To general partners for amounts they are claiming as creditors* (*e.g.*, for loans).

        (5) *To general partners for their share of the profits.* Although these are paid before capital contributions, as a practical matter, no profits will be paid if capital cannot fully be returned.

        (6) *To general partners for their capital contributions.*

    b. **RULPA:** [§615] The RULPA differs from the ULPA by putting partner creditors on par with nonpartner creditors, preserving partners' rights to distributions declared before dissolution, and treating general partners and limited partners alike. RULPA section 804 provides for distributions in the following order:

        (1) *To creditors, including general and limited partners who are creditors*, in satisfaction of liabilities of the limited partnership other than liabilities for distributions to partners upon withdrawal or for interim distributions (*i.e.*, periodic distributions provided for in the partnership agreement);

        (2) Except as provided in the partnership agreement, *to general and limited partners and former partners in satisfaction of liabilities for interim distributions* and to former partners to satisfy distributions owing them upon the partners' withdrawal; and

        (3) Except as provided in the partnership agreement, *to general and limited partners first for the return of their contributions and second*

for partnership profits and property, in the proportions in which the partners share in distributions.

4. **Cancellation of Certificate:** [§616]   Upon the dissolution and winding up of the limited partnership, a certificate of cancellation must be filed. [ULPA §24; RULPA §203]

J.   FOREIGN LIMITED PARTNERSHIPS [§617]

The RULPA provides that a foreign limited partnership may file with the state to qualify to do business in the state. The law of the state of organization governs internal organization. A foreign limited partnership cannot maintain an action in court until it registers with the state, but it may defend. [RULPA §§901, 902, 907]

Notes

Notes

Notes

Notes

Notes

Publications Catalog

Publishers of America's Most Popular Legal Study Aids!

All Titles Available At Your Law School Bookstore.

Gilbert Law Summaries are the best selling outlines in the country, and have set the standard for excellence since they were first introduced more than twenty-five years ago. It's Gilbert's unique combination of features that makes it the one study aid you'll turn to for all your study needs!

Accounting and Finance for Lawyers
Professor Thomas L. Evans, University of Texas

Basic Accounting Principles; Definitions of Accounting Terms; Balance Sheet; Income Statement; Statement of Changes in Financial Position; Consolidated Financial Statements; Accumulation of Financial Data; Financial Statement Analysis.
ISBN: 0-15-900382-2   Pages: 136 $19.95

Administrative Law
By Professor Michael R. Asimow, U.C.L.A.

Separation of Powers and Controls Over Agencies; (including Delegation of Power) Constitutional Right to Hearing (including Liberty and Property Interests Protected by Due Process, and Rulemaking- Adjudication Distinction); Adjudication Under Administrative Procedure Act (APA); Formal Adjudication (including Notice, Discovery, Burden of Proof, Finders of Facts and Reasons); Adjudicatory Decision Makers (including Administrative Law Judges (ALJs), Bias, Improper Influences, Ex Parte Communications, Familiarity with Record, Res Judicata); Rulemaking Procedures (including Notice, Public Participation, Publication, Impartiality of Rulemakers, Rulemaking Record); Obtaining Information (including Subpoena Power, Privilege Against Self-incrimination, Freedom of Information Act, Government in Sunshine Act, Attorneys' Fees); Scope of Judicial Review; Reviewability of Agency Decisions (including Mandamus, Injunction, Sovereign Immunity, Federal Tort Claims Act); Standing to Seek Judicial Review and Timing.
ISBN: 0-15-900000-9   Pages: 278 $20.95

Agency and Partnership
By Professor Richard J. Conviser, Chicago Kent

Agency: Rights and Liabilities Between Principal and Agent (including Agent's Fiduciary Duty, Right to Indemnification); Contractual Rights Between Principal (or Agent) and Third Persons (including Creation of Agency Relationship, Authority of Agent, Scope of Authority, Termination of Authority, Ratification, Liability on

Agents, Contracts); Tort Liability (including Respondeat Superior, Master-Servant Relationship, Scope of Employment). Partnership: Property Rights of Partner; Formation of Partnership; Relations Between Partners (including Fiduciary Duty); Authority of Partner to Bind Partnership; Dissolution and Winding up of Partnership; Limited Partnerships.
ISBN: 0-15-900327-X   Pages: 149 $17.95

Antitrust
By Professor Thomas M. Jorde, U.C. Berkeley, Mark A. Lemley, University of Texas, and Professor Robert H. Mnookin, Harvard University

Common Law Restraints of Trade; Federal Antitrust Laws (including Sherman Act, Clayton Act, Federal Trade Commission Act, Interstate Commerce Requirement, Antitrust Remedies); Monopolization (including Relevant Market, Purposeful Act Requirement, Attempts and Conspiracy to Monopolize); Collaboration Among Competitors (including Horizontal Restraints, Rule of Reason vs. Per Se Violations, Price Fixing, Division of Markets, Group Boycotts); Vertical Restraints (including Tying Arrangements); Mergers and Acquisitions (including Horizontal Mergers, Brown Shoe Analysis, Vertical Mergers, Conglomerate Mergers); Price Discrimination—Robinson-Patman Act; Unfair Methods of Competition; Patent Laws and Their Antitrust Implications; Exemptions From Antitrust Laws (including Motor, Rail, and Interstate Water Carriers, Bank Mergers, Labor Unions, Professional Baseball).
ISBN: 0-15-900328-8   Pages: 210 $18.95

Bankruptcy
By Professor Ned W. Waxman, College of William and Mary

Participants in the Bankruptcy Case; Jurisdiction and Procedure; Commencement and Administration of the Case (including Eligibility, Voluntary Case, Involuntary Case, Meeting of Creditors, Debtor's Duties); Officers of the Estate (including

Trustee, Examiner, United States Trustee); Bankruptcy Estate; Creditor's Right of Setoff; Trustee's Avoiding Powers; Claims of Creditors (including Priority Claims and Tax Claims); Debtor's Exemptions; Nondischargeable Debts; Effects of Discharge; Reaffirmation Agreements; Administrative Powers (including Automatic Stay, Use, Sale, or Lease of Property); Chapter 7-Liquidation; Chapter 11-Reorganization; Chapter 13-Individual With Regular Income; Chapter 12-Family Farmer With Regular Annual Income.
ISBN: 0-15-900442-X   Pages: 311 $21.95

Business Law
By Professor Robert D. Upp, Los Angeles City College

Torts and Crimes in Business; Law of Contracts (including Contract Formation, Consideration, Statute of Frauds, Contract Remedies, Third Parties); Sales (including Transfer of Title and Risk of Loss, Performance and Remedies, Products Liability, Personal Property Security Interest); Property (including Personal Property, Bailments, Real Property, Landlord and Tenant); Agency; Business Organizations (including Partnerships, Corporations); Commercial Paper; Government Regulation of Business (including Taxation, Antitrust, Environmental Protection, and Bankruptcy).
ISBN: 0-15-900005-X   Pages: 277 $17.95

California Bar Performance Test Skills
By Professor Peter J. Honigsberg, University of San Francisco

Hints to Improve Writing; How to Approach the Performance Test; Legal Analysis Documents (including Writing a Memorandum of Law, Writing a Client Letter, Writing Briefs); Fact Gathering and Fact Analysis Documents; Tactical and Ethical Considerations; Sample Interrogatories, Performance Tests, and Memoranda.
ISBN: 0-15-900152-8   Pages: 216 $18.95

Civil Procedure
By Professor Thomas D. Rowe, Jr., Duke University, and Professor Richard L. Marcus, U.C. Hastings

Territorial (Personal) Jurisdiction, including Venue and Forum Non Conveniens; Subject Matter Jurisdiction, covering Diversity Jurisdiction, Federal Question Jurisdiction; Erie Doctrine and Federal Common Law; Pleadings including Counterclaims, Cross-Claims, Supplemental Pleadings; Parties, including Joinder and Class Actions; Discovery, including Devices, Scope, Sanctions, and Discovery Conference; Summary Judgment; Pretrial Conference and Settlements; Trial, including Right to Jury Trial, Motions, Jury Instruction and Arguments, and Post-Verdict Motions; Appeals; Claim Preclusion (Res Judicata) and Issue Preclusion (Collateral Estoppel).
ISBN: 0-15-900429-2   Pages: 410 $22.95

Commercial Paper and Payment Law
By Professor Douglas J. Whaley, Ohio State University

Types of Commercial Paper; Negotiability; Negotiation; Holders in Due Course; Claims and Defenses on Negotiable Instruments (including Real Defenses and Personal Defenses); Liability of the Parties (including Merger Rule, Suits on the Instrument, Warranty Suits, Conversion); Bank Deposits and Collections; Forgery or Alteration of Negotiable Instruments; Electronic Banking.
ISBN: 0-15-900367-9   Pages: 166 $19.95

Community Property
By Professor William A. Reppy, Jr., Duke University

Classifying Property as Community or Separate; Management and Control of Property; Liability for Debts; Division of Property at Divorce; Devolution of Property at Death; Relationships Short of Valid Marriage; Conflict of Laws Problems; Constitutional Law Issues (including Equal Protection Standards, Due Process Issues).
ISBN: 0-15-900422-5   Pages: 161 $18.95

Conflict of Laws

By Dean Herma Hill Kay, U.C. Berkeley

Domicile; Jurisdiction (including Notice and Opportunity to be Heard, Minimum Contacts, Types of Jurisdiction); Choice of Law (including Vested Rights Approach, Most Significant Relationship Approach, Governmental Interest Analysis); Choice of Law in Specific Substantive Areas; Traditional Defenses Against Application of Foreign Law; Constitutional Limitations and Overriding Federal Law (including Due Process Clause, Full Faith and Credit Clause, Conflict Between State and Federal Law); Recognition and Enforcement of Foreign Judgments.
ISBN: 0-15-900424-1   Pages: 250 $20.95

Constitutional Law

By Professor Jesse H. Choper, U.C. Berkeley

Powers of Federal Government (including Judicial Power, Powers of Congress, Presidential Power, Foreign Affairs Power); Intergovernmental Immunities, Separation of Powers; Regulation of Foreign Commerce; Regulation of Interstate Commerce; Taxation of Interstate and Foreign Commerce; Due Process, Equal Protection; "State Action" Requirements; Freedoms of Speech, Press, and Association; Freedom of Religion.
ISBN: 0-15-900375-X   Pages: 312 $21.95

Contracts

By Professor Melvin A. Eisenberg, U.C. Berkeley

Consideration (including Promissory Estoppel, Moral or Past Consideration); Mutual Assent; Defenses (including Mistake, Fraud, Duress, Unconscionability, Statute of Frauds, Illegality); Third-Party Beneficiaries; Assignment of Rights and Delegation of Duties; Conditions; Substantial Performance; Material vs. Minor Breach; Anticipatory Breach; Impossibility; Discharge; Remedies (including Damages, Specific Performance, Liquidated Damages).
ISBN: 0-15-900014-9   Pages: 278 $21.95

Corporations

By Professor Jesse H. Choper, U.C. Berkeley, and Professor Melvin A. Eisenberg, U.C. Berkeley

Formalities; "De Jure" vs. "De Facto"; Promoters; Corporate Powers; Ultra Vires Transactions; Powers, Duties, and Liabilities of Officers and Directors; Allocation of Power Between Directors and Shareholders; Conflicts of Interest in Corporate Transactions; Close Corporations; Insider Trading; Rule 10b-5 and Section 16(b); Shareholders' Voting Rights; Shareholders' Right to Inspect Records; Shareholders' Suits; Capitalization (including Classes of Shares, Preemptive Rights, Consideration for Shares); Dividends; Redemption of Shares; Fundamental Changes in Corporate Structure; Applicable Conflict of Laws Principles.
ISBN: 0-15-900342-3   Pages: 282 $21.95

Criminal Law

By Professor George E. Dix, University of Texas

Elements of Crimes (including Actus Reus, Mens Rea, Causation); Vicarious Liability; Complicity in Crime; Criminal Liability of Corporations;

Defenses (including Insanity, Diminished Capacity, Intoxication, Ignorance, Self-Defense); Inchoate Crimes; Homicide; Other Crimes Against the Person; Crimes Against Habitation (including Burglary, Arson); Crimes Against Property; Offenses Against Government; Offenses Against Administration of Justice.
ISBN: 0-15-900217-6   Pages: 271 $20.95

Criminal Procedure

By Professor Paul Marcus, College of William and Mary, and Professor Charles H. Whitebread, U.S.C.

Exclusionary Rule; Arrests and Other Detentions; Search and Seizure; Privilege Against Self-Incrimination; Confessions; Preliminary Hearing; Bail; Indictment; Speedy Trial; Competency to Stand Trial; Government's Obligation to Disclose Information; Right to Jury Trial; Right to Counsel; Right to Confront Witnesses; Burden of Proof; Insanity; Entrapment; Guilty Pleas; Sentencing; Death Penalty; Ex Post Facto Issues; Appeal; Habeas Corpus; Juvenile Offenders; Prisoners' Rights; Double Jeopardy.
ISBN: 0-15-900376-8   Pages: 244 $20.95

Estate and Gift Tax

By Professor John H. McCord, University of Illinois

Gross Estate; Allowable Deductions Under Estate Tax (including Expenses, Indebtedness, and Taxes, Deductions for Losses, Charitable Deduction, Marital Deduction); Taxable Gifts; Deductions; Valuation; Computation of Tax; Returns and Payment of Tax; Tax on Generation-Skipping Transfers.
ISBN: 0-15-900425-X   Pages: 298 $20.95

Evidence

By Professor Jon R. Waltz, Northwestern University, and Roger C. Park, University of Minnesota

Direct Evidence; Circumstantial Evidence; Rulings on Admissibility; Relevancy; Materiality; Character Evidence; Hearsay and the Hearsay Exceptions; Privileges; Competency to Testify; Opinion Evidence and Expert Witnesses; Direct Examination; Cross-Examination; Impeachment; Real, Demonstrative, and Scientific Evidence; Judicial Notice; Burdens of Proof; Parol Evidence Rule.
ISBN: 0-15-900385-7   Pages: 342 $22.95

Federal Courts

By Professor William A. Fletcher, U.C. Berkeley

Article III Courts; "Case or Controversy" Requirement; Justiciability; Advisory Opinions; Political Questions; Ripeness; Mootness; Standing; Congressional Power Over Federal Court Jurisdiction; Supreme Court Jurisdiction; District Court Subject Matter Jurisdiction (including Federal Question Jurisdiction, Diversity Jurisdiction);

Pendent and Ancillary Jurisdiction; Removal Jurisdiction; Venue; Forum Non Conveniens; Law Applied in the Federal Courts (including Erie Doctrine); Federal Law in the State Courts; Abstention; Habeas Corpus for State Prisoners; Federal Injunctions Against State Court Proceedings; Eleventh Amendment.
ISBN: 0-15-900232-X   Pages: 270 $21.95

Future Interests & Perpetuities

By Professor Jesse Dukeminier, U.C.L.A.

Reversions; Possibilities of Reverter; Rights of Entry; Remainders; Executory Interest; Rules Restricting Remainders and Executory Interest; Rights of Owners of Future Interests; Construction of Instruments; Powers of Appointment; Rule Against Perpetuities (including Reforms of the Rule).
ISBN: 0-15-900218-4   Pages: 162 $19.95

Income Tax I - Individual

By Professor Michael R. Asimow, U.C.L.A.

Gross Income; Exclusions; Income Splitting by Gifts, Personal Service Income, Income Earned by Children, Income of Husbands and Wives, Below-Market Interest on Loans, Taxation of Trusts; Business and Investment Deductions; Personal Deductions; Tax Rates; Credits; Computation of Basis, Gain, or Loss; Realization; Nonrecognition of Gain or Loss; Capital Gains and Losses; Alternative Minimum Tax; Tax Accounting Problems.
ISBN: 0-15-900421-7   Pages: 279 $21.95

Income Tax II - Partnerships, Corporations, Trusts

By Professor Michael R. Asimow, U.C.L.A.

Taxation of Partnerships (including Current Partnership Income, Contributions of Property to Partnership, Sale of Partnership Interest, Distributions, Liquidations); Corporate Taxation (including Corporate Distributions, Sales of Stock and Assets, Reorganizations); S Corporations; Federal Income Taxation of Trusts.
ISBN: 0-15-900384-9   Pages: 210 $19.95

Labor Law

By Professor James C. Oldham, Georgetown University, and Robert J. Gelhaus

Statutory Foundations of Present Labor Law (including National Labor Relations Act, Taft-Hartley, Norris-LaGuardia Act, Landrum-Griffin Act); Organizing Campaigns, Selection of the Bargaining Representative; Collective Bargaining (including Negotiating the Agreement, Lockouts, Administering the Agreement, Arbitration); Strikes, Boycotts, and Picketing; Concerted Activity Protected Under the NLRA; Civil Rights Legislation; Grievance; Federal Regulation of Compulsory Union Membership Arrangements; State Regulation of Compulsory Membership Agreements; "Right to Work" Laws; Discipline of Union Members; Election of Union Officers; Corruption.
ISBN: 0-15-900340-7   Pages: 221 $19.95

Legal Ethics

By Professor Thomas D. Morgan, George Washington University

Regulating Admission to Practice Law; Preventing Unauthorized Practice of Law; Contract Between Client and Lawyer (including Lawyer's Duties Regarding Accepting Employment, Spheres of Authority of Lawyer and Client, Obligation of Client to Lawyer, Terminating the Lawyer-Client Relationship); Attorney-Client Privilege; Professional Duty of Confidentiality; Conflicts of Interest; Obligations to Third Persons and the Legal System (including Counseling Illegal or Fraudulent Conduct, Threats of Criminal Prosecution); Special Obligations in Litigation (including Limitations on Advancing Money to Client, Duty to Reject Certain Actions, Lawyer as Witness); Solicitation and Advertising; Specialization; Disciplinary Process; Malpractice; Special Responsibilities of Judges.
ISBN: 0-15-900026-2   Pages: 221 $20.95

Legal Research, Writing and Analysis

By Professor Peter J. Honigsberg, University of San Francisco

Court Systems; Precedent; Case Reporting System (including Regional and State Reporters, Headnotes and the West Key Number System, Citations and Case Finding); Statutes, Constitutions, and Legislative History; Secondary Sources (including Treatises, Law Reviews, Digests, Restatements); Administrative Agencies (including Regulations, Looseleaf Services); Shepard's Citations; Computers in Legal Research; Reading and Understanding a Case (including Briefing a Case); Using Legal Sourcebooks; Basic Guidelines for Legal Writing; Organizing Your Research; Writing a Memorandum of Law; Writing a Brief; Writing an Opinion or Client Letter.
ISBN: 0-15-900436-5   Pages: 162 $17.95

Multistate Bar Examination

By Professor Richard J. Conviser, Chicago Kent

Structure of the Exam; Governing Law; Effective Use of Time; Scoring of the Exam; Jurisdictions Using the Exam; Subject Matter Outlines; Practice Tests, Answers, and Subject Matter Keys; Glossary of Legal Terms and Definitions; State Bar Examination Directory; Listing of Reference Materials for Multistate Subjects.
ISBN: 0-15-900246-X   Pages: 776 $24.95

Personal Property

Gilbert Staff

Acquisitions; Ownership Through Possession (including Wild Animals, Abandoned Chattels); Finders of Lost Property; Bailments; Possessory Liens; Pledges; Trover; Gift; Accession; Confusion (Commingling); Fixtures; Crops (Emblements); Adverse Possession; Prescriptive Rights (Acquiring Ownership of Easements or Profits by Adverse Use).
ISBN: 0-15-900360-1   Pages: 118 $14.95

Professional Responsibility

(see Legal Ethics)

gilbert
LAW SUMMARIES
AMERICA'S BEST SELLING OUTLINES

Property
By Professor Jesse Dukeminier, U.C.L.A.

Possession (including Wild Animals, Bailments, Adverse Possession); Gifts and Sales of Personal Property; Freehold Possessory Estates; Future Interests (including Reversion, Possibility of Reverter, Right of Entry, Executory Interests, Rule Against Perpetuities); Tenancy in Common; Joint Tenancy; Tenancy by the Entirety; Condominiums; Cooperatives; Marital Property; Landlord and Tenant; Easements and Covenants; Nuisance; Rights in Airspace and Water; Right to Support; Zoning; Eminent Domain; Sale of Land (including Mortgage, Deed, Warranties of Title); Methods of Title Assurance (including Recording System, Title Registration, Title Insurance).

ISBN: 0-15-900426-8   Pages: 445 $22.95

Remedies
By Professor John A. Bauman, U.C.L.A., and Professor Kenneth H. York, Pepperdine University

Damages; Equitable Remedies (including Injunctions and Specific Performance); Restitution; Injuries to Tangible Property Interests; Injuries to Business and Commercial Interests (including Business Torts, Inducing Breach of Contract, Patent Infringement, Unfair Competition, Trade Defamation); Injuries to Personal Dignity and Related Interests (including Defamation, Privacy, Religious Status, Civil and Political Rights); Personal Injury and Death; Fraud; Duress, Undue Influence, and Unconscionable Conduct; Mistake; Breach of Contract; Unenforceable Contracts (including Statute of Frauds, Impossibility, Lack of Contractual Capacity, Illegality).

ISBN: 0-15-900325-3   Pages: 349 $22.95

Sale and Lease of Goods
By Professor Douglas J. Whaley, Ohio State University

UCC Article 2; Sales Contract (including Offer and Acceptance, Parol Evidence Rule, Statute of Frauds, Assignment and Delegation, Revision of Contract Terms); Types of Sales (including Cash Sale Transactions, Auctions, "Sale or Return" and "Sale on Approval" Transactions); Warranties (including Express and Implied Warranties, Privity, Disclaimer, Consumer Protection Statutes); Passage of Title; Performance of the Contract; Anticipatory Breach; Demand for Assurance of Performance; Unforeseen Circumstances; Risk of Loss; Remedies; Documents of Title; Lease of Goods; International Sale of Goods.

ISBN: 0-15-900367-9   Pages: 196 $19.95

Secured Transactions
By Professor Douglas J. Whaley, Ohio State University

Coverage of Article 9; Creation of a Security Interest (including Attachment, Security Agreement, Value, Debtor's Rights in the Collateral); Perfection; Filing; Priorities; Bankruptcy Proceedings and Article 9; Default Proceedings; Bulk Transfers.

ISBN: 0-15-900231-1   Pages: 191 $18.95

Securities Regulation
By Professor David H. Barber, and Professor Niels B. Schaumann, William Mitchell College of Law

Jurisdiction and Interstate Commerce; Securities Act of 1933 (including Registration Requirements and Exemptions); Securities Exchange Act of 1934 (including Rule 10b-5, Tender Offers, Proxy Solicitations Regulation, Insider Transactions); Regulation of the Securities Markets; Multinational Transactions; State Regulation of Securities Transactions.

ISBN: 0-15-9000437-3   Pages: 421 $22.95

Torts
By Professor Marc A. Franklin, Stanford University

Intentional Torts; Negligence; Strict Liability; Products Liability; Nuisance; Survival of Tort Actions; Wrongful Death; Immunity; Release and Contribution; Indemnity; Workers' Compensation; No-Fault Auto Insurance; Defamation; Invasion of Privacy; Misrepresentation; Injurious Falsehood; Interference With Economic Relations; Unjustifiable Litigation.

ISBN: 0-15-900220-6   Pages: 400 $22.95

Trusts
By Professor Edward C. Halbach, Jr., U.C. Berkeley

Elements of a Trust; Trust Creation; Transfer of Beneficiary's Interest (including Spendthrift Trusts); Charitable Trusts (including Cy Pres Doctrine); Trustee's Responsibilities, Power, Duties, and Liabilities; Duties and Liabilities of Beneficiaries; Accounting for Income and Principal; Power of Settlor to Modify or Revoke; Powers of Trustee Beneficiaries or Courts to Modify or Terminate; Termination of Trusts by Operation of Law; Resulting Trusts; Purchase Money Resulting Trusts; Constructive Trusts.

ISBN: 0-15-900039-4   Pages: 238 $20.95

Wills
By Professor Stanley M. Johanson, University of Texas

Intestate Succession; Simultaneous Death; Advancements; Disclaimer; Killer of Decedent; Elective Share Statutes; Pretermitted Child Statutes; Homestead; Formal Requisites of a Will; Revocation of Wills; Incorporation by Reference; Pour-Over Gift in Inter Vivos Trust; Joint Wills; Contracts Relating to Wills; Lapsed Gifts; Ademption; Exoneration of Liens; Will Contests; Probate and Estate Administration.

ISBN: 0-15-900040-8   Pages: 262 $21.95

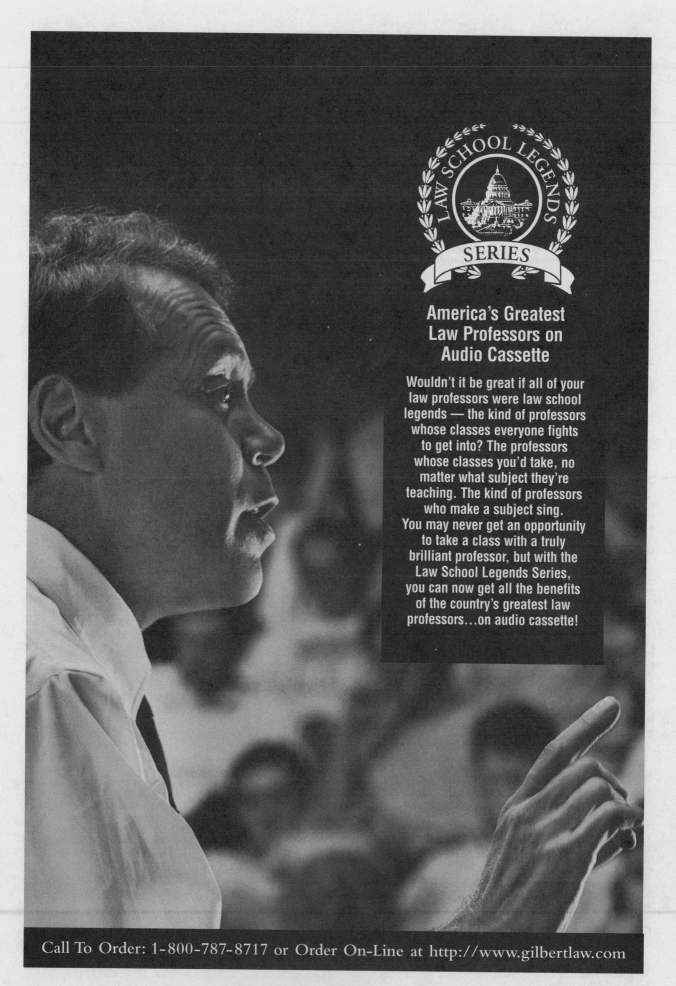

Criminal Procedure

By Professor Charles H. Whitebread
USC School of Law

TOPICS COVERED: Incorporation Of The Bill Of Rights; Exclusionary Rule; Fruit Of The Poisonous Tree; Arrest; Search & Seizure; Exceptions To Warrant Requirement; Wire Tapping & Eavesdropping; Confessions (Miranda); Pretrial Identification; Bail; Preliminary Hearings; Grand Juries; Speedy Trial; Fair Trial; Jury Trials; Right To Counsel; Guilty Pleas; Sentencing; Death Penalty; Habeas Corpus; Double Jeopardy; Privilege Against Compelled Testimony.

3 Audio Cassettes
ISBN: 0-15-900281-8 $39.95

Evidence

By Professor Faust F. Rossi
Cornell Law School

TOPICS COVERED: Relevance; Insurance; Remedial Measures; Settlement Offers; Causation; State Of Mind; Rebuttal; Habit; Character Evidence; "MIMIC" Rule; Documentary Evidence; Authentication; Best Evidence Rule; Parol Evidence; Competency; Dead Man Statutes; Examination Of Witnesses; Present Recollection Revived; Past Recollection Recorded; Opinion Testimony; Lay And Expert Witness; Learned Treatises; Impeachment; Collateral Matters; Bias, Interest Or Motive; Rehabilitation; Privileges; Hearsay And Exceptions.

5 Audio Cassettes
ISBN: 0-15-900282-6 $45.95

Family Law

Professor Roger E. Schechter
George Washington University Law School

TOPICS COVERED: Marital Relationship; Formalities And Solemnization; Common Law Marriage; Impediments; Conflict Of Laws; Non-Marital Relationship; Void And Voidable Marriages; Annulment; Divorce; Separation; Full Faith And Credit; Temporary Orders; Property Division; Community Property Principles; Equitable Distribution And Reimbursement; Marital And Separate Property; Alimony; Child Support; Enforcement Of Orders; Antenuptial And Postnuptial Agreements; Separation And Settlement Agreements; Custody; Visitation Rights; Termination Of Parental Rights; Adoption; Illegitimacy; Paternity Actions.

3 Audio Cassettes
ISBN: 0-15-900283-4 $39.95

Federal Courts

Professor John C. Jeffries
University of Virginia School of Law

TOPICS COVERED: History Of The Federal Court System; "Court Or Controversy" And Justiciability; Congressional Power Over Federal Court Jurisdiction; Supreme Court Jurisdiction; District Court Subject Matter Jurisdiction—Federal Question Jurisdiction, Diversity Jurisdiction And Admiralty Jurisdiction; Pendent And Ancillary Jurisdiction; Removal Jurisdiction; Venue; Forum Non Conveniens; Law Applied In The Federal Courts; Federal Law In The State Courts; Collateral Relations Between Federal And State Courts; The Eleventh Amendment And State Sovereign Immunity.

3 Audio Cassettes
ISBN: 0-15-900372-5 $39.95

Federal Income Tax

By Professor Cheryl D. Block
George Washington University Law School

TOPICS COVERED: Administrative Reviews; Tax Formula; Gross Income; Exclusions For Gifts; Inheritances; Personal Injuries; Tax Basis Rules; Divorce Tax Rules; Assignment Of Income; Business Deductions; Investment Deductions; Passive Loss And Interest Limitation Rules; Capital Gains & Losses; Section 1031, 1034, and 121 Deferred/Non Taxable Transactions.

4 Audio Cassettes
ISBN: 0-15-900284-2 $45.95

Future Interests

By Dean Catherine L. Carpenter
Southwestern University Law School

TOPICS COVERED: Rule Against Perpetuities; Class Gifts; Estates In Land; Rule In Shelley's Case; Future Interests In Transferor and Transferee; Life Estates; Defeasible Fees; Doctrine Of Worthier Title; Doctrine Of Merger; Fee Simple Estates; Restraints On Alienation; Power Of Appointment; Rules Of Construction.

2 Audio Cassettes
ISBN: 0-15-900285-0 $24.95

Law School Exam Writing

By Professor Charles H. Whitebread
USC School of Law

TOPICS COVERED: With "Law School Exam Writing," you'll learn the secrets of law school test taking. Professor Whitebread leads you step-by-step through his innovative system, so that you know exactly how to tackle your essay exams without making point draining mistakes. You'll learn how to read questions so you don't miss important issues; how to organize your answer; how to use limited exam time to your maximum advantage; and even how to study for exams.

1 Audio Cassette
ISBN: 0-15-900287-7 $19.95

Professional Responsibility

By Professor Erwin Chemerinsky
USC School of Law

TOPICS COVERED: Regulation of Attorneys; Bar Admission; Unauthorized Practice; Competency; Discipline; Judgment; Lawyer-Client Relationship; Representation; Withdrawal; Conflicts; Disqualification; Clients; Client Interests; Successive And Effective Representation; Integrity; Candor; Confidences; Secrets; Past And Future Crimes; Perjury; Communications; Witnesses; Jurors; The Court; The Press; Trial Tactics; Prosecutors; Market; Solicitation; Advertising; Law Firms; Fees; Client Property; Conduct; Political Activity.

3 Audio Cassettes
ISBN: 0-15-900371-7 $39.95

Real Property

By Professor Paula A. Franzese
Seton Hall Law School

TOPICS COVERED: Estates—Fee Simple, Fee Tail, Life Estate; Co-Tenancy—Joint Tenancy, Tenancy In Common, Tenancy By The Entirety; Landlord-Tenant Relationship; Liability For Condition Of Premises; Assignment & Sublease; Easements; Restrictive Covenants; Adverse Possession; Recording Acts; Conveyancing; Personal Property.

4 Audio Cassettes
ISBN: 0-15-900289-3 $45.95

Remedies

By Professor William A. Fletcher
University of California at Berkeley, Boalt Hall School of Law

TOPICS COVERED: Damages; Restitution; Equitable Remedies; Tracing; Rescission and Reformation; Injury and Destruction of Personal Property; Conversion; Injury to Real Property; Trespass; Ouster; Nuisance; Defamation; Trade Libel; Inducing Breach of Contract; Contracts to Purchase Personal Property; Contracts to Purchase Real Property (including Equitable Conversion); Construction Contracts; and Personal Service Contracts.

4 Audio Cassettes
ISBN: 0-15-900353-9 $45.95

Sales & Lease of Goods

By Professor Michael I. Spak
Chicago Kent College of Law

TOPICS COVERED: Goods; Contract Formation; Firm Offers; Statute Of Frauds; Modification; Parol Evidence; Code Methodology; Tender; Payment; Identification; Risk Of Loss; Warranties; Merchantability; Fitness; Disclaimers; Consumer Protection; Remedies; Anticipatory Repudiation; Third Party Rights.

3 Audio Cassettes
ISBN: 0-15-900291-5 $39.95

Secured Transactions

By Professor Michael I. Spak
Chicago Kent College of Law

TOPICS COVERED: Collateral; Inventory; Intangibles; Proceeds; Security Agreements; Attachment; After-Acquired Property; Perfection; Filing; Priorities; Purchase Money Security Interests; Fixtures; Rights Upon Default; Self-Help; Sale; Constitutional Issues.

3 Audio Cassettes
ISBN: 0-15-900292-3 $39.95

Securities Regulation

By Professor Therese H. Maynard
Loyola University Law School
NEW
4 Audio Cassettes
ISBN: 0-15-900359-8 $39.95

Torts

By Professor Richard J. Conviser
Chicago Kent College of Law

TOPICS COVERED: Essay Exam Techniques; Intentional Torts—Assault, Battery, False Imprisonment, Intentional Infliction Of Emotional Distress, Trespass To Land, Trespass To Chattels, Conversion; Defenses. Defamation—Libel, Slander; Defenses; First Amendment Concerns; Invasion Of Right Of Privacy; Misrepresentation; Negligence—Duty, Breach, Actual And Proximate Causation, Damages; Defenses; Strict Liability, Products Liability; Nuisance; General Tort Considerations.

4 Audio Cassettes
ISBN: 0-15-900185-4 $45.95

Wills & Trusts

By Professor Stanley M. Johanson
University of Texas School of Law

TOPICS COVERED: Attested Wills; Holographic Wills; Negligence; Revocation; Changes On Face Of Will; Lapsed Gifts; Negative Bequest Rule; Nonprobate Assets; Intestate Succession; Advancements; Elective Share; Will Contests; Capacity; Undue Influence; Creditors' Rights; Creation Of Trust; Revocable Trusts; Pourover Gifts; Charitable Trusts; Resulting Trusts; Constructive Trusts; Spendthrift Trusts; Self-Dealing; Prudent Investments; Trust Accounting; Termination; Powers Of Appointment.

4 Audio Cassettes
ISBN: 0-15-000201-X $45.95

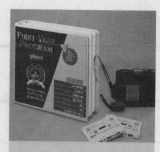

Law School Legends Series
FIRST YEAR PROGRAM

Includes Five Law School Legends Titles:

■ **Civil Procedure**
By Professor Richard D. Freer
Emory University Law School

■ **Contracts**
By Professor Michael I. Spak
Chicago Kent College Of Law

■ **Criminal Law**
By Professor Charles H. Whitebread
USC School of Law

■ **Real Property**
By Professor Paula A. Franzese
Seton Hall Law School

■ **Torts**
By Professor Richard J. Conviser
Chicago Kent College of Law

Plus—

■ **Law School Exam Writing**
By Professor Charles H. Whitebread
USC Law School

All titles are packaged in a convenient carry case. $250 if purchased separately. $195 if purchased as a set. Save $55.

ISBN: 0-15-900306-7   Set $195

If you accidentally damage a tape within five years from the date of purchase we'll replace it for FREE— No questions asked!

NO QUESTIONS ASKED.

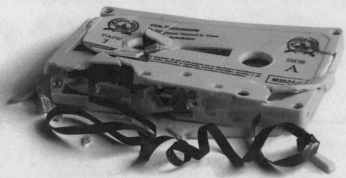

We stand behind our products... even if someone stands on them!

With the Law School Legends Series you get America's Greatest Law Professors on audio cassette — plus one of the best audio tape guarantees in the business! If you accidentally damage a Law School Legends tape within 5 years from the date of purchase, we'll replace it for free — **no questions asked!**

The Law School Legends Series
America's Greatest Law Professors on Audio Cassette

Available in Many Popular Titles. All Titles Fully Indexed for Quick Reference.

Administrative Law	Constitutional Law	Family Law	Real Property
Agency & Partnership	Contracts	Federal Courts	Remedies
Antitrust Law	Copyright Law	Federal Income Tax	Sale & Lease of Goods
Bankruptcy	Corporations	First Year Program	Secured Transactions
Civil Procedure	Criminal Law	Future Interests	Securities Regulation
Commercial Paper	Criminal Procedure	Law School Exam Writing	Torts
Conflict of Laws	Evidence	Prof. Responsibility	Wills & Trusts

Call To Order: 1-800-787-8717 or Order On-Line at http://www.gilbertlaw.com

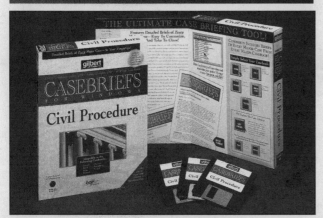
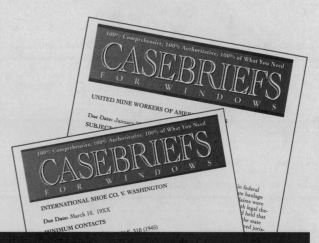

on the Internet!

Employment Guides

A collection of best selling titles that help you identify and reach your career goals.

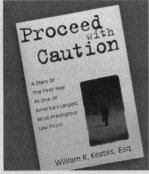

Guerrilla Tactics for Getting the Legal Job of Your Dreams
Kimm Alayne Walton, J.D.

Whether you're looking for a summer clerkship or your first permanent job after school, this revolutionary book is the key to getting the job of your dreams!

Guerrilla Tactics for Getting the Legal Job of Your Dreams leads you step-by-step through everything you need to do to nail down that perfect job! You'll learn hundreds of simple-to-use strategies that will get you exactly where you want to go. You'll Learn:

- The seven magic opening words in cover letters that ensure you'll get a response.
- The secret to successful interviews every time.
- Killer answers to the toughest interview questions they'll ever ask you.
- Plus Much More!

Guerrilla Tactics features the best strategies from the country's most innovative law school career advisors. The strategies in *Guerrilla Tactics* are so powerful that it even comes with a guarantee: Follow the advice in the book, and within one year of graduation you'll have the job of your dreams ... or your money back!

Pick up a copy of *Guerrilla Tactics* today ... you'll be on your way to the job of your dreams!

ISBN: 0-15-900317-2   **$24.95**

Proceed With Caution: A Diary Of The First Year At One Of America's Largest, Most Prestigious Law Firms
William R. Keates

Prestige. Famous clients. High-profile cases. Not to mention a starting salary approaching six figures.

In *Proceed With Caution*, the author takes you behind the scenes, to show you what it's really like to be a junior associate at a huge law firm. After graduating from an Ivy League law school, he took a job as an associate with one of New York's blue-chip law firms.

He also did something not many people do. He kept a diary, where he spelled out his day-to-day life at the firm in graphic detail.

Proceed With Caution excerpts the diary, from his first day at the firm to the day he quit. From the splashy benefits, to the nitty-gritty on the work junior associates do, to the grind of long and unpredictable hours, to the stress that eventually made him leave the firm — he tells story after story that will make you feel as though you're living the life of a new associate.

Whether you're considering a career with a large firm, or you're just curious about what life at the top firms is all about — *Proceed With Caution* is a must read!

ISBN: 0-15-900181-1   **$17.95**

The Official Guide To Legal Specialties
Lisa Shanholtzer

With *The Official Guide To Legal Specialties* you'll get a behind the scenes glimpse at dozens of legal specialties. Not just lists of what to expect, real life stories from top practitioners in each field. You'll learn exactly what it's like to be in some of America's most desirable professions. You'll get expert advice on what it takes to get a job in each field. How much you'll earn and what the day-to-day life is really like, the challenges you'll face, and the benefits you'll enjoy. With *The Official Guide To Legal Specialties* you'll have a wealth of information at your fingertips!

Includes the following specialties:

Banking	Intellectual Property
Communications	International
Corporate	Labor/Employment
Criminal	Litigation
Entertainment	Public Interest
Environmental	Securities
Government Practice	Sports
Health Care	Tax
Immigration	Trusts & Estates

ISBN: 0-15-900391-1   **$17.95**

Beyond L.A. Law: Inspiring Stories of People Who've Done Fascinating Things With A Law Degree
National Association for Law Placement

Anyone who watches television knows that being a lawyer means working your way up through a law firm — right?

Wrong!

Beyond L.A. Law gives you a fascinating glimpse into the lives of people who've broken the "lawyer" mold. They come from a variety of backgrounds — some had prior careers, others went straight through college and law school, and yet others have overcome poverty and physical handicaps. They got their degrees from all different kinds of law schools, all over the country. But they have one thing in common: they've all pursued their own, unique vision.

As you read their stories, you'll see how they beat the odds to succeed. You'll learn career tips and strategies that work, from people who've put them to the test. And you'll find fascinating insights that you can apply to your own dream, whether it's a career in law or anything else!

From Representing Baseball In Australia. To International Finance. To Children's Advocacy. To Directing a Nonprofit Organization. To Entrepreneur.

If You Think Getting A Law Degree Means Joining A Traditional Law Firm — Think Again!

ISBN: 0-15-900182-X   **$17.95**

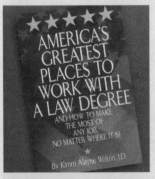

America's Greatest Places To Work With A Law Degree
Kimm Alayne Walton, J.D.

"Where do your happiest graduates work?"

That's the question that author Kimm Alayne Walton asked of law school administrators around the country. Their responses revealed the hundreds of wonderful employers profiled in *America's Greatest Places To Work With A Law Degree*.

In this remarkable book, you'll get to know an incredible variety of great places to work, including:

- Glamorous sports and entertainment employers — the jobs that sound as though they would be great, and they are!
- The 250 best law firms to work for between 20 and 600 attorneys.
- Companies where law school graduates love to work and not just as in-house counsel.
- Wonderful public interest employers – the "white knight" jobs that are so incredibly satisfying.
- Court-related positions, where lawyers entertain fascinating issues, tremendous variety, and an enjoyable lifestyle.
- Outstanding government jobs, at the federal, state, and local level.

Beyond learning about incredible employers, you'll discover:

- The ten traits that define a wonderful place to work ... the sometimes surprising qualities that outstanding employers share.
- How to handle law school debt, when your dream job pays less than you think you need to make.
- How to find — and get! — great jobs at firms with fewer than 20 attorneys.

And no matter where you work, you'll learn expert tips for making the most of your job. You'll learn the specific strategies that distinguish people headed for the top ... how to position yourself for the most interesting, high-profile work ... how to handle difficult personalities ... how to negotiate for more money ... and what to do now to help you get your next great job!

ISBN: 0-15-900180-3   **$24.95**

About The Author

Kimm Alayne Walton is the author of numerous books and articles including two national best seller's — *America's Greatest Places To Work With A Law Degree* and *Guerrilla Tactics For Getting The Legal Job Of Your Dreams*. She is a renowned motivational speaker, lecturing at law schools and bar associations nationwide, and in her spare time, she has taken up travel writing, which has taken her swimming with crocodiles in Kakadu, and scuba diving with sharks on the Great Barrier Reef.

E-mail the Job Goddess with your own legal job search questions!

Visit www.gilbertlaw.com for details.

Call To Order: 1-800-787-8717 or Order On-Line at http://www.gilbertlaw.com

Employment Guides

A collection of best selling titles that help you identify and reach your career goals.

The National Directory Of Legal Employers
National Association for Law Placement

The National Directory of Legal Employers brings you a universe of vital information about 1,000 of the nation's top legal employers— *in one convenient volume!*

It includes:

- Over 22,000 job openings.
- The names, addresses and phone numbers of hiring partners.
- Listings of firms by state, size, kind and practice area.
- What starting salaries are for full time, part time, and summer associates, plus a detailed description of firm benefits.
- The number of employees by gender and race, as well as the number of employees with disabilities.
- A detailed narrative of each firm, plus much more!

The National Directory Of Legal Employers has been the best kept secret of top legal career search professionals for over a decade. Now, for the first time, it is available in a format specifically designed for law students and new graduates. *Pick up your copy of the Directory today!*

ISBN: 0-15-900434-9 $39.95

SAMPLE PAGE

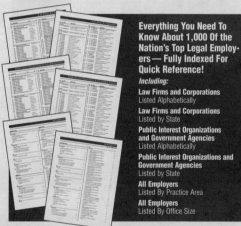

Everything You Need To Know About 1,000 Of the Nation's Top Legal Employers — Fully Indexed For Quick Reference!

Including:

Law Firms and Corporations
Listed Alphabetically

Law Firms and Corporations
Listed by State

Public Interest Organizations and Government Agencies
Listed Alphabetically

Public Interest Organizations and Government Agencies
Listed by State

All Employers
Listed By Practice Area

All Employers
Listed By Office Size

Company Information

1. *Name, Address, and Phone Number Of Hiring Partner*
2. *Demographics*
3. *Primary Practice Areas*
4. *Benefits*
5. *Pro Bono*
6. *Public Interest Fellowships*
7. *Minority Recruitment Efforts*
8. *Non-Discrimination Policy*
9. *Narrative*

Employment Information

10. *Office Size*
11. *Total Firm Size*
12. *Job Opportunities*
13. *Summer Associate Information*
14. *Application Timeline For Summer Associates*
15. *Hiring Criteria For All Job Openings*
16. *Salary Information*
17. *Other Compensation*
18. *Other Data*
19. *Partnership Data*
20. *Other Offices*
21. *Campus Interviews*

The Best Of The Job Goddess
Kimm Alayne Walton, J.D.

In her popular **Dear Job Goddess** column, legal job-search expert Kimm Alayne Walton provides the answers to even the most difficult job search dilemmas facing law students and law school graduates. Relying on career experts from around the country, the Job Goddess provides wise and witty advice for every obstacle that stands between you and your dream job!

ISBN: 0-15-900393-8 $14.95

SAMPLE COLUMN

Business Card Resumes: Good Idea, Or Not?

Dear Job Goddess,

One of my friends showed me something called a "business card resume." What he did was to have these business cards printed up, with his name and phone number on one side, and highlights from his resume on the other side. He said a bunch of people are doing this, so that when they meet potential employers they hand over these cards. Should I bother getting some for myself?

Curious in Chicago

Dear Curious,

Sigh. You know, Curious, that the Job Goddess takes a fairly dim view of resumes as a job-finding tool, even in their full-blown bond-papered, engraved 8-1/2x11" incarnation. And here you ask about a business card resume, two steps further down the resume food chain. So, no, you *shouldn't* bother with business card resumes. Here's why.

Think for a moment, Curious, about the kind of circumstance in which you'd be tempted to whip out one of these incredible shrinking resumes. You're at a social gathering. You happen to meet Will Winken, of the law firm Winken, Blinken, and Nod, and it becomes clear fairly quickly that Will is a) friendly, and b) a potential employer. The surest way to turn this chance encounter into a job is to use it as the basis for future contact. As Carolyn Bregman, Career Services Director at Emory Law School, points out, "Follow up with a phone call or note, mentioning something Winken said to you." You can say that you'd like to follow up on whatever it is he said, or that you've since read more about him and found that he's an expert on phlegm reclamation law and how that's a topic that's always fascinated you, and invite him for coffee at his convenience so you can learn more about it. What have you done? *You've taken a social encounter and* turned it into a potential job opportunity. And that makes the Job Goddess very proud.

But what happens if you, instead, whip out your business card resume, and say, "Gee, Mr. Winken, nice meeting you. Here's my business card resume, in case you ever need anybody like me." *Now* what have you done? You have, with one simple gesture, wiped out any excuse to follow up! Instead of having a phone call or a note from you that is personalized to Winken, you've got a piddling little standardized card with your vital statistics on it. Ugh. I know you're much more memorable, Curious, than anything you could possibly fit on the back of a business card.

So there you have it, Curious. Save the money you'll spend on a business card resume, and spend it later, when you have a *real* business card to print, reading, "Curious, Esq. Winken, Blinken, and Nod, Attorneys at Law."

Yours Eternally,

The Job Goddess

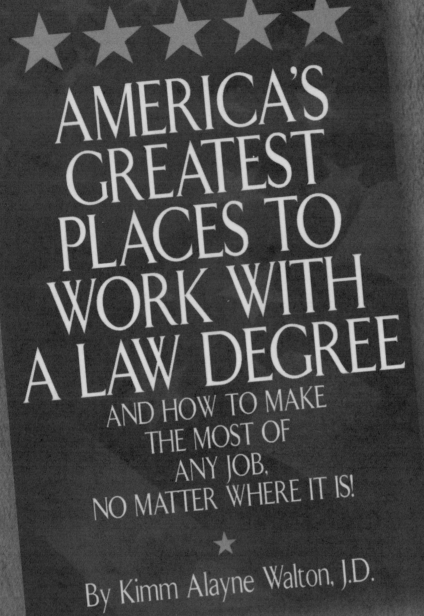